RUSSIAN SKETCHES

ALEXANDER DAVYDOFF

RUSSIAN SKETCHES

MEMOIRS

Foreword Marc RAEFF
Introduction John M. DAX

HERMITAGE
1984

Alexander Davydoff

RUSSIAN SKETCHES

Memoirs

Translated from Russian by Olga Davydoff-Dax

Copyright © 1984 by Olga Davydoff-Dax

Library of Congress Cataloging in Publication Data
Davydov, Aleksandr, 1881-1955.
   Russian sketches.

Translation of : Vospominaniia.
1. Davydoff family. 2. Davydov, Aleksandr, 1881-1955.
3. Intellectuals—Russian S.F.S.R.—Biography.
4. Russians—France—Paris—Biography. 5. Russians.
Americans—New York (N.Y.)—Biography. I.Title.
CT1217.D38D3813   1984   947.08'092'4   84—22586

ISBN 0-938920-56-1

Cover design by Serge Hollerbach
Tailpieces by O.D.D.
Published by HERMITAGE
P.O. BOX 410
Tenafly, N.J. 07670, U.S.A.

To my husband,

Without his efficient, devoted and loving help, this book would never have seen the light of day.

Alexander Vassilievich DAVYDOFF

1881 — 1955

To my treasure, my darling daughter, in memory of her « knight ».

New York   Al. Davydoff

July 1950

FOREWORD

Now and then we experience the surprise and excitement of encountering someone who is a living link with a past so remote as to seem impossible of direct access. This is the case of Aleksander Vassil'evich Davydoff who, born in 1881, and until his death in 1955, was a direct link to the Decembrist movement of the first quarter of the 19th century. Indeed, as a youngster and adolescent he had known the widow of the Decembrist Vassilii L'vovich Davydoff, his great grandmother who died in 1894 at the age of 92. Moreover, the author of these Memoirs had also spent many a summer at the family estate of Kamenka, in South Western Ukraine, that had received the visits of A. S. Pushkin and his friends in the 1820s and those of P. I. Tchaikovsky and his brother and sister in the 1880s. And in his Memoirs, alas published posthumously thanks to the devoted efforts of his daughter, A. V. Davydoff has left us a series of vivid and warm-hearted vignettes of the progressive-minded, cultured elite of imperial Russia.

The significance of the Decembrists, a seminal group of the younger generation of the Russian elite in the first quarter of the 19th century, for the subsequent intellectual and political history of Russia is not to be measured alone by their attempt at bringing about a radical transformation of the imperial system. For, as is well known, they failed in their abortive revolt on 14 December 1825—hence their name—on Senate Square in St. Petersburg (and a subsequent mutiny in the Ukraine) at the time of the succession crisis attendant upon Emperor Alexander I's sudden death. But the psychological impact of their aspirations and plans, as well as their martyrdom (and mythology) proved to be no mean force in the cause of Russia's political emancipation. At the time, the secret societies of the Decembrists represented what was most liberal and intellectually dynamic in Russian society. It is no accident that both A. Pushkin and A. Griboedov were closely associated with them, even though they themselves were not members of the conspiratorial societies. The literature on the Decembrist movement is dauntingly vast and includes many memoirs of the participants who survived until the amnesty granted them by Alexander II. The memoirs, however, were written long after the events, often from a self-serving perspective, and they focus almost exclusively on the organization, ideology, and actions of the secret societies leading up to the events of 14 December 1825. In their memoirs we find but rare glimpses of the personal and family circumstances of the Decembrists—a gap that is not filled by the numerous monographic studies that have come off the Russian presses since the early years of the present century. A. V. Davydoff's reminiscences and sketches of his forebears and of life on his ancestral estates help to fill this gap, while also providing delightful vignettes of the cultivated noble elite of Russia in the 19th century.

Reading about this elite one is struck by the intertwining of family and ethnic backgrounds that helps to explain the dynamism, openness and variety of Russian culture in the 19th and early 20th centuries. This is a particularly important aspect that foreigners and many academic students of Russian culture often tend to overlook or to minimize because of the obvious primacy of the language, literature, and traditions of the Great Russians. But it is good to be reminded that this primacy was achieved only thanks to the participation—albeit reluctant and formal—of many other ethnic and cultural traditions. A. V. Davydoff's memoirs show vividly the contributions, for example, of the Polish and Jewish elements in the Ukraine or of the Baltic Germans in Moscow and St. Petersburg. As with any social group, the Russian noble elite's characteristic traits and outlook were largely shaped by the upbringing and education imparted to its members. While we have a substantial literature

10

on the imperial school system and many memoirs of those pupils and students who later became prominent in the professions or revolutionary movement, we have relatively little on the upbringing and schooling of the «average» member of the nobility in the last decades of the imperial regime. Here again A. V. Davydoff's reminiscences fill the gap by their lively and arresting, albeit too brief, descriptions of his primary and secondary schooling in Moscow. Finally, the unfortunately incomplete memoirs also throw some light on the Russo-Japanese war of 1904-1905 and the very first stages of the revolutions of 1917 in the countryside of the Crimea, from the perspectives of the volunteer soldier in the former instance and of the noble estate manager in the latter.

I did not have the good fortune of knowing A. V. Davydoff personally. This I regret very much, and not only because he could have shared valuable information on his ancestors, the Decembrists (on whom I had done some work). But I missed the opportunity of making the acquaintance of a distinguished representative of the cultivated and liberal elite of imperial Russia. From his memoirs A. V. Davydoff emerges as a generous, independently thinking and open-minded gentleman who embodied all that was best in Russia before 1917. It would have been fascinating to learn how men like A. V. Davydoff coped with the revolution and civil war and rebuilt their existence in the West. Alas, illness and death prevented him from telling us about those periods of his life. All those interested in the history, literature, and culture of 19th century Russia, however, are much in debt to his daughter, Olga Aleksandrovna Davydoff-Dax, who has seen to the publication of her father's memoirs in both Russian and English/French, and provided them with rare illustrations from family archives. A couple of chapters on her recent visits to her family's homes round out the book. These descriptions also breathe her father's open-mindedness and concern for the human side of things and situations. The Decembrist tradition lives on abroad; let us trust that is has not disappeared in Russia either.

MARC RAEFF

INTRODUCTION

*O*utside *Russia very few people know about the attempted revolution of December 1825 when idealistic young nobles tried to liberalize the autocratic tsarist regime. Two of the leading members of this group were Vassili Lvovich Davydoff and Prince Serge Petrovitch Trubetskoy. One of the sons of Vassili Davydoff married one of the daughters of Serge Trubetskoy and their son was the father of Alexander Davydoff, the author of this book. It is therefore important to give, for the non-Russian reader, a brief outline of what came to be known as the Decembrist revolution.*

As is well known, Catherine the Great entertained a long correspondence with foreign thinkers, particularly Voltaire, Diderot and the Encyclopedists and this contributed to introduce liberal ideas into Russian society. Later on, the Napoleonic wars and the occupation of France enabled the young Russian officers to come in contact with French society and the literary salons where the liberal theories of the French revolution were freely discussed. When they returned to their country they realized all the more, and were shocked by, the conditions that existed there.

The hopes that these young officers had nourished when Alexander I had come to power were crushed when he reinforced the autocratic character of his regime and named as minister the ultra-reactionary Arakcheev. They got into the habit of meeting to discuss the liberal ideas they had discovered abroad, whether those of the French revolution or of the Italian Carbonari or even the German Tugendbund.

Thus secret societies were formed, which, because of disagreements between their members, changed names and structures several times. Finally two closely linked societies emerged. In St. Petersburg, the Northern Society had as its leading members Alexander and Nikita Muraviev, Kondraty Ryleev, Prince Eugene Obolensky and Prince Serge Trubetskoy. The Southern Society had its headquarters in Tulchin in the Ukraine. Its head was the most extremist of the future revolutionaries, Pavel Ivanovitch Pestel. The most active of his followers were Serge Muraviev-Apostol and Michael Bestujev-Riumin. Prince Serge Volkonsky and Vassili Davydoff were the heads of one of the most important regional branches, which was located in the Davydoff family estate near the village of Kamenka south of Kiev.

The majority of these men only wished to temper the autocratic tsarist regime and create a sort of constitutional monarchy. Only Pestel and his friends considered eliminating the tsar and setting up a truly republican state.

When Alexander I died suddenly on November 19, 1825, in circumstances that have remained mysterious to this day, neither Society was ready for action. However, a confused situation was created by the fact that the legitimate heir, Constantine, who was governor-general of Poland, had secretly renounced his rights to the throne in a secret manifesto, thus placing his brother Nicholas as next in succession without even close members of the tsar's entourage being aware of the fact, and the plotters decided they had to take advantage of this and act without delay. They told the men of their regiments that Nicholas was a usurper and that, at the ceremony that was to take place on the Senate Square, they should only swear allegiance to Constantine.

Thus on the fateful day of December 14, 1825 the troops were divided into two groups on the Senate Square, the troops loyal to Nicholas on one side, and the rebel troops facing them on the other. Unfortunately for the latter several of their chiefs, among others Serge Trubetskoy, took fright at the last moment and did not appear on the Senate Square, leaving the soldiers with no directives and no commanding officers. They thought that many of the «loyal» troops would come over to their side after nightfall, so just stood around waiting in what got to be

14

known as «the Standing Revolution». This delay proved fatal as Nicholas finally ordered his artillery to open fire on the mutinous soldiers. They were mowed down along with many civilians who had gathered to watch. Within hours the leaders of the insurrection were arrested and imprisoned in the Peter and Paul fortress.

In the South, Pestel had already been arrested on the day before the attempted insurrection after having been denounced to the tsarist authorities. Serge Muraviev-Apostol and Michael Bestujev-Riumin rallied their troops and attempted a military action but they also were mowed down by the artillery of the loyal troops. Thus ended the decembrist revolution.

Of the 579 persons arrested, 290 were acquitted, 134 were found guilty of minor acts and scattered among regiments on the outposts of the Empire or placed under police surveillance after being stripped of their ranks. 4 of the plotters were extradited and 20 died either before or during the trial. 5 were condemned to death by hanging—Pestel, Muraviev-Apostol, Bestujev-Riumin, Ryleev and Kakhovsky who had killed count Miloradovitch, the governor-general of Moscow, on the Senate Square. 31, among whom were Serge Trubetskoy and Vassili Davydoff, were condemned to hard labor in Siberia for life. The remainder were exiled to Siberia for various terms.

On July 13, 1826, the 5 men condemned to death were hanged and those exiled to Siberia left St. Petersburg in chains. 11 of their wives joined them. The first to do so was Katacha, the wife of Serge Trubetskoy. The wife of Serge Volkonsky, Maria Nikolaevna, born Raevskaia, a niece of Vassili Davydoff, caught up with her. The wife of Vassili Davydoff was pregnant and joined him later leaving her six children born before the exile to the care of friends in St. Petersburg.

After several years of hard labour in the Siberian mines, when the trying conditions they were subjected to were gradually relaxed, the condemned men were able to have their own homes and concentrate on educating the local inhabitants, developing agriculture and improving sanitary conditions, among other activities. Thus an intelligentsia unkown until then in Siberia was implanted there permanently. When, on August 26, 1856, Alexander II became Tsar he amnestied the Decembrists *and gave them back their rights, their privileges and their titles, but by that time only 25 to 30 of the exiles were still living and most of them chose to remain in Siberia.*

The attempted revolution of December 14, 1825 finally achieved no practical result except that Nicholas I lost all confidence in the liberal minded nobles and the young officers and increased his autocratic regime. In spite of this, although they had destroyed nothing and created nothing, the Decembrists were glorified by the revolutionaries of the following century as victims of autocratic injustice. Their legend stimulated political agitation.

The adventurous enterprise of the Decembrists may be considered as the prelude of a long struggle between autocracy and democracy in Russia. Their contribution may appear slender but they had defied traditional old Russia. Sadly the so-called democracy that followed on the fall of autocracy was unrecognizable from the one that the Decembrists had preached...

JOHN M. DAX

PREFACE

M y father's memoirs he should have been the one to publish them. The book was practically ready and some of the chapters had appeared in the Russian paper of New York, the Novoye Russkoye Slovo. But in June father fell ill.

Unfortunately we had never spoken of the book. I only knew that father was writing and preparing it but I was not interested in it at all then and he, by that time, was too tired.

Father corresponded with a lot of well-known writers, slavists, professors of universities, and our home was often the place of literary gatherings. But, in October 1955, father died.

It is I, his daughter, who am now publishing his book in memory of him.

29 years have elapsed. Many things have changed in our world but Russia, the Soviet Union, remains this immense territory, this vast and infinite land, this enormous bear that attracts and frightens us. And yet many things are still as they were in the times of the Marquis de Custine's visit to Russia in 1839.

My father was a liberal conservative and he often spoke of the fact that it was others who moved in one direction or another while he remained somewhere in the center.

Father was kind, generous and open-minded. I share his ideas and his opinions, and if one looks back at the past, at the time of the Decembrists, I can't help but think what a pity it is that the plans, the objectives of these idealistic young men did not succeed. If they had, many things in this world to-day might be different, perhaps better, who knows?

I first published this book in Russian, in its original form, without any changes, hurrying to do so in order that the few remaining old Russian émigrés and those who still remember my father could read it. I would also be very happy if it could be read in Russia, because I know how much the Russians are interested and curious about bygone times and how eager they are to know the truth.

From the reader, I ask comprehension and acceptance of the lack of continuity of the chapters which I have voluntarily left as father wrote them, not changing one iota and not «arranging» them. Each chapter has its own frame and its independent life. There is no special order. Only the linking thread, a perspective, that of my father on the people, the places and the events that he lived and experienced...

Olga DAVYDOFF DAX

KAMENKA

«You, the Raevskys and Orlov
And the happy memories of Kamenka»
A.S. Pushkin («To V.L. Davydoff»)

Deeply buried in cherry trees, the houses of the old village of Kamenka[1] sprawl along both banks of the swampy river Tiasmin. Only their roofs are visible, their gay whiteness contrasting sharply with the greenness of the trees. Yellow sun-flowers rise from tressed corn-cob fences that separate small gardens. From this greenery shoot skyward the spires of two churches, the Nikolaevsky and the Pokrovsky[2], which give their names to the two sections of the village.

Small, tightly packed, Jewish hovels line both sides of the dirty village streets and the shabby synagogue with its school rises above them. On each side of the main street one-story brick buildings have Jewish shops that sell all sorts of wares from those useful both to landowners and to peasants, to champagne, perfume and white kid gloves. Close by these shops a sign indicates a Jewish inn with crooked windows and a dilapidated entrance. In a neighboring lane the coloured glass jars of the local pharmacy shine through the windows of a brick building.

If you cross the bridge over the Tiasmin and turn left towards the Nikolaevsky quarter, you may see, profiled on

---

1. The privilege of founding a Jewish community was given by Augustus III, King of Poland in 1756.
2. St Nicholas and the Intercession.

the hilltop the large buildings of a sugar refinery, and just above the river, at the entrance to the refinery, a white tower in Russian Empire style with a red weather-vane on its roof. This is an abandoned water-mill where Sherwood, the man who betrayed the Decembrist plot, used to work. The sugar refinery stands on the very edge of the Tiasmin where it enters a rocky gorge that gave its name to Kamenka.

On the other side of the bridge a wide alley climbs up the hillside through the large park of a private estate and leads to a courtyard surrounded by small houses and, in its center, an unfinished brick building built in the style of a medieval castle.

There is nothing striking about the countryside around Kamenka. In summer, fields of wheat and oats and the green leaves of beets cover the endless steppe. The horizon is cut up by the grim heights of the distant Carpaths and oaktrees grow in deep ravines called «iare», though there are only a few large oak forests.

That is how I remember Kamenka.

One might think that Kamenka is in no way different from any of the other villages and hamlets of Western Ukraine. Fate willed otherwise and Kamenka became a part not only of the history of the Ukraine where it symbolised the fight of the local Cossacks against the Poles, but also of the history of Russia itself and of its cultural past, and became known to all educated Russians.

Kamenka is situated 45 versts [3] from the old country town of Tchigirin whose bailiff in the XVIth century was Bogdan Khmelnitsky [4]. Bogdan won his first victory over the Polish hetmans at the locality known as «the Yellow Waters» where the Tiasmin flows into the Dniepr.

Deep in the Gruchev forest, close to Kamenka, rose once upon a time the old Matroninsky monastery, surrounded by ancient fortifications. It was founded by Paul, bishop of Pereyaslavl, ten years before Batu Khan's invasion [5]. It got its name

---

3. 1 verst = 1,067 km.
4. Bogdan Khmelnitsky (1593-1657): hetman of the Ukrainian Cossacks. He led their revolt against the Poles in 1648.
5. Batu Khan: Mongol Prince, founder of the Golden Horde.

20

from Princess Matrona, who owned the locality at that time. The monastery was completely destroyed by the Tatars and it was only in 1568 that a chapel was built on its emplacement. Prince Jan Jablonovsky, owner of Tchigirin at the start of the 18th century, gave ownership of the land to the monastery without binding it to the Uniate Church. This did not prevent Father Melhissediek from rising against the Poles and from blessing the swords of Jeleznia and Gonte at the time of the Uman massacres [6].

At the end of the Polish domination, and even into the first half of Catherine's reign, Kamenka belonged to a well-known family of Polish magnates, the Princes Liubomirsky. At that time, in spite of the honors that had been showered on him, his incredible wealth and the vastness of his domains, Potemkin's ambition knew no bounds and he dreamed of a crown that would make him Catherine's equal and end once and for all the intrigues of her latest favorite, Zubov. The country where he could make these dreams come true with the least difficulty was Poland because in Poland sovereignty could be got by election. However the first step was to become a Polish magnate, that is to say own land in the kingdom. With this in mind, Potemkin bought from the Princes Liubomirsky for six million roubles the district of Smeliansk which included Smela and Kamenka. We do not know if Potemkin ever visited his Ukrainian estates but we may be sure that he never stayed there long. Before he died he bequeathed to his favorite niece, the attractive Sachenka Engelhardt, whom he had married to Count Branitsky, the famous domain of White Church which, at the time of the 1917 revolution, still included 900,000 dessiatines [7] of land, and to the children of his sister Samoilova, whose husband had been best man at his wedding to Catherine, Smela and Kamenka along with several other estates. His nephew Alexander Nikolaevitch inherited Smela and his niece Ekaterina Nikolaevna Kamenka.

---

6. The Cossacks massacred the Poles and the Jews at Uman in 1768.
7. 1 dessiatine = 1.1 hectare.

Ekaterina Samoilova's destiny was quite out of the ordinary. It was shaped early in her life by her father and by Empress Catherine. They married her to Nicholas Simenovitch Raevsky at such a young age that, for a long time after her wedding, she still played with her dolls which she would hastily hide when she heard the bells of the troïka that was bringing her husband home. This marriage did not last long. N.S. Raevsky died in 1771 from wounds he had received near Chumla, leaving Ekaterina Nikolaevna a young widow with two sons. Her widowhood only lasted a short time. One year after the death of her first husband she made a love marriage with Major-General Lev Denisovitch Davydoff.

Lev Denisovitch was of Tatar origin. His ancestor «Murzah» Mintchak, son of «Murzah» Kossaia, had left the Golden Horde at the start of the 15th century and had arrived at the court of Grand Duke Vassili Dimitrievitch I where, at the time of the Holy Baptism, he was given the name Simeon. Having become a Christian convert he was named Simon Kossaievich Mintchakov. According to the customs of that time he received a gift of land. One of the estates was in the region of Novgorod and the others near Moscow, close to Borodino [8]. Simon Kossaievich had two sons, David and Uvar. From the first descend the Davydoffs, from the second the counts Uvarov. The first generation of Davydoffs were called Davydoff Mintchakoff, and it seems that they had the title of Prince for their coat-of-arms is set on a «princely coat» with a noble crown. Nothing remarkable occurred in the Davydoff family until the appearance of Lev Denisovitch. He was the first Davydoff to attain a high post when he became «Oberkriegscommissar». Catherine named him aide-de-camp.

After she took possession of Kamenka in 1790, Ekaterina Nikolaevna did not live there regularly until the death of her husband at the start of the 19th century when she settled in Kamenka permanently and remained there until her death in 1825.

---

8. L. Tolstoy in his description of Borodino in «War and Peace» writes: «Several thousand dead and wounded lay in their uniforms on the fields and meadows that belonged to the Davydoffs and to their serfs.

After her arrival in peaceful and remote Kamenka it was pervaded by the sweet breath of Catherine's reign. The enormous house that existed at that time on the right-hand side of the park sprang to life. Friends and acquaintances, relatives from St. Petersburg, Moscow, Smela and White Church, as well as neighboring landowners, became habitués. However, life at Kamenka did not reach its peak until 1816 when the Russian troops returned from abroad at the end of the Napoleonic wars. It is only then, when the children and the grandchildren of Ekaterina Nikolaevna returned from their distant campaigns abroad that there was heard in Kamenka the «gay sound of country family life».

To the habitués of Kamenka were added the friends and the comrades-at-arms of the sons and the grandsons of Ekaterina Nikolaevna. At that time the second army was stationed in the Ukraine. The general staff had its headquarters in Tulchin in the province of Podolsk while the regiments were dispersed among the villages and boroughs. The generals, the commanding officers and the other officers of the second army often visited Kamenka. One may get an idea of what life was like there at that time from a letter written to N.F. von Meck by P.I. Tchaikovsky who, as we shall see further on, was a frequent visitor to Kamenka: «To-day Alexandra Ivanovna Davydova [9] told me in detail about the life Pushkin led in Kamenka. According to her, Kamenka was then a marvelous large manor where people lived in princely style. Life was led on a grand scale with an orchestra, singers, bards etc.». This was not difficult to achieve as Ekaterina Nikolaevna was so wealthy that with the initials of her many estates one could compose the sentence: «Lev loves Ekaterina».

Of Ekaterina Nikolaevna's two sons by her marriage to Raevsky only Nicholas was still living, Nicholas, the famous hero of the wars against Napoleon, the brave of braves whose name is glorified in Russian military history by many feats, notably at the battle of Borodino and at the capture of Paris. He had two sons, Alexander and Nicholas, and four daughters. The two sons were friends of Pushkin, and Alexander is Pushkin's

---

9. The author's great-grandmother, the widow of Vassili Lvovich Davydoff.

«Demon». Of the daughters, Ekaterina, engaged to general Orlov, was noted for her charm and beauty, and Maria later married the Decembrist Serge Grigorievich Volkonsky.

By her marriage to Lev Davydoff, Ekaterina Nikolaevna had four children, three sons and a daughter. The eldest son, handsome Peter, known as «le beau» was married to Countess N.V. Orlova and was Marshal of the Imperial Court. He lived permanently in St. Petersburg and only rarely came to Kamenka. The youngest of the Davydoff children, Sophie, was married to the first governor of Taurid, Major-General A.M. Borozdin, and lived in Simferopol. With Ekaterina Nikolaevna at Kamenka lived her second son Alexander, his wife and three children, and her youngest son Vassili, who was not married.

A well-known gourmet of his time, Alexander Lvovich Davydoff was renowned for his enormous obesity. A piece the shape of his stomach had to be cut out of the table in front of his seat, otherwise he would not have been able to reach the food in his plate. His cult of good food was such that when he went to Paris he would take his cook along with him and when he went to a restaurant he would send his cook to the kitchen to show the French chefs what sort of food he liked. One day when he was going to the Crimea by sea he invited Pushkin to go with him, but Pushkin was unable to do so and answered him with the following verses:

> «Impossible, my fat Aristippus,
> Although I love your conversation,
> Your friendliness and your hoarse voice,
> Your good taste and your rich dinners,
> I cannot sail with you
> To the shores of southern Taurid...»

These verses show that Pushkin liked Alexander Lvovich, but this did not prevent him from teasing him and calling him «the magnificent cuckold». The reason for this nickname was that Alexander Lvovich's wife, née de Gramont, from the Duc de Gramont's family, was not noted for her faithfulness. According to her contemporaries, everyone swooned at her feet, from the generals to the cornets. Even Pushkin was attracted by her, judging from the verses he dedicated to «the Coquette».

24

It seems that her interest in him did not last long, for the epigram «Someone else has got my Aglaé» which he dedicated to her shows his vexation. His attraction to Aglaé did not prevent Pushkin from running after her daughter Adèle, aged twelve, and intimidating her with his passionate looks. He did not really attach much importance to this last infatuation, as is shown by his poem dedicated to Adèle «Play, Adèle, ignore sorrow...» which expresses mainly a feeling of enthusiasm for the pretty and nice child.

«An intelligent little devil», thus Pushkin named Ekaterina Nikolaevna's youngest son Vassili, the future Decembrist. In society he was known as «le Richard» and his contemporaries said of him that he was unique in his culture, his intelligence, his wit and his kindness but that he had a weak character. According to Prince V.P. Gorchakov he loved to be known as a man of simple tastes. I have kept two snapshots of him, one taken in his youth and the other a short time before his death. On the first one we see a handsome young man with clear-cut features, hair brushed back, a small moustache, high eyebrows and soft dreamy eyes. The second one, taken in Siberia, shows an old man with lifeless eyes and a vacant look broken by the privations and sufferings of his life in Siberia. In their stories, my aunts, who worshipped the memory of their father, stressed his faith and his infinite kindness. At the time of which I am writing he was not married and was having an affair with one of his mother's serfs, Alexandra Ivanovna Potapova [10]. This liaison, however, was not like the usual ones between master and servant. A very strong bond united them which had lasted for several years and which finally culminated in their legal marriage only one year before the arrest and exile of Vassili Lvovich, for such a marriage was unthinkable during his mother's lifetime. This love between my great-grandfather and my great-grandmother was so strong and real that, along with other wonderful Russian women, she followed her husband to Siberia, sharing with him all the miseries of his life until he died in Krasnoyarsk. I had the good fortune to know her. She died at Kamenka at the age of 92 when I was already 14, surrounded by her large

---

10. Some soviet sources say that she was not a serf but the daughter of a low class civil servant.

family who worshipped her like a saint. Her main traits were a true Christian humbleness and a great kindness. When one looked at her or listened to her, she did not seem to be a woman but an angel for whom nothing earthly existed. And yet she had needed a great strength of will and character to follow her husband to Siberia, leaving behind six children born before the exile, then having and bringing up seven more during the exile, to give her husband the strength his weak character lacked and to help him support better than he did his unhappy fate.

In addition to Ekaterina Nikolaevna's direct offspring, a large number of nephews lived in her house in Kamenka. One can easily imagine the gay life that all these young people led in Ekaterina Nikolaevna's rich household. However, this mode of life did not reflect the life of the provincial landowners such as it existed at that time in Russia. Ekaterina Nikolaevna herself, her relatives and her guests belonged to that circle of society that had already been affected by the new tendencies of that time. The education that the representatives of that circle had received was radically different from the one their parents had been given before the reign of Catherine the Great. Brought up by French tutors, they had grown up under the influence of French literature, particularly of the works of the Encyclopedists. Another factor that contributed to their development was the freemasonry that was prevalent in Russia in Catherine's time.

If the older people in Kamenka were interested in foreign literature as well as in the budding Russian one, in philosophical debates and in music, among the younger elements who lived in Kamenka or who visited there, other interests were developing. This youth grew up at the time of «the wonderful start of Alexander's days» and had to suffer the Napoleonic wars. For them what characterized this epoch was the climate in which the Decembrist movement was born. As we know this movement was directly linked to Kamenka. The headquarters of the Southern Society was in Tulchin and local seats were scattered in other areas of the South West. One of these seats was in Kamenka and its president was Vassili Lvovich Davydoff. While in Ekaterina Nikolaevna's salon, on the ground floor of the house, mundane conversations were in progress, in Vassili Lvovich's room the conspirators were studying the plans for the coup d'état.

Pushkin wrote to P.N. Gnedich about his stay in Kamenka: «I am staying in the country at the Davydoffs, those charming and intelligent hermits. I spend my time between aristocratic dinners and democratic debates. Our group, now dispersed, was, only a short time ago, a varied and gay mixture of original minds, of people well known in our Russia and strange for a newcomer. Few women, lots of champagne, many bons mots, lots of books and a little poetry. You will easily understand me if I tell you that, seduced by all this, I paid little attention to the rumors from St. Petersburg.»

In addition to his role of president of the Kamenka group, Vassili Lvovich, who, because of his previous posting with the Hussars of the Imperial Guard, had many friends and comrades in the regiments of the Guard who were members of the Northern Society, was the link between them and the Duma in Tulchin. Couriers from one or the other Society were constantly arriving in Kamenka to study plans and measures that had to be taken in common. These couriers stayed a few days in Kamenka and took part in «the aristocratic dinners», then went to Vassili Lvovich's room where they made fiery speeches while champagne flowed. Not all of the people present were members of the Secret Society but all were in sympathy with their ideas without always knowing of the existence of the group. Prince P.A. Viazemsky, speaking of the fact that Pushkin was not one of the conspirators, writes: «He lived and caught fire in this burning and volcanic atmosphere. More or less all of us breathed this air and were troubled and excited by it».

Among the habitués of «the democratic debates» during the Kamenka evenings were Alexander Lvovich, N.N. Raevsky and his two sons, General Orlov, Prince S.G. Volkonsky, and, among the numerous guests, Okhotnikov, Yakushkin and Pushkin. Of all these only the Raevsky sons, General Orlov, Prince Volkonsky, Okhotnikov and Yakushkin were members of the Secret Society.

Pushkin and the Decembrist Yakushkin recall these meetings, Pushkin in his message to Vassili Lvovitch, Yakushkin in his memoirs.

Pushkin wrote to Vassili Lvovich Davydoff:

> «I cannot help but remember,
> Davydoff, your wine...
> Here is another Eucharist
> When you and your brother
> In front of the chimney
> Donning the gown of democracy
> To liberation filling our cups
> With an icy and frothless wine
> To the health of «They» and «It» [11]
> To the dregs, to the last drop
> We drank».

Yakushkin relates the last evening he spent in Kamenka: «When I arrived in Kamenka I thought I would know no one and I was pleasantly surprised when Pushkin, who happened to be there, rushed up to me with open arms. At that time in Kamenka there were General N.N. Raevsky and his son Alexander, Orlov and Okhotnikov. The last evening, V.L. Davydoff, Okhotnikov and I decided, so as to confuse Raevsky regarding our membership in the Secret Society, to act in the following manner. To make it seem more plausible, we named Raevsky president. With a half-joking half-serious air he controlled the general trend of the talks... After many discussions, Orlov asked the following question: «What good could come out of the creation of a secret society in Russia?» He himself set forth the arguments for and against a secret society. V.L. Davydoff and Okhotnikov agreed that very little good would result. Pushkin on the other hand demonstrated with fire how useful such a society would be for Russia. After having asked the president the authorization to speak, I tried to demonstrate how impossible it was for a secret society to be of the slightest use in Russia. Raevsky started to prove the contrary and enumerated the cases where a secret society could be useful and successful. In answer to this remark I said: «It is not difficult for me to prove that you are joking. One remark will suffice: if a society such as you have described were to exist right now, you would certainly not be ready to become one of its members». «On the contrary», he replied, «I would certainly join it». «In that case», I said to him, «give me your hand». So he held out his hand—and I

---

11. «They» = the Italian Carbonari. «It» = Liberty.

burst out laughing, saying to Raevsky «Of course, all this is only a joke». The others also laughed except A.L. Davydoff «the magnificent cuckold», who was dozing, and Pushkin, who was very upset. Before this incident he had thought that the secret society already existed or that at the very least it was about to be formed there and then and that he would become a member of it, but when he found out that it was all a joke he rose and, red-faced and tearful, said: «I have never been so unhappy as at this moment. I could already see my life ennobled and a great destiny ahead of me, and it was all a joke!» At that moment he was truly magnificent.

A great deal has been written about the reasons why Pushkin was not allowed to attend the evening debates of the Secret Society at Kamenka. Personally I think that my grandfather Piotr Vassilievich, his brother Nicholas and their elder sister Elisaveta, had judged the situation quite correctly. According to them, it seems that on the one hand the conspirators could not count on Pushkin's discretion and feared that, although he could be counted upon to keep his promise not to divulge the secret, he might nevertheless, with his temperament, either in a poem or by a word uttered without thinking during a conversation, put the ruling powers on the track of the Secret Society. They also felt that if Pushkin took part in the conspiracy and it was discovered, both he and his genius would be condemned which would be an irretrievable loss for Russia.

Pushkin arrived in Kamenka from Kishinev in November 1820 with General Orlov who commanded the troops stationed in the Kishinev area. He had probably been invited by the Raevskys with whom he had traveled to the Caucasus after spending some time in the Crimea at Gurzuf. Apart from the friendship that linked him to the Raevsky sons, Alexander and Nicholas (he dedicated to Nicholas «the Prisoner of the Caucasus» which he wrote in Kamenka), Pushkin was attracted to them perhaps by one of the purest and most noble of sentiments, his love for their sister Maria, the future wife of the Decembrist Volkonsky. This love started in the Caucasus and perhaps even in the Crimea, and expressed itself at first in some of the well-known verses of Eugene Onegin where he speaks of «a woman's small feet», and, later, when Maria Nikolaevna had joined her husband in Siberia, in «Poltava», which he dedicated to her.

This feeling however did not prevent Pushkin from making advances to Aglaé Davydoff and making eyes at her daughter Adèle, as well as taking part in «the democratic debates» and above all writing. Apart from «the Prisoner of the Caucasus», he wrote at Kamenka «I have outlived my desire...» and several other poems which he gave to V.L. Davydoff. They were taken by the police authorities when Vassili Lvovich was arrested and disappeared forever.

The brilliant period of Kamenka's history did not last long, barely ten years. Early in 1825 Ekaterina Nikolaevna died, and in the month of January of the following year, after the December 14 uprising had been crushed, Vassili Lvovitch Davydoff and Prince Serge Grigorievich Volkonsky were arrested. Alexander Lvovich died in 1833 and his wife returned to France where she later married the famous Marshal Horace Sebastiani. The Raevskys moved to an estate that had been given them to share in a sector of Kamenka already in 1805, «Boltychka», and Vassili Lvovich's wife followed him to Siberia, leaving her children in the care of Countess Tchernitcheva-Kruglikova who lived in St. Petersburg. Of these six children four, two boys and two girls, had been born before wedlock, and two sons, my grandfather Piotr and my great uncle Nicholas, after their parents' marriage and before their exile. Ekaterina Nikolaevna bequeathed Kamenka to Vassili Lvovich which is why, after he was sent into exile, Kamenka was given to his two legitimate sons and was not confiscated.

Count Bobrinsky, owner of Smela and husband of Ekaterina Nikolaevna Samoilova's niece, was named guardian of these infant heirs. He must have given very little of his time to Kamenka for, according to my grandfather, during his childhood and his youth full powers were in the hands of managers who not only did not look after the interests of the infant owners but even literally plundered the estate. During that period, I don't know for what reason, the large house of Kamenka was completely destroyed as well as the colonnaded pavillion which stood on the left side of the park and where Pushkin liked to write lying flat on the billiard table. Until the main house was destroyed, the managers of the estate would organize drinking parties with their neighbors on the terraces where in olden times members of the «aristocratic society» would meet. The champagne that remained in the cellars flowed freely and was even given to the horses, while a choir of serfs sang Little-Russian songs. This sort of management ended by completely ruining the estate and the young owners were threatened with a total loss. What saved them were their unfortunate experiences in their posts in St. Petersburg. Having finished the school of Ensigns of the Guard the eldest, Piotr, became officer of the Cavalry of the Guard, and the youngest, Nicholas, officer of the Preobrajenski regiment. However, neither of the brothers remained long in the army. Piotr had to leave the army because of his impossible pranks and Nicholas because of his insolent attitude towards the Imperial heir, the future Emperor Alexander II. When Nicholas I was told that the cornet of the Cavalry of the Guard Piotr Davydoff had galloped up the Nevski Prospekt from the Admiralty to the Lavra of Alexander Nevski in a three-horse carriage and had then appeared naked on horseback at the first rank of the parade in the camp, he had only laughed and said: «Send him to see his father in Siberia». This was a light punishment as my grandfather went to Krasnoyarsk a free man and could return whenever he wished. For his father in exile it was a great joy to see his son again. Thus Nicholas I, who was known for his severity, acted magnanimously towards the son of the Decembrist. His heir Alexander Nikolaevich, who later was to amnesty the Decembrists, acted in a totally different manner towards my uncle Nicholas. At a parade of the Preobrajenski regiment that he was inspecting, he shouted to my great-uncle who had made some mistake or other: «Lieutenant Davydoff, you lie always and about everything». Whereupon my uncle had no choice but to tender his resignation.

After spending less than one year in Siberia, my grandfather returned with a wife, the daughter of the Decembrist S.P. Trubetskoy, the beautiful Elisaveta, and settled with her in their estate of Sably in the Crimea, while my great-uncle

Nicholas went to Kamenka to look after the estate—which saved it. Nicholas found that the situation in Kamenka was absolutely disastrous and devoted himself entirely to putting it back into shape. He adopted a spartan mode of life which he kept until the end of his life. There was no longer any question of «the gay sound of country family life» in Kamenka. Nothing was left of its wealth. My uncle was a bachelor and lived alone. He had to think not only of his own income but also of that of his brothers and sisters who lived in St. Petersburg as well as of that of his father and of his family in Siberia. Under the supervision of his uncle Bobrinsky, who was an experienced administrator of land and a pioneer of the culture of the sugar beet in the Ukraine, Nicholas started by putting the agriculture in order, then he built a sugar factory. The affairs of the estate soon improved and in a few year's time the brothers were not only able to cover their own needs and those of their father, they also put money aside for their brothers and sisters born in Siberia.

After burying her husband in Krasnoyarsk in 1855, my great-grandmother Alexandra Ivanovna returned from Siberia with her children. She settled in Kiev and only spent the summer months in Kamenka. However a little life did return to Kamenka. The Davydoff family was reunited. Alexandra Ivanovna gathered around her all her children, those born before and those born after the exile of their father to Siberia. At that time only eleven of her thirteen children were still alive.

After a short time, uncle Nicholas, whose main interest had never been the running of the estate, succeeded in doing what he had always wanted to do—devote his life to the study of philosophical, social and political subjects. Having noticed that the eldest of the brothers born in Siberia, Lev, seemed to be gifted for the management of the estate, in agreement with his brother and co-owner of the estate, my grandfather Piotr Vassilievich, he arranged to transfer this management to Lev while he himself devoted all his time to his favorite studies, which was all the easier for him as Kamenka possessed a large library.

I remember very well uncle Kolia, as we called him. He died in 1916 at the age of 90 when I was already 35. As I got to know him better he struck me as a person quite out of the ordinary. Physically he was not tall but wiry. He was never ill and, in his youth, had been very strong and muscular. All his movements, his gait, his gestures, were resolute and sharp and expressed the strength of will he had inherited from his mother. Psychologically he was a strange mixture of extreme conservatism and of 18th century ideas he had got from his father's books. When I listened to him or looked at him I would think of him as the last Voltairian, but this did not fit with his extreme political conservatism. I never heard him utter an atheistic remark, but, by the same token, I do not remember ever seeing him go to church, even at Easter. On the other hand he spoke without hiding his loathing for the liberal ideas of that time. It seems to me that, having inherited from his father a great intelligence and sharpness of mind and having been given in his youth an excellent education that he had perfected by his readings, he was very lonely in his present surroundings. He deeply loved his mother, his sisters and his brothers and he did not want to hurt their great piety by his atheistic opinions, although they agreed entirely on political matters. I have often wondered how the opinions of the Decembrist children, at least those of my family, could differ so deeply from those of their parents. For a long time it was totally incomprehensible to me that the children of people who, because of their liberal ideas, has been sentenced to hard labor and had still remained true to their ideals, could differ so completely from their parents while still revering their memory. I remember how suprised I was on reading in his book «the Decembrists» Prince S.M. Volkonsky's touching story about his father. The latter had been sent to Siberia by Emperor Alexander II with the manifesto of the amnesty and, having arrived at night at Irkutsk from Angarsk, he had knocked on the door of his father's home and, to the question «Who goes there» had answered «I have brought the pardon». It seemed strange to me that people who had ruined their lives because they wanted to overthrow the imperial power could receive with joy their pardon from this same power. I must admit there was a time when I suspected that these persons had forsaken their ideals and had repented. However the veneration that surrounded the memory of the

Decembrists and that persisted in Russian society even in the most radical spheres made me change my mind. Nowadays the words of the son of the Decembrist Volkonsky strike me as the final chapter of a long drama lived by Russia from the start of the reign of Emperor Alexander I to the accession to the throne of Alexander II. The manifesto brought to Irkutsk on a dark night meant the end of a long period of Russian history and marked the dawn of a new era rising over Russia. Pushkin wrote of the Decembrists:

> Your hardships will not have been in vain
> Nor meaningless your aspirations

and he was not mistaken. The son of «the policeman of Europe» started his liberal reign by admitting the rights of those who, thirty years earlier, had thought as he did and by extending his hand to them. Instead of «pardon» the Volkonsky son might have said «reconciliation». For the children of the Decembrists their fathers' affair was closed and truth had been found to be on their side. They did not have to fight the reigning power and the elevated spirituality and disinterested sacrifice of their fathers inspired in them a profound respect.

To complete the portrait of uncle Nicholas, I must describe his character. After meeting him and speaking to him for the first time, one might have thought that he was a wicked man, possessive and intolerant, and it is only when one got to know him better that one discovered his charm and his kindness of heart. Even to a person who did not share his views he would only say «nonsense» while striking the ground with his cane, then surprise him by the depth of his views and the vastness of his knowledge. His kindness did not only manifest itself by his great charity but also by the fact that he never criticized anyone. When someone, even a close relative, committed an act that went against his rules of ethics and honor, he acted as if he knew nothing about it and did not change his attitude towards him.

Uncle Nicholas had one particular trait which, in fact, was quite prevalent among Russian landowners in the Ukraine. He hated the Poles, of whom there were many among the neighboring landowners. He called them «liahy» [12] and never allowed them in his house. The reason for this hate was the memory of the Polish uprising in 1863. Although they found no support among the local orthodox peasant population, the Polish landowners managed to form small bands which attacked the police and the estates of neighboring Russians. The latter had to take measures for their protection. Uncle Nicholas, who had no firearms, armed his servants with pikes made in the Kamenka blacksmith's forge and he himself patrolled the estate at night. This affair ended without any further incident and Kamenka was never attacked, but, in memory of those times, my great uncle kept two pikes for a long time thereafter.

My great uncle also had other idiosyncracies, such as an exaggerated preoccupation for his health. As he enjoyed excellent health, he felt it was his duty to look after it and, for that purpose, every day, three times a day, he would take his temperature and jot it down in a notebook along with other remarks about his health. These notebooks accumulated over the years and when one asked him what his temperature had been for instance on December 3, 1865 at 3 p.m. he would take down the corresponding notebook from the shelf and give the precise answer. The extraordinary thing is that his temperature was always normal. With the same idea in mind, he insisted that the doctor in charge of the sugar factory visit him every day and prescribe some medicine. Not knowing what to do, the doctor came to an agreement with the pharmacist that, whatever was written on the prescription that my uncle would send him, he should only give him some syrup diluted in water. It so happened that one day the doctor was obliged to prescribe a real medicine in solution form which had to be taken in drops. He made a special note on the prescription and the medicine was delivered by the pharmacist. My uncle however, who was used to taking his syrups by the soup spoon, did the same for the solution to be taken in drops—which, incidentally, did him no harm.

Sweet, dear uncle Kolia, even now I can see you arriving from your «little green house» for 5 o'clock tea at the big house

---

12. An untranslatable scornful word for «Poles».

where your mother and your sisters lived. I can see your silhouette, short but wiry, your strong face, your firm step, cane in hand. I can see the gleam in your intelligent black eyes and your charming kind smile when you proffered your smooth clean-shaven cheek for me to kiss. How neat you were, how you smelled good of a certain soap...

In 1860 uncle Lev Vassilievich Davydoff married Alexandra Ilyinishna Tchaikovskaia and brought his wife to Kamenka. This event turned another page in the history of Kamenka and linked its name to that of Piotr Ilyich Tchaikovsky. Fate willed that after Pushkin another Russian genius should immortalize the name of Kamenka, not only because this genius went there often and even made it his permanent residence for a while, but also because the people who lived there, the Davydoffs, became his closest and dearest friends.

What did Piotr Ilyich find in Kamenka and in the Davydoffs that he should love them like his parents? First of all, it was not Kamenka with its uncomfortable house and its small annexes clustered against each other on the smelly and swampy Tiasmin close to a dirty, dusty, small Jewish village, nor was it the surrounding countryside, that could attract one who had known the splendors of N.F. von Meck's Brailov estate and who had travelled extensively abroad. Nor was it the Davydoffs with their modest and monotonous mode of life, their retrograde ideas and their lack of interest in music, who could, at first sight, satisfy a person as refined, cultured and erudite as Piotr Ilyich. Finally, in spite of the widespread opinion that Piotr Ilyich appreciated highly the popular arias of the Ukraine and was inspired by them for several of his works, the truth is, as we now know, that as far as he was concerned he was disappointed in them. What he heard in Kamenka was devoid of all originality and was not equal to the arias of «Great-Russia». Only the piano piece «Russian Scherzo», inspired by the song that was sung under his window by women gardeners, and the theme of the second symphony which Piotr Ilyich named «the Crane», were taken from Ukrainian songs of that same name. Even the well-known

36

songs of the «lirnik», the blind beggars of the Ukraine, who sang its past glory, did not find any particular echo in him. He only used one of them for the first part of his piano concerto opus 23.

Nevertheless, wherever Piotr Ilyich found himself, in the luxury of Brailov, in the countryside near St. Petersburg, in Paris, in Italy, in Switzerland, he was always attracted by Kamenka. Already after his first stay there he had written to his sister: «Never in my life have I spent such a pleasant summer». And again, while staying with the Davydoff family in the estate of the Miatlevs near Peterhoff, he wrote: «Life isn't bad at all at the Miatlevs and were it not for the thought of Kamenka which gnaws at me constantly I could find this life quite pleasant». And even in Paris, he dreams of Kamenka: «I cannot but admit», he writes, «that for a working artist an ambiance as noisy and as rowdy as Paris is far less suitable than any lake such as Tunskoe, without mentioning the very smelly banks of dear Tiasmin which has the good fortune to flow in front of the house where certain charming people who are dear to me live».

Along with this constant thought of Kamenka which one finds in Piotr Ilyich's letters, there are the most affectionate and tender words for its inhabitants. For instance, my great-grandmother Alexandra Ivanovna and her daughters, my aunts Elisaveta and Alexandra, are never called anything but «our angels», «our three doves». In that same letter he wrote to his sister from the Miatlev estate he says: «What wonderful people, those Davydoffs. This is nothing new for you, but for me it is difficult to stop talking about them. I had never lived in so great an intimacy with them as now, and each minute their infinite kindness surprises me». Neither was Piotr Ilyich put off by the grim looks of uncle Nicholas. As is testified by Modest Ilyich, very shortly after their first meeting Piotr Ilyich discovered under Nicholas's external appearances his true nature and so succumbed to his charm that he adopted his reactionary views.

I saw Piotr Ilyich in Kamenka in the last years of his life, when he went there rarely. I was then very young and naturally could not understand him and the reasons that attracted him to Kamenka and to my family. In spite of this, the fact of living in the same atmosphere that Piotr Ilyich breathed, and of being very close to those he loved so dearly, made a lot of things more understandable. The people who lived in Kamenka told me a great many things about Piotr Ilyich, and of his life there and, later on, when I returned to visit his sister's family, particularly her children, my uncles and aunts, whom I knew so well, I got to know and even feel this atmosphere. For me there is no doubt that the major reason for Piotr Ilyich's love for Kamenka lay in himself, in his penchants, his interests, his tastes. At Kamenka and in the Davydoff family he found everything that was essential to him. Piotr Ilyich loved a family life and was deprived of it. As an artist he needed freedom and did not have it in St. Petersburg. He found both these elements in Kamenka. First of all, his favorite sister Alexandra Ilyinishna lived there and her cloudless marriage delighted and charmed him. There lived her children whom he loved so much and for whom he was «darling uncle Petia». Furthermore, the other Davydoffs were kind and simple and showed him so much affection without meddling in his private life. In Kamenka Piotr Ilyich could concentrate on his work without being disturbed, go out, chat with uncle Nicholas on political and philosophical subjects, invent games and jokes for the children, make them study music, or chat peacefully with his «doves» and take part in their sewing work. He could take long walks every day in the woods around Kamenka, Zrubants, Tarapune, Pliakovsky and its oak trees, or organize picnics in the big forest where those bonfires he loved so much were lit and which one went to in large four-horse coaches. «My God, what wouldn't I give to find myself right away in the «Big Wood», wrote Piotr Ilyich to his sister from Sodena. «I can see myself dragging dry branches, leaves and twigs for the bonfire on the small hill. I can see you with Lev and the children around the tablecloth with the samovar, the bread and butter. I can see the horses resting. I can smell the fragrance of the hay. I can hear the charming cries of the children. How wonderful all that is!». When I write these lines, I can see everything that Piotr Ilyich has described as if it were there alive in front of me. I myself have been to the «Big Wood», or, as we used to call it, «the

Boltych», in that same coach, maybe at the same time as he, and my childish cries could be heard on the hillside, and the hay smelled the same and the samovar was boiling...

In Kamenka, Piotr Ilyich also found something else that pleased his intellectual tastes. Of all the epochs of Russian history, Piotr Ilyich was most interested in Catherine's and particularly in the early 19th century. In the library at Kamenka he found all the writings that had occupied the minds of the intellectuals of the late 18th century, and Kamenka itself, and, among its inhabitants, my great-grandmother Alexandra Ivanovna and her eldest daughter Elisaveta, were living witnesses of the events of Alexander I's reign. They had actually seen and known Pushkin whom Piotr Ilyich loved so much. The friendship between Piotr Ilyich and the Davydoff family started in St. Petersburg, where he had lived for many years, through talking with aunt Lisa who, while her mother was in Siberia, was brought up in the house of Countess Tchernitcheva-Kruglikova were she met all the famous people of that time, Pushkin, Gogol and others. My great-grandmother Alexandra Ivanovna could tell Piotr Ilyich what life was like in Kamenka when Pushkin was there and when the Decembrists met.

If the Ukrainian folklore had little influence on Piotr Ilyich, Kamenka's past history and especially the shadow of Pushkin which hung over it exerted without question a powerful influence on him. It is not without reason that he composed in Kamenka the whole 1812 ouverture, and, when he finished Eugene Onegin, he played it from start to finish for the first time in front of the Davydoff family. Of course I was not there on that occasion but it is not difficult for me to imagine Piotr Ilyich sitting at the piano which stood in front of the window in the left-hand corner of the dining room of what we used to call «the Big House» in Kamenka. I can also see the audience sitting in Empire chairs and armchairs around the table. There is uncle Nicholas with his long cherrywood cigarette holder, there are aunt Elisaveta Vassilievna and aunt Alexandra Vassilievna with their mother, a stooped wizened old woman, all three in plain grey dresses with a cape, and there are uncle Lev and aunt Sasha.

At that time, as I have already said, neither the big house of Kamenka nor the colonnaded pavilion which Pushkin liked, existed any more, but the grotto on the right side of the park was still there. Piotr Ilyich loved to sit in it and it may have been there that the vision of Tatiana and Eugene came to him. In that grotto, aunt Elisaveta Vassilievna convinced him that he should not change the ending of Onegin as Modest Ilyich had suggested, and not force Tatiana to leave her husband for the love of Onegin...

If towards the end of his life Piotr Ilyich went more and more seldom to Kamenka it was because he could not find there any more what his tormented soul was searching for. The older members of the Davydoff family were aging. My great-grandmother outlived Piotr Ilyich but, although she kept a remarkable freshness of mind and memory until the end of her life, physically she was very diminished and it was not possible to have any long conservations with her any more. All the thoughts of her daughters, my aunts, were concentrated on the care of their «Mamenka» as they called her. At that time, we small boys were taken to our great-grandmother only once a day and only for half an hour after lunch. But the main reason why Piotr Ilyich stayed away from Kamenka was the illness of his sister Alexandra Ilyinishna which caused her intolerable pains that were only calmed by morphine or some other analgesic. I remember that, under the effect of these drugs, she seemed sometimes quite abnormal. Piotr Ilyich, with his extreme sensitivity, could not bear his sister's condition and, knowing he could not help her, he preferred not to see her.

However, there was another thing that temporarily attracted Piotr Ilyich to Kamenka. That was his love for his nephew, the son of his sister, Vladimir, better known under the nickname of Bob. This love was probably Piotr Ilyich's strongest bond. It started when Bob was still a child and it manifested itself at that time by the fact that, of all his sister's children, Bob was the one Piotr Ilyich spoiled the most. Later on, when the young boy grew up and became an adorable young man, intelligent and talented, Piotr Ilyich became attached to him with all his heart. We know that Piotr Ilyich dedicated several of his compositions to Bob, among them the most extraordinary of all his works, the 6th Symphony. In addition he passed on to Bob also that extraordinary refinement of aesthetic feeling that became his most beautiful characteristic.

When, in the late Eighties, Bob left to study in St. Petersburg and settled in Modest Ilyich's house, the last link that held Piotr Ilyich to Kamenka snapped and he found another place of retirement, Klin.

KATACHA TRUBETSKAIA

Her story by her great-grandson

Die you will, but the tales of your suffering
Will live on in loving hearts
And at midnight your grandchildren,
Sighing from the innermost of their soul,
Will keep on talking about you with their friends.
They will show them your unforgettable features
And to the memory of the great-grandmother
Who perished in the heart of nowhere
The brimming cups will be emptied.

N. A. Nekrassov «Russian Women»

In front of me two portraits. One, a miniature painted over 130 years ago in Paris. The other a daguerreotype taken 100 years ago in Irkutsk. The first one represents a very young girl with a tender and soft face, blue eyes, blond hair and regular features, the other an old lady seated in an armchair, rather buxom, whose face reflects the kindness of her soul. These two portraits are of the same woman. The first one is the young Countess Ekaterina Ivanovna Laval when she was only nineteen. The second one is Princess Ekaterina Ivanovna Trubetskaia a short time before her death in 1854.

These two portraits remind me of the distant years of my youth and I see another old lady sitting on a settee in the drawing-room of her estate, «Sably», in the Crimea and telling me the story of her mother's life in remote Siberia. She is the daughter of Ekaterina Ivanovna Trubetskaia, my grandmother

43

Elisaveta Sergeevna Davydova. She did not speak to me only of her mother's life in exile. She also told me about life in St. Petersburg, about her parents and her sisters, her ancestors and all the people she used to meet in her parents' home. But above all she loved to talk about what her mother had endured after the events of 1825 and how, after surmounting innumerable obstacles, she had followed her husband to his forced labor in Siberia and had never left him.

There are people whose names enter and remain in history not only because their destiny is unique but also because their origins are extraordinary and because their names evoke wonderful historical figures of the past. To this group of people belongs Princess Ekaterina Ivanovna Trubetskaia, or rather, as her parents and her close friends called her, Katacha.

Nekrassov, in his poem dedicated to Katacha and to Maria Nikolaevna Volkonskaia, called her «the Russian Woman», and indeed she was by her way of thinking which was typically Russian, though one could not in truth say that she was really Russian. She would have been considered an ordinary French woman if she had not proved throughout her life that she had a Russian soul. Her father was indeed a French immigrant, Jean Charles François Laval de la Loubrerie, a nobleman from Marseilles who had first served his king with the Hussars of Bercheny before being posted to the French Embassy in Constantinople. He left this post to join Conde's army in 1791 and, in 1795, he signed up as a captain in the Russian army from which he eventually resigned to go to St. Petersburg where he found a job as professor of French at the naval college while at the same time giving private French lessons to Russian families. Katacha inherited her Russian soul from her mother whose origins were truly extraordinary.

One day Peter the Great, finding himself by the Volga, wished to cross over to the other side. Three strong young locals ferried him across on their boat. Their looks and their working ability appealed to Peter who, when they reached the other bank, invited them to dinner at his table. During the meal he questioned them about who they were, how they lived and whether they were pleased with their life. They answered that they were peasants and old believers who made their living as ferrymen and did not complain about their mode of life. Two of them were brothers, Ivan and Iakov Tverdychev, and the third one was their brother-in-law Ivan Semenovich Miasnikov. From what they said, Peter gathered that they were brave, intelligent and resourceful and he asked them why they were content with a job which paid so little and had no future when at that very moment in the Ural it was so easy to become rich like Demidov who had discovered iron ore in that region. The ferrymen answered that they would be delighted to try their luck but that they did not even have the modest means that Demidov had had when he started his venture. Whereupon Peter gave them 500 roubles and by the time he died they owned already, not counting their capital, 8 factories and 76,000 serfs.

Ivan Tverdychev died childless. His brother's daughter who had married Gavril Ilyich Bibikov, died young, also childless. Thus the entire fortune of the ferrymen was inherited by the four daughters of Ivan Miasnikov—Irene Beketeva, Daria Pachkova, Agrafine Durassova and Ekaterina, the youngest daughter, who was not married.

One day Potemkin happened to be in Simbirsk with Catherine's secretary Grigori Vassilievich Kozitsky, for a «presentation of petitions» and stayed with the Miasnikovs. The guests were received by Ekaterina Ivanovna who was a typical Volgian girl, pretty and pleasantly plump. On an impulse Potemkin married her there and then to Kozitsky. The young married couple settled in St. Petersburg, where Ekaterina Ivanovna, in spite of her lack of education and her ignorance of any foreign language, managed to make for herself a decent place in the brilliant court of Catherine II thanks to her innate intelligence and to the sharpness of her mind. By marrying Kozitsky she had been admitted into official orthodoxy.

When Kozitsky died in 1775 Ekaterina Ivanovna found herself a young widow of 29 with two daughters, Alexandra and Anna. These children were given an education worthy of their rank. Although, according to contemporaries, the youngest girl Anna looked like a maid-servant, she was nevertheless the first one to marry. She married an ex-diplomat who had been posted in Dresden and in Turin, Prince Alexander Mikhailovich Beloselsky-Belozersky. He received an enormous dowry which greatly helped to straighten out his personal affairs. This dowry included, in addition to land and factories, ten million roubles and the Krestovsky island in St. Petersburg. Prince Beloselsky-Belozersky was a widower and had one daughter by his first marriage, the famous Princess Zenaida Alexandrovna Volkonskaia, wife of Prince Nikita Grigorievich Volkonsky, the brother of the Decembrist. After the Decembrist uprising she did not hide her disapproval of the measures taken by the reigning power against the conspirators and, with the permission of Nicholas I, emigrated to Rome where she became a catholic convert. She owned in Rome the famous Villa Volkonsky where she entertained Russian writers and artists like Gogol, Ivanov and many others.

Ekaterina Ivanovna Kozitskaia's elder daughter, Alexandra Grigorievna, took a long time before getting married. She was already 27 when she fell in love with a French immigrant, a nobleman from Marseilles, Ivan Stepanovich Laval. He also fell in love and it seemed that there could be no obstacle to their happiness but Ekaterina Ivanovna adamantly refused to agree to their marriage. A friend advised them to apply directly to the Tsar Paul I and ask him for his help, which they did. Paul asked Ekaterina Ivanovna to state the reasons why she would not agree to their marriage. She answered: «Not of our faith. We do not know where he comes from. He does not have a high rank.» The Emperor announced his decision: «He is a Christian. I know him. For a Kozitsky his rank is quite high enough.» Therefore «let them be married» and he added «let them be married within the next half hour.» Although Laval did not receive a dowry as important as that of Beloselsky-Belozersky, nevertheless it was a very decent one. Apart from twenty million roubles he received the famous factory of Archangelsk in the Urals, a large amount of land and part of the Aptekarsky Island in St. Petersburg with a splendid country house on the Neva.

After their marriage the newly-weds looked around for a house in St. Petersburg. They bought from A.N. Stroganov a plot of land on the English Quay near the Senate Square and built on it a house according to the plans of the architect Thomas de Tomon. This house became famous for its architecture and for the art treasures it contained, and also because it became the meeting place for famous people of that time such as Pushkin, Mitskievich, Griboedov, Lermontov, Kozlov, Mme de Stael and Joseph de Maistre. It was in this house that on May 16, 1818 Pushkin read his «Boris Godunov» to Griboedov and Mitskievich. It was in this house that, during a ball on February 16, 1840, because of Princess Chtcherbatova, Lermontov and the son of a French diplomat, Ernest Baranton, had an argument that ended in a duel. Pushkin in his «Bronze Horseman» writes about this house:

> On Peter's Square a house has risen
> With, on its elevated porch,
> Two guardian lions
> As if alive, with upraised paw.
> There sat, astride the marble beast,
> Arms crossed, head bare and deathly pale
> Eugene....

The treasures collected by the Lavals had a unique artistic value. The pictures included three Rembrandts and many works by French artists of the late 18th and early 19th centuries. One of the rooms had a mosaic floor dating back to Nero's time. The most marvelous elements in this collection were the Etruscan and Egyptian antiques. A great many of these art treasures are now in the Hermitage.

The Lavals lived in this house until their death, Ivan Stepanovich on April 20, 1846, his wife on December 19, 1850.

On March 29, 1814, the day Paris was captured by the allies, the Lavals were in London where at that time lived the future King of France Louis XVIII. Alexandra Grigorievna, hearing that the pretender was in financial difficulties, sent him, via Duke Blacas, 300,000 francs. The future King thanked her by giving her a miniature portrait of himself and in 1817 made her husband a Count.

The Lavals had six children, four girls and two boys. Their

son Paul, born in 1811, died that same year. The other son, Vladimir, born in 1806, committed suicide in 1825 after losing at cards. On the daughters' side, Zinaida, born in 1803, married twice: the first time Count Lebzeltern, Austrian Ambassador to the Imperial Court of Russia; then, after his death in 1854, an Italian poet, Joseph Campagna. Her daughter by her marriage to Lebzeltern married the Vicomte des Cars. One of their daughters, Countess Jeanne Cossé Brissac, had a daughter who married Prince de Robech, Count de Lévis Mirepoix. In the latter's castle «La Morosière» is buried Countess Zinaida Ivanovna Lebzeltern. Another daughter of the Lavals, Sophie, nicknamed Frison, who after her mother's death inherited the house on the English Quay, married Count Bork, Master of Ceremonies and Director of the Imperial Theatres. Alexandra Laval, who was brought up by her grandmother Kozitsky, married Count S.G.F. Korvin Kossakovsky, Senator, savant and publicist.

A unique fate awaited the eldest of the Laval daughters Ekaterina. She was born in 1800. Little is known about her childhood apart from the statement by her elder sister Zinaida that she was «fundamentally gay, honest, impetuous and acutely sensitive and was known for her great heart and her kindness.» At her father's insistence she was given an exceptionally good education. She spoke and wrote Russian, French, English, Italian and German. Joseph de Maistre in a letter to Alexandra Grigorievna Laval wrote: «Mettez moi, je vous prie, aux genoux de cette grave Catache, notre maîtresse à tous sur le participe passé».

After the Restoration, Countess Alexandra Grigorievna Laval spent a great deal of time in Paris. One winter she rented the Hotel Lobau and received there the Tout-Paris. In 1819, at Tatiana Borisovna Potemkina's home, Katacha met Tatiana's nephew Prince Serge Petrovich Trubetskoy. He was the son of Prince Piotr Sergeevitch Trubetskoy by his first marriage to Her Most Serene Princess Daria Alexandrovna Gruzinskaia. Prince Serge Trubetskoy was born on July 29, 1790 and when he first met Katacha he was already 30. He was a tall man, slim, with dark eyes and curly hair, very intelligent and cultured, whose features recalled his Georgian mother. This likeness may be seen on the miniature made in Paris as well as on the photograph taken in his old age, both of which I have in my possession.

Katacha and Trubetskoy fell in love and with the blessing of their parents were married a short time later. Their wedding took place on 16/28 May 1820 at the Russian church on the place Vendôme where at that time stood the Russian Embassy. After their marriage the young couple returned to St. Petersburg and settled in the Laval's house where Katacha's parents had arranged an apartment where they could live completely independently. Their happiness knew no bounds but it was to be short lived. Terrible events awaited them which, although they did not separate them, completely ruined their lives.

Prince Trubetskoy was brought up and educated at a time when the young elements of Russian nobility, the only cultured milieu of Russian society at that time, were under the influence of the ideas of the French revolution and of the Encyclopedists. These young men grew up during «the wonderful start of Alexander's days» and the long time they spent abroad, particularly in Paris, developed in them democratic ideas and liberal tendencies. Prince Trubetskoy was not only full of these ideas, he was also one of the first to try and bring them to reality. In 1816, on his return to St. Petersburg from abroad, he first became a member of the masonic lodge «the Three Virtues», then, in 1817, he founded with Alexander and Nikita Muraviev the first secret society which was known as «the Union for the Salvation of the True and Faithful Sons of the Nation», the statute of which was written by Pestel. In 1818 the society's name was changed to «Union of Welfare», the constitution of which was written by Alex and Michael Muraviev, P. Kolochyn and Prince S.P. Trubetskoy and was based on the Tugenbund constitution. In 1822 the Union of Welfare was dissolved and in its place was created in St. Petersburg the Northern Society in which Prince S.P. Trubetskoy occupied a prominent post.

The Trubetskoy's apartment in the Lavals' house where, not to mention eminent people of that time, the Emperor himself and his entire family came, was obviously the perfect foolproof meeting place for the plotters. In that house, in his wife's bathroom, Trubetskoy kept a hand printing press. In their apartment Katacha was introduced to Pestel, Ryleev, Prince Volkonsky and other friends of her husband. Nevertheless, Katacha never suspected what was going on in her home until one day, after overhearing an unwise conversation, she understood what her husband's intentions were. She tried to make him change his mind by showing him with force what was in store for him, and her efforts seemed to be not entirely in vain, or so it seemed to her, for the plotters assured her she had nothing to worry about as they had taken all necessary precautions.

On December 14, 1825 in the entrance hall of the Lavals' house, Pushin and Ryleev begged Trubetskoy, who had been named the day before head of the group, to go out on the Senate Square with the rebellious troops, but he, having lost faith in the success of the insurrection, did not listen to his comrades and hid with his wife in the home of the Austrian Ambassador Count Lebzeltern, his brother-in-law, where he was arrested.

With her husband's arrest ended forever the happy and carefree life of Katacha. Trubetskoy was questioned by Nicholas I himself who promised to spare his life and ordered that his wife be informed of this immediately in writing. Thus Katacha, whose major fear, that of losing her husband, had been dispelled, had only one thought from there on, to not be separated from him despite his exile. To achieve this she first had to convince her parents that she had to leave them, perhaps forever, and then get the Emperor Nicholas I to authorize her to follow her husband to Siberia. Katacha's mother did everything she could to prevent her from leaving but her father, once he understood that her decision was dictated by her sense of duty, accepted the idea and convinced his wife.

The problem of Nicholas I's authorization was a much more difficult one to solve. The Emperor wanted the Decembrists to be forgotten and whatever happened he did not want their fate to be glorified by the heroism of their wives. Katacha was the first wife of a Decembrist to have decided to follow her husband and it was up to her to open the way to others.

When the attempts made by her parents and by her influential friends failed to achieve any results, Katacha decided to take matters in her own hands and went to see the Empress. The young Empress received very kindly the wife of the State criminal. She understood Katacha as soon as she spoke but at first she advised her to change her mind. The two women cried as they embraced. Finally the Empress said to Katacha: «You are right to want to follow your husband, yes, you certainly are right. In your place I would not have hesitated to do the same thing. I promise you I will beg the Emperor to help you and your friends».

The Empress was true to her word. Nicholas received Katacha and at the end of their talk said to her: «Well, go then and tell the others they can go too... I will not forget you.»

In July 1826 Katacha left St. Petersburg and her parents' home forever. Princess Alina Volkonskaia wrote to her mother: «I have seen Katacha. She is leaving for Siberia as if she were going to a party». Katacha herself thought that «God would take away his blessing and his goodness from her if she were to leave her husband». Like all travels to Siberia at that time, hers was a difficult one. The difficulties and the hardships were aggravated by the fact that she would accept no rest and never stopped anywhere. Her father's secretary, the Frenchman Vaucher, who accompanied her though he spoke not a word of Russian, rode with her but his resistance gave out and he fell ill. At last Katacha reached Irkutsk where another trial awaited her. Although Nicholas I had allowed her to follow her husband, he had at the same time given secret orders to the governor of Irkutsk, Ivan Bogdanovich Tseidler, to try and discourage her by every possible means. For that purpose he should describe to Katacha in the most fearful terms the life that awaited her in Siberia and scare her by his descriptions of the rigors of her journey to the silver mines of Blagodatski which she would have to make on foot with the group of exiled men. After listening stoically to the governor's warnings, Katacha remained firm. The governor then asked her to sign a paper by which she would renounce, both for herself and for her future children, all the rights that were hers by birth. When she signed this paper without hesitation, the governor told her she could leave and that everything he had said to her was only to try and dissuade her from proceeding further.

Katacha joined her husband at the silver mines of Blagodatski where Volkonsky, Obolensky, Yakubovich, Davydoff, the Borissov brothers and Artamon Muraviev also worked. She arrived there with Princess Maria Nikolaevna Volkonskaia who had caught up with her at the Big Factory of Nertchinsk. There is no need to describe in detail the reuniting of these two wonderful women with their husbands. For the two of them, apart from being reunited with their loved ones, it was the victorious culmination of a hard fight against innumerable obstacles. If Katacha had had to overcome the will of Nicholas I, Princess M.N. Volkonskaia had had to break the resistance of her father and of her two brothers who did everything they could to prevent her from leaving. It is not without reason that Nekrassov associated their names in his poem «The Russian Women».

At the Blagodatski mines the Decembrists had to work under the most trying conditions for one year until the end of the construction of their new lodgings at the Petrovsk factory, which was being built under the supervision of General Leparsky. This governor had been chosen especially by Nicholas I to be the Decembrists' gaoler and he became their guardian angel. Nicholas I had a chivalrous side to his character that excluded all idea of vengeance once he had punished the rebels. That is why he put them in the care of a human and generous man. It is said that, before leaving for Siberia, General Leparsky was received by the Emperor and, after an interview that lasted over an hour, he appeared looking very excited and happy.

The life of the wives of the Decembrists in Siberia was not an easy one. Material conditions were very difficult at first and only improved very slowly. It is true that at the Petrovsk factory they did manage to buy and build small houses which were all situated on a street facing the prison that got to be known as «the Ladies street», but they lacked money because their families were only allowed to send them 250 roubles a year and a few parcels. A servant was out of the question and

52

they had to improve their husbands' nourishment at all costs as what they were given was quite insufficient for the hard labor they were subjected to. Katacha and Princess Maria Volkonskaia for a long time only ate bread and drank kvass without their husbands' knowledge. Later on, when this got to be known in St. Petersburg, they were allowed to receive 3000 roubles a year and entire convoys of effects and provisions.

In spite of the rigors of her life, Katacha had many children. On February 5, 1830 a girl, Sashinka, who later married N.R. Rebinder. Then another girl, Lisanka, the future wife of the son of the Decembrist V.L. Davydoff, Piotr, my grandfather. On December 10 1835 a son, Nikita, who died in 1840. Then, on May 6 1837, another girl, Zinaida, who married N.D. Sverbeev and who died during the time of the bolsheviks in Orel on June 24 1924. Her son, Serge Nikolaevich Sverbeev, my godfather, was the last Ambassador of the Imperial Court of Russia to Berlin. A second son, Vladimir, died in Irkutsk in 1839. Much later, in 1843, Katacha gave birth to a third son Ivan who died on his return to Russia in 1874. The title of Prince was restored to him by an addendum of the Senate. He had married Princess V.S. Obolenskaia who, after his death, married Count Golenichev-Kutuzov. Katacha's last child was a girl, Sophie, who was born on June 15 1844.

S.P. Trubetskoy's sentence to hard labor was reduced considerably and in 1839 he was assigned to Oek near Irkutsk and later allowed to live in Irkutsk itself. Here the life of the Decembrists became almost normal especially after the nomination of governor Muraviev.

All that Katacha felt, suffered and endured she considered to be a test imposed by God and she thanked him for it. She wrote to her sister Lebzeltern «The thought of God and the thought of death are two powerful guardians of goodness». She never complained, neither when the catastrophe occurred nor later during the most painful trials she had to endure in exile, and she never regretted having left of her own free will the happy life she had led in her parents' home. She writes about this at the end of her life: «One of the major reasons of my gratitude to God is that He arranged things in such a way that all that had to do with my family and with the early affections of my childhood do not awaken in me any thoughts and feelings other than love and peace». About her life in exile she writes to Narichkina: «Our private life is always the same—the children's studies, our worries about them—those are our principal preoccupations». Not a word about the great work that the Decembrists were accomplishing and of which the grandson of the Decembrist Prince S.M. Volkonsky speaks: «They became nests of culture, the focus of divine light. In each family several children from the neighborhood lived and were educated». In their early childhood they were under the surveillance of and educated by the wives of the Decembrists. Later the husbands took over their education. Through family cultural life they acceded to science and art, and were formed and matured intellectually and morally.

Katacha did not have the good fortune to live until the happy day of «the pardon». She was unwell the last year of her life and died peacefully on December 14, 1854 in the arms of her husband and of her daughter Zinaida, the only daughter who had not left her birth place.

In July 1904, while serving with the first battalion of the infantry regiment of Tchembarsk, I took advantage of a prolonged halt in Irkutsk to go and kneel before my great-grandmother's grave. In the main courtyard of the Voznesiensky monastery, facing the entrance, I found her grave before which, for exactly fifty years, not one of this great Russian lady's descendants had knelt. One of the officers from my company who was interested in the history of the Decembrists and who owned a camera, accompanied me on this pilgrimage. He took a picture of me standing in front of the ironwork that surrounds the grave. I sent two of these pictures to my grandmother Elisaveta Sergeevna Davydova in her Crimean estate of Sably. Later, she told me she had indeed received them but when, after her death, I looked for them among the mass of photos and documents that had been plundered by the bolsheviks in the house of Sably, I could not find them...

SABLY

Countess Alexandra Grigorievna Laval, who had suffered a stroke a few days before, died in St. Petersburg on December 19, 1850. Muraviev, governor of Irkutsk, who happened to be in St. Petersburg at that time, heard that she was dying, went to see her and persuaded her to make a will which would assure the future of Katacha and of her children. Alexandra Grigorievna followed his advice and made a will whereby she left her entire fortune to her daughters. The estate in the province of Penza, which covered 15,355 dessiatines and included 2,978 souls, was given to Katacha along with 4,000 dessiatines of land in the Crimea. The Penza estate had been inherited from Ekaterina Ivanovna Kozitskaia, while the Crimean one, Sably, had been bought by Countess A.G. Laval, or, to be more precise, by her manager on February 29, 1828 at an auction sale in St. Petersburg under very special circumstances. Countess A.G. Laval's doctor had advised her to take sea-baths in the Crimea and as at that time there was no decent hotel in that part of Russia and it was impossible to rent a comfortable house, the Countess ordered her manager to buy an estate with its outbuildings. Without leaving St. Petersburg, the manager bought Sably without even knowing exactly where this property was located. When the Countess arrived in the newly acquired estate, she discovered that, if by a very clear day one could see the sea, it was in fact 40 versts distant as the crow flies. However, as it stood in a magnificent region, was large and yielded good returns, the Countess decided to keep it. When Katacha's second daughter married my grandfather

P.V. Davydoff, Katacha gave it to her as a wedding present and the young couple, after a brief stay in Kamenka, settled down in Sably.

My grandfather Piotr Vassilievich Davydoff had a great physical resemblance to his brother Nicholas, the only difference being that he had a definite tendency to be overweight. Their characters, on the other hand, were totally different. Much less intelligent than his brother and less inclined to the study of serious subjects, he had inherited from his father his kind heart and his lack of will power. I have already said how in his youth he had not been innocent of certain pranks.

My grandmother Elisaveta Sergeevna was the opposite of her mother. She had inherited her looks from her Georgian grandmother. Tall, with black hair, bright eyes and regular features, she had been very beautiful in her youth. Her character was also quite different from that or her mother, the tender and kind Katacha. Temperamental, ambitious, wilful and quick tempered, she was not known for her kindness and was not easy to live with. Intelligent and not devoid of malice she reached her objective by intrigue when she could not succeed otherwise. She was educated at the University of Irkutsk and had not been a particularly bright student. It is easy to understand why she took complete possession of her weak husband and made him do everything she wanted. One day, my mother said to my grandfather that she could not stand the insolent attitude of her mother-in-law towards her, and he answered: «Bear with it, Olia, I have done so for so many years!»

My grandparents had three children: my father Vassili Petrovitch, born in 1852, and two daughters, Zinaida, married to Dubliansky, and Ekaterina, married to Prince Dolgoruky. Because of her character, my grandmother was unable to give her children an education in any way normal. In their childhood they were afraid of her and did not love her and when they reached adulthood the daughters, who had made poor marriages, lied regularly to their parents and tried by every conceivable means to get them to give them more money. As for my father, my grandmother loved him passionately but with an egotistical maternal love in which entered more vanity than tenderness. She destroyed in him the few vestiges of will power that he had. Nevertheless my grandparents, after an incident that I will relate later, gave my father the estate of Yurchikha in full ownership and a life interest in the estate of Sably on condition that they be allowed to live there the rest of their lives.

My grandparents lived in Sably one may say their whole life. They settled there in 1852 and it was only during the Crimean war, when their house was turned into a military hospital, that they left to live for two years in Kamenka. When they grew old, they used to spend the winter months in Simferopol, closer to doctors and to local society. They both died in that city, my grandfather in 1912, a few days after they had celebrated their diamond wedding anniversary, and grandmother in February 1918 when the bolsheviks were spreading terror and celebrating their capture of the town.

Thus my grandparents spent 60 years of their life in Sably. They led a quiet and basically happy life. They were very wealthy and never knew poverty, lacked nothing and lived in a dignified manner, ignoring all luxury. Misfortunes befell them, relatives died, contemporaries also, but in a certain way this affected them little. Masses and funeral services were celebrated, then everything returned to normal. They had few worries except when their daughters asked for more money, whereupon a council of neighboring friends would convene and almost always the decision was reached to refuse it to them. In summer the daughters and their children would arrive and for a while the house would spring to life. When they were in town their friends often visited them but they rarely came to Sably for the simple reason that they were not invited there, I don't know why.

My grandfather never took part in any local life. Although he had lived such a long time in Sably, he was never elected to the zemstvo, nor was he chosen as a representative of the noble families, though his means and the respect he enjoyed gave him every right to be. I think my grandmother was opposed to his leading an active public life for fear that she might then lose her authority over him. Grandfather did not even take part in the elections of the nobility. And yet they both took a great interest in certain elections, especially grandmother who, with a great deal of daring, discussed the chances of the various candidates, never failing to express her opinion of each, which was usually far from flattering.

At the start of their life in the Crimea, when they were young, my grandparents had had a lot of friends. These were highly placed civil servants from St. Petersburg who belonged to their milieu, or locals, neighboring landowners and more or less influential families, but, with time, the ranks of these friends became thinner and the circle of their friends decreased. Grandmother was a great snob. She did not easily make friends nor receive in her home. Furthermore, contrary to what often happens to old people, as grandmother grew older she did not become gentler and kinder, and this not only did not attract new friends but even decreased the number of visits of her grandchildren.

It seems to me that I must have been 12 or 13 when I first visited Sably with my brother Piotr. The estate, the park and the surrounding landscape produced on me an enchanting effect and the tenderness and kindness of my grandfather touched me. Unfortunately everything was spoilt by I don't know what disturbing feeling which was provoked in me by my grandmother's lack of sincerity. However, everything around me in the Crimea was so new to me, the impressions were so wonderful, that this annoyance was short-lived. First of all naturally we visited the South coast and Sebastopol and were enchanted by it. Then we were fascinated by the exotic appearance of the inhabitants of the Crimea. In the Crimea at that time one could count 35 different races among which first place was held by the Tatars. Our old folk would tell us many interesting and amusing things about their customs in particular the «Murzahs», the noble Tatars. But the main theme of my grandparents' tales was Siberia and the life led by their parents. Along with the older children of the Decembrists, they held very conservative views but the memory of their parents was sacred. Grandmother spoke especially of her mother, of her kindness and of her faith, of her love for her children and how she worried about them. She remembered the Institute of Irkutsk and her headmistress

Kusmina who had earlier been her teacher. Her father, her friends and their children were also very often the subject of their conversations. She showed us drawings and paintings of life in Siberia as well as daguerreotypes and miniatures...

ST. BARTHOLOMEW

One day, shortly after my arrival in New York, I read in the New York Times that the Wildenstein Gallery had bought some old paintings from the Golman collection. According to the newspaper, among these paintings was Rembrandt's St. Bartholomew which in olden times had belonged to the Princes Trubetskoy. This article awoke so many memories in me that I immediately called Wildenstein and asked him if he would allow me to take a look at the painting he had just bought. After I had given him my name he very kindly invited me to go and see him the following week when the St. Bartholomew would have been restored and placed in the setting it deserved.

On the appointed day, when I arrived Wildenstein took me to a special room on the second floor where, on one of the walls, hung the painting I had not seen for such a long time. But who would have recognized it? Instead of a painting darkened by the passage of time of a middle-aged man with dark hair and a morose expression, I saw a luminous painting flooded by the light of ingeniously set electric lamps. Rembrandt's famous «lights and shadows» stood out clearly against the background and only the face with its unique expression looked at me as it used to do. I stood silently for a long time in front of the painting. Wildenstein understood and was also silent. Finally I started telling him the story that I thought would interest him.

It was a long time ago, I began, over fifty years, when as a small boy I used to go every year to the Crimea to visit my Davydoff grandparents in their Sably estate. In this unpretentious house the walls of the drawing-room and of my grandfather's study were covered with paintings which, to my inexperienced young eyes, appeared old and uninteresting. It was only later that I started taking an interest in them. When I was about 14 I questioned my grandfather about them. It turned out that they had all been inherited by my grandmother from her mother Princess Ekaterina Ivanovna Trubetskaia, the wife of the famous Decembrist. Before that they had been part of the collection of her grandfather Count Laval whose house in St. Petersburg on the English Quay had been, at the start of the 19th century, a real museum. When I asked my grandfather who had painted the portrait that hung behind his desk in his study, he answered it was by Rembrandt and was one of the paintings that had belonged to Count Laval, the name of which had been forgotten. Seeing that I was curious about her paintings my grandmother showed me the list of them and their estimated value at the time when her grandfather's collection was divided among his heirs. Among these paintings was a nameless Rembrandt valued at 1000 roubles. Grandmother told me that Count Laval, during his frequent visits to Paris, used to buy paintings and one day had bought three Rembrandts for 1500 roubles.

The years went by, grandmother grew older and she decided to divide her paintings among her grandchildren while she was still living, with the agreement that they would remain with her until her death. The Rembrandt, which was the most valuable of all the paintings, was given to my elder brother V.V. Davydoff. It remained hanging on the same wall, often even when the owners were away and there was no one to watch over it.

It was during those years that there started in different countries of Europe thefts of paintings from private collections and from state galleries. I was already of adult age and as I lived in St. Petersburg I used to see a lot of people connected with the Hermitage. I also read foreign art reviews. Among my friends a rumor spread, very soon confirmed by the art reviews, that the specialists on Rembrandt had not been able to find all his paintings and that one of them, entitled

62

St. Bartholomew or the Assassin, was missing. The only thing that was known about its whereabouts was that it was somewhere in Russia, but no one knew exactly where. I got the idea that this Rembrandt was the one that hung in Sably. The increase in the number of thefts of paintings and the interest raised by the lost Rembrandt incited me to remain on my guard and an unexpected incident confirmed my fears.

One day, I don't remember in what year, my grandparents were having lunch in Sably. With them at the table was a guest, the old Senator A.D. Sverbeev. They were just finishing their meal when a carriage with four unknown men entered the courtyard. The butler went to receive the new arrivals and quickly returned to say that a Professor Schwartz from Munich wished to see Mrs. Davydoff. As grandmother did not speak German and furthermore did not like to meet strangers, she asked A.D. Sverbeev to see them and ask them what they wanted. Professor Schwartz turned out to be a well-known specialist on Rembrandt and he immediately came to the point and stated that after a long research he had been able to establish that the lost Rembrandt was in Sably. At his request A.D. Sverbeev showed him the picture and even allowed him to take it down from the wall and examine it more closely. Before he had even finished examining it, Professor Schwartz announced that this painting was not by Rembrandt, the proof being the absence of signature. However, he added, I am nevertheless prepared to buy it from you for 15,000 roubles.

A.D. Sverbeev answered that nobody had asked him to come from so far to examine the painting and that his opinion was of no interest at all to them as Mrs. Davydoff had irrefutable proof on that matter. «Furthermore» he said, «this is not an antique dealer's shop and Mrs. Davydoff does not sell her paintings».

Professor Schwartz, who had come specifically to buy at a ridiculously low price from provincial Russians who knew nothing about the matter this extremely rare painting, realized that he was losing this excellent deal, lost his self-control and committed an unpardonable mistake. He suggested to the old and dignified Senator, who was quite well off, that he receive a commission of 1000 roubles for his help in the sale of the painting. The result of this insolent suggestion was immediate. A.D. Sverbeev called the butler and ordered him to accompany the undesirable guests to the door.

However, this incident had much greater consequences for grandmother and for us, her grandchildren. The location of the Rembrandt had been discovered and the danger of keeping it with other valuable paintings in a country estate became obvious. Grandmother asked us to take our paintings immediately, which we did with great pleasure. But whereas my second brother and myself refused to part with ours, my elder brother, who was not interested in old paintings and needed money for the expansion of his agricultural companies, decided to sell the Rembrandt. He went to Berlin where, on my advice, he saw my friends the bankers Mendelssohn and asked them whom he should see to sell his painting. The Mendelssohns referred him to the English firm Agnew. They even offered to arrange an interview with a member of this firm at their bank as one of the Agnew partners happened to be in Berlin. It would be easy to bring the painting there without any risk. This was done and after Agnew had examined the painting he said to my brother that it was in all likelihood by Rembrandt but that, because of the absence of a signature, it would be better to show it to an expert like Professor Bode, curator of the Kaiser Friedrich Wilhelm museum. The latter was of the opinion that the lower part of the picture had been painted over and that to determine its authenticity it had to be restored, which meant to say that the whole non-Rembrandt layer of paint had to be removed. In view of the risks involved in this work he asked a very high price for it, 8000 marks. Agnew suggested to my brother that they share the expense and that, if the operation was successful and the signature should appear, he pay him 500,000 marks for the picture. If my brother did not agree to this offer he, Agnew, was prepared to take the whole risk upon himself and pay for the restoring, in which case he would pay my brother 300,000 marks right away. Having bargained for a further 50,000 marks my brother accepted this second offer.

A few months later I read in the review «Die Kunst» that the restoration had been a complete success, that on the left

Uncle Kolia's Green House in Kamenka
Now A.S. Pushkin & P.I. Tchaikovsky Museum

The river Tiasmin

The Water-mill
KAMENKA

The Grotto

I

Ekaterina Nikolaevna SAMOILOVA
1755 — 1825

Piotr Lvovitch DAVYDOFF
1777 — 1842

II

Denis Vassilievich DAVYDOFF
Colonel of the Russian Aghtir Hussars
« The Black Captain »
1784 — 1839
(painted by A. Orlowski)

The grave of
Denis DAVYDOFF
Novo-Dyevitchi
Convent — Moscow

III

Vassili Lvovich DAVYDOFF
Decembrist
1792 — 1855
(ca 1820)

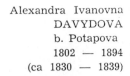

Alexandra Ivanovna
DAVYDOVA
b. Potapova
1802 — 1894
(ca 1830 — 1839)

IV

Vassili Lvovich DAVYDOFF
(ca 1853)

Alexandra Ivanovna DAVYDOVA
(ca 1860)

Alexandra Ivanovna
DAVYDOVA
in Kamenka
(ca 1890)

The Davydoff's home in Krasnoyarsk

The grave of A.I. Davydova
by the roadside
Kamenka

The grave of V.L. Davydoff
Krasnoyarsk

Piotr Vassilievich DAVYDOFF
The author's grandfather
1825 — 1912

Nikolai Vassilievich DAVYDOFF
The author's uncle
1826 — 1916

The three TRUBETSKOY sisters
Elisaveta, Alexandra, Zinaida

Lev Vassilievich DAVYDOFF
& Alexandra Ilyinishna
b. Tchaikovskaia

KAMENKA
The Monument to the Decembrists
On the left : V.L. Davydoff

KAMENKA
Early 19th century

A.S. PUSHKIN & Decembrists in Kamenka

Aunt Sacha and Aunt Lisa
going to church on Xmas eve
(water-color by M.A. Davydova)

Christmas eve in Kamenka — 1905
(water-color by M.A. Davydova)

Picnic in the Big Wood
(water-color by M.A. Davydova)

The Davydoffs leaving for Nice
January 1910
(water-color by M.A. Davydova)

Uncle Kolia's daily walk
in the garden of the Green House
Kamenka — 1914
(water-color by M.A. Davydova)

Uncle Kolia and relatives
1906
(water-color by M.A. Davydova)

side of the picture had appeared the whole signature «Rembrandt van Rijn 1657» and that the man who had been shown holding a book turned out, after the superficial layer of paint had been removed, to be holding in fact a knife. It was «St. Bartholomew» or, as he was called because of the knife in his hand, «the Assassin», the painting that had been sought for so long. It was also mentioned that Agnew had sold the painting in America to Golman for 700,000 marks.

Wildenstein listened attentively to my tale and it was only when I spoke of the restoration that his face expressed surprise. Obviously he knew nothing about it. When I had finished he opened a fat book at a marked page and showed me the list of owners of the Rembrandt before Mr. Golman. I read: Princess Laval, Princess Trubetskoy, Prince Davydoff.

«All this is quite correct», I told him, «except that Countess Laval was not a Princess and we Davydoffs were never Princes». We both laughed and he showed me to the door.

MOSCOW

Moscow...How that name can start
A tumult in the Russian heart!

A.S. Pushkin - «Eugene Onegin»

I was born on September 29, 1881 (old style) in Tambov where
my father was then a civil servant working for the Governor.
I remember nothing about Tambov because in 1884 my mother
moved to Moscow with her three sons and settled there. My
father went to live in the Tchigirin district of the province of
Kiev.

My parents did not reside long in Tambov—from 1879
to 1884. Before then they had lived in St. Petersburg where my
father was an officer in a battalion of the Cavalry. He left
St. Petersburg and his regiment because of a whim of his
mother, my grandmother Elisaveta Sergeevna Davydova, who,
as I have said, lived with my grandfather Piotr Vassilievich
Davydoff in her estate of Sably in the Crimea. My grandmother,
who had a despotic and temperamental character, loved my
father and was very proud of his career in the first regiment
of the Russian Imperial Guard, but she could not accept his
marriage to my mother. As she could not object to my mother's
origins—she was born the Most Serene Princess Olga Lieven—
she criticized her for not having any dowry. The truth is that
she was afraid that her son, once he was married, would fall

under his wife's influence and would no longer be submissive to her own will.

Having settled the debts, in truth very small, of my aunt's husband, a person of no interest whatever, my grandmother used this as a pretext to write and tell my father that she could no longer afford to pay his expenses in St. Petersburg and ordered that he and his family go and live with her in the country. If he should disobey she threatened to stop all financial help. My parents were forced to accept and my mother, a young woman full of «joie de vivre», found herself with her husband and two small children, my elder brothers, under the same roof as her mother-in-law, whom she hated. As might be expected, the effects of such a situation made themselves felt very rapidly. The young couple's life became intolerable. My father, who had a weak character, was unable to adopt the right attitude between his mother and his wife, and my mother, who had inherited the Lieven pride, would not give in to her mother-in-law. The inevitable occurred. Very shortly and after many disputes, the breaking point was reached and my parents left Sably without a penny, for my grandmother stopped all financial aid. My father had to find a job, which he did at 30 roubles a month as a civil servant in the Section of Special Affairs of the Tambov governorship.

Needless to say life with this minimal income and two children was very hard, even in those times, and it was then, at quite the wrong moment, that I made my entry into the world... In spite of their straitened circumstances and of the privations, my mother's pride not only prevented her from making it up with her mother-in-law or from asking her own family for help, it also made her stop her husband from doing so. It is then that a miracle occurred.

One night, after a very fervent evening prayer—and my mother was deeply religious—exhausted by her day's work, she dropped off to sleep and had a strange dream. In this dream she saw St. Cyril and St. Methodius who told her that her prayer had been heard, that she should buy an icon that represented them and give a mass for them in her home. After that, so they said, everything would turn out all right. The following morning my mother did everything she had been told to do and the help that been promised by the saints came very quickly and in a very unexpected manner. My father received a letter from his aunt, Zinaida Sergeevna Sverbeeva, my grandmother's sister, informing him that having learnt in what straitened circumstances he found himself, she had expressed her regrets to her sister that she was unable to provide for her son's needs, adding that the only possible explanation was my grandmother's lack of financial means, and that therefore she, Zinaida, had decided to give my father 3,000 roubles a year. Sweet aunt Zina knew her sister very well and her extreme vanity. The reaction to aunt Zina's intercession occurred as predicted. My father immediately received from the domain of Kamenka the stewardship of Yurchikha which included 1,150 dessiatines [1] of arable land and 1,750 dessiatines of a wonderful oak forest.

It seemed as if my parent's practical problems had been solved and that their life would now take a turn for the better, but unfortunately this change in their life came too late. Their marriage had already been ruined. My father had reacted badly to his separation from his regiment and from his circle of friends in St. Petersburg. Being of a passionate and weak nature, he was unable to stand up to this great change and found other interests to occupy his life. He tried to busy himself and calm his spirits by plunging into a life of dissipation, and the disagreements that arose between him and my mother ended in their separation. My father left to manage his estate in the province of Kiev while my mother and we three children left for Moscow to stay with my mother's elder sister who was a spinster.

It is difficult to say what would have happened if my grandmother had not so brutally changed the course of our family life. One can't be certain that it would have taken a different turn but one can certainly say that, as my father would have continued to serve in his regiment and to frequent with my mother the society of St. Petersburg that was very close to them, and as furthermore he would have been kept under control by the discipline of his regiment and of his

---

1. 1 dessiatine = 1.1 hectares = 2.7 acres.

comrades, he would not have destroyed his family life as he did and he would have made a career, if not exceptional, at least a normal one as a Guard officer and my mother would not have left her circle of friends. As far as we three sons are concerned, our destiny would certainly have been completely different. We would have grown up and been brought up in the atmosphere of St. Petersburg, so different from that of Moscow, and our friends would have been the sons of those families among which lived my father and my mother. My brothers, enrolled at an early age by order of Emperor Alexander II in the Corps of Pages, would in all probability have served in the regiment of the Guard, and I would have entered one of the ministries as a civil servant. I think that this would have probably been a better thing for my brothers, but as far as I am concerned I do not regret that my life took a different turn. What it lost in ease it gained in interest and diversity.

*

In Moscow, if you take the Pokrovka you will arrive at the Zemliano Val. There, if you cross the bridge that passes over the railway junction of the lines to Nikolaevsk and Kursk, then, when you reach the church of Nikita the Martyr, turn right into a small street the name of which escapes me, you will find yourself in that part of Moscow known as «the Field of Peas». I have never known the historical origin of this name. In all probability, in the old times of Peter the Great, the foreigners who lived in this district cultivated peas. The history of this suburb of Moscow is shown by the names of the streets and of its landmarks. After taking the Street of Resurrection that starts at the church of the same name at the end of the Street of Peas, you reach the German and Lefortov streets, then, after crossing the bridge over the Yauza, you reach the Collegiate Chamber of Val, the Annenghoff wood and the Vladimir barrier. The Lefortov and German streets are well known for their role in Peter the Great's youth. In that part of town lived foreigners who, at that time, were called «Germans» and were Peter's first contact with the West, its culture and its civilization. The Yauza bridge is mentioned by Tolstoy in «War and Peace» when he describes the meeting between Rostopchine and Kutuzov during the retreat of the Russian army when it passed through Moscow. I do not remember the origin of the name given to the Collegiate Chamber of Val, I only know that it used to be a very old Muscovite fortress. The Vladimir barrier and the road of the same name that starts there, used to be well-known to the inhabitants of Moscow because the convicts who were sent to Siberia on foot used to pass there. In a popular song that describes the fate that awaited the convicts and the murderers, the words go «You will pass through Vladimir...».

The river Yauza and its small affluent the Tchetchora flow through the Field of Peas. Once upon a time Peter's boots strode over their green and gravelly banks and their waters were clear and limpid. During my time all the waste and impurities of the factories on its banks already polluted the Yauza. Its waters reflected every color of the rainbow and spread nauseating smells. The small river Tchetchora that flowed under the second Moscow Gymnasium and alongside the park of the Elisabeth Institute for Young Girls acted as a closed canal in which was dumped the rubbish from the two taverns and the factory that stood between the schools.

The Field of Peas covered a vast area but it had very few inhabitants. On each side of the streets, amid parks and gardens, sometimes even kitchen gardens, rose small two-story wooden houses. Factories and manufacturing houses were only found on a few of these streets. The three schools and their large parks took up a large amount of space. They were the Mejevo Institute, the kindergartens of the Nikolaevsky Institute for small girls and the Elisabeth Institute for young girls. Because of the extensiveness and small number of inhabitants of Moscow at that time, suburbs like the Field of Peas were quite provincial in character. On the cobbled roads, the pavements of which were dotted with small stone posts, rolled noisy coaches and sometimes also long convoys carrying goods from the neighboring railway stations from which, in the evening, when the noise of the town subsided, sounded the whistle of trains. Policemen, whom a lot of people still called, according to an old custom, «gate-keepers», stood day

71

and night at the crossroads, and, under the front porch of each house, at night, dozed porters who in winter were dressed in heavy lamb coats.

Although the Field of Peas was a quiet and safe place, one could occasionally hear at night calls for help from passers-by who were being attacked by robbers. These cries would wake us up and make our young hearts beat faster.

In winter, when it snowed and the noise of the cab-wheels was muffled, the streets were plunged into a silence that surprised our ears, accustomed to the summer noises. Because of the snow that had fallen the rooms were light and it was pleasant to hear the crunching of the snow under the boots of the pedestrians and the crackling of the logs in the Dutch stoves. What a joy it was for us boys to ride on a sleigh drawn by a lively trotter on the rolled down snow-covered road. We seemed to fly through the air and how proud we were when we overtook another «solitary» in which sat a fat merchant. When during our outings we walked down German Street, lined with shops and stores, how pleasant was the smell, in warm weather, when the door of the grocery shop with its squeaky pulley would open to let through a client. The most colorful houses were the taverns which were mostly in isolated small wooden houses with green signs on which were written in gold letters amusing slogans such as «Don't linger», «One for the Road» etc. Through their frosted windows one could see tradesmen seated at tables drinking innumerable cups of tea while munching lumps of sugar that they held between their fingers, or cabmen and coachmen washing down their fried eggs and sausages with the contents of «a small flask». Sometimes the door would be flung open with a loud bang and there would appear, all dressed in white with a raspberry-colored belt behind which was tucked an oilcloth-bound note book, waiters throwing out a workman or a foreman who had drunk too much. Often one heard sounds of quarrels coming from the taverns and awful swear words. A policeman and sometimes the police inspector himself would arrive and the whole group of drunken «guests» would leave under police escort for the nearest police station where they were kept until they sobered up, when they were released without further punishment. It was only when a particularly quarrelsome drunk refused to obey the orders of the agent of the law and resisted that the policemen would take measures to convince him «in a fatherly way», but the whole affair would end there.

In the Field of Peas lived mainly lower middle-class people, workmen, tradesmen, lower civil servants, craftsmen, grocers and schoolteachers who taught in the local schools. Many churchmen also resided there because, as everyone knows, Moscow in those times was overcrowded with churches of which there were, as the saying went, «forty times forty». All these people lived off their work and rarely went «into town», as one then said, and «the thunder of the orators and the sound of the chatter» only rarely reached them. Life went by quietly and peacefully and only events like marriages or funerals attracted crowds of curious neighbors. The ones that attracted the most people were the military funerals that were attended by local troops with their regimental band. The most interesting were the funerals of generals because for them all three army corps attended—the infantry, the cavalry and the artillery. Everyone's attention was focused on the deceased's decorations and on the most important members of the general staff. At weddings the crowd would talk not so much of the beauty of the bride as of the size of her dowry and what it consisted of. It was said of the bridegroom that he was a sensible man who surely would not beat his wife.

Winter in Moscow was pleasant but spring had no reason to be envious of it. It is true that it often arrived late and kept us waiting a long time. It is also true that its fight with the winter was not an easy one and often it did not end before the latter had succeeded in halting its triumphal entry for a short time. However, once its victory was complete, with what beauty and what force it installed itself. For us boys it had its own special charm as it meant that the school year would soon be over and the holidays start and we would shortly be off to the country. Already on March 9, when the bakeries started to sell the special twisted loaves of bread shaped like birds' heads called «skylarks», we would start to look out impatiently for spring. At first it came slowly. Outside there was still the «sleigh lane» that deteriorated a little more each day. It still froze at night but in the daytime the air was already milder. We yearned so much to remove as fast as possible our winter «disguise» and inaugurate the lighter spring one. At last armies of janitors would appear on the streets armed with picks and shovels and with horse-drawn sleighs, and the snow would start to be removed. This work, which used to be called «Vlassov's spring» from the name of the famous Moscow police commissioner, had to be finished in three days. The streets were freed of their winter coat and, oh joy!, in the street passed the first horse-drawn carriage. How many glances through the double windows, how many discussions to decide whether to harness the sleigh or the carriage...

RAZUMOVSKY AND THE LIEVEN FAMILY

At the end of the Street of Peas, not far from a square close to the church of the Ascension, stood, at the time of which I write, submerged in the surrounding gardens, the old palace of Elisabeth's magnate, Count Razumovsky. I only lived in this palace a very short time and I only remember its exterior. I recall that it had a facade of red brick and a large courtyard giving onto the street and, at the far end, a perron of honor. I remember the terrace giving onto the park, all covered with flowers. I remember the large park that extended right to the river Yauza, with deep depressions that in olden times had been ponds. Of the interior of the palace I only recall the drawing room of our apartment and the church—the very same one where Natasha Rostova had knelt and listened to the prayer for the victory of the Russian army and had experienced patriotic sentiments for the first time.

It was to this palace that my mother brought us, me and my two brothers, from Tambov in 1884. In those times it had been turned into the kindergarten section of the Nikolaevsky Institute of Moscow, of which my aunt, the Most Serene Princess Elena Alexandrovna Lieven, was the head. With my arrival in Moscow started the first phase of my life which was spent entirely in the ambiance of the Lieven family. I must therefore make a parenthesis and describe this family.

The Lieven family starts with the dean of the Kaupo tribe which had adopted the Christian faith in 1186. This dean was made a noble by Pope Celestine III at Avignon in 1202. The first person to take the name Lieven was Nicholas Rheingold

Lieven who, in 1653, was Governor of Ezelsky and who, with his brother Berendson-Ottonom, was elevated to the rank of Baron. His brother's son was a friend of Charles XII, the King of Sweden, and accompanied him on his military campaigns. Rheingold Lieven's descendant, Yogan-Christophore whose Russian name was Ivan Romanoff, was, in Catherine's time, Governor of Arkhangelsk. It was under this Empress that the intimate friendship of the Lieven family with the house of Romanoff started, a friendship that lasted until the end of its reign.

In 1783, Empress Catherine II wanted to find a governess for her two grand-daughters, the daughters of Grand Duke Paul Petrovich, and a tutor for her two youngest grandsons, Constantine and Nicholas. At the recommendation of Braun, Governor of Riga, the post of governess was offered to Baroness Charlotte Karlovna Lieven, née von Gaugreben, whose husband, Major-General Baron Otto Heinrich Lieven had died in 1781. Baroness Ch. K. Lieven was not well-off and lived in Mitau where she brought up her sons. Ernest Daudet in his book on the life of Princess Daria Christophorovna Lieven («the Life of an Ambassadress») says that when Braun went to see her to hand her the Empress's request he found her in a state of great penury and her children ran around barefoot.

Baroness Charlotte Karlovna Lieven was an intelligent and energetic woman. Her moral qualities and her honest character rapidly enabled her to occupy a place apart in the family of Paul Petrovich who held her in high regard. She was the person closest to Empress Maria Feodorovna whose children considered her, until the end of her life, a member of the family. In 1799 she was named «Lady of the State» and decorated with the Order of Catherine of the First Degree. On February 22, 1799 she was given the hereditary title of Countess. On the day of Emperor Alexander I's coronation she received a bracelet with the portrait of the Imperial couple, and in 1824 a gold chain with the portrait of Alexander I. Finally, on the day of the coronation of Emperor Nicholas I, she was elevated to the rank of Princess and in December of that same year she was given the title «Most Serene». Charlotte Karlovna died on February 24, 1828 and was buried in Courland in her estate of Mezoten.

The eldest of Charlotte Karlovna's sons, Prince Karl Andreevich Lieven, was born on February 1 1767. He enlisted in the army in 1788 and was successively Potemkin's aide-de-camp, commander-in-chief of the Preobrajenski regiment, member of the State Council, commanding officer of a regiment that bore his name, curator of the University of Dorpat and minister of Education. He died in Courland on December 31, 1844. According to his family he was a very cultured and liberal man for that time but was known for his bad temper.

Charlotte Karlovna's second son, Prince Christopher Andreevich Lieven, was born in Kiev on May 6, 1774 and made a brilliant career both in the army and in civilian life. In 1797 he was aide-de-camp to Emperor Paul I and in 1805 took part in the battle of Austerlitz. He was Ambassador to Berlin in 1809 and to London in 1812. In a speech in Parliament, Lord Grey praised his qualities and expressed the gratitude of the British government. When he returned to Russia in 1834 he was honored by the special confidence of Emperor Nicholas I who named him tutor of the heir Alexander Nikolaevich, the future Emperor Alexander II. He died in Rome on December 29, 1838 while traveling with the Grand Duke as his tutor.

Prince Christopher Andreevich Lieven was married to Countess Daria Christophorovna Benkendorff, sister of the famous chief of police. She was a remarkable woman both by her intelligence and by her savoir-faire in society. She occupied an important position in London where she ran a real political salon which had a great diplomatic influence. Her friendship was sought after by all the famous people of that time. Her intimacy with Metternich is well known and later she had a long affair with Guizot. She did not return to Russia with her husband and died in Paris on January 15, 1857. She is buried with her mother-in-law in Mezoten.

Charlotte Karlovna's third son, Ivan Andreevich, was born in 1778 and died a Major-General in 1848.

Prince Karl Andreevich Lieven had four sons: André, Alexander (my grandfather), Karl and Feodor.

When my great-grandfather Karl Andreevich Lieven retired, he moved with his family to Courland. Only one of his sons, my grandfather, did not follow him. He had married a Russian, Ekaterina Nikitichna Pankratieva, and lived at first in St. Petersburg, then for a while in Taganrog where he was governor and finally settled in Moscow where he became Senator. Through his marriage to a Russian and his long career as a civil servant he had become completely russianized in contrast to his brothers and their families who lost all contact with anything Russian and couldn't even speak the language. Only one of the sons of Prince André Lieven, George, worked for a short time at the Ministry of Foreign Affairs.

Fate intervened on December 14, 1825 when my great-grandfather Vassili Lvovich Davydoff was on the side of the Decembrists and my grandfather Prince Alexander Karlovich Lieven was commanding officer of a company of the regiment of the Guard of Moscow. He struck with his sword the officer who commanded the right wing of his company, forced his men to swear allegiance to Emperor Nicholas I and led them to the Winter Palace. For this deed he was named aide-de-camp.

My grandfather was chivalrous and kind, honest, straightforward and entirely devoted to the Tsar and to his country. Innocent of all malice, he could not accept that it should exist in others and, above all, in any member of his family. One can therefore imagine how great was his disappointment when, after the death of his father, not having gone to Courland for the sharing out of the inheritance and having entire confidence in his brothers he only received 200,000 roubles out of an enormous fortune that comprised many millions. Faithful to the traditions of the family, he did not argue and was not even angry with his brothers.

Because of this injustice, when my grandfather died he only left his children a small inheritance which included the estate of «Sinee» in the suburbs of Moscow and houses in Moscow itself in the small «street of the dead» in the parish of «Uspenia na Mogiltsach». All these properties were sold and the proceeds divided among the children. Each one received the modest sum of 100,000 roubles. However, by that time the two elder daughters had died and of the remaining children five were already settled. Only aunt Lina, who was not married, had to look for a job. She addressed herself to Empress Maria Alexandrovna whose governess she had been and asked her to find her a job, whereupon the Empress named her head of the Razumovsky Institute.

As my Lieven grandmother had died when my mother was only ten years old, she was brought up by aunt Lina. Because of his modest means it was difficult for my grandfather to give my mother a comprehensive education. She did however learn to speak French and German well, and knew everything that a young «society» girl should know. She certainly had a remarkable upbringing. Aunt Lina inculcated her with a deep faith and with the rules of ethics and honor that where the most salient traits of her character. When the time came she took her out into the world of society, dressing her and herself on her modest income. At a ball my mother met my father who had come to visit his parents who were then staying in Moscow and shortly after she married him.

Because of these special circumstances of their lives, the relationship between the two sisters drew them very close together. They loved each other dearly and my mother kept forever a filial devotion to the elder sister who had brought her up. That is why when my mother's family life broke up, aunt Lina asked her to come and stay with her, which she accepted with joy, and I, at the age of 3, found myself at the Razumovsky Institute.

Aunt Lina was, like all the Lievens, tall with blond hair and blue eyes. One could not say she was pretty and when I first saw her she was already past forty and showed the Lieven tendency to put on weight. The traits of her character were reflected in her face. She was, in the good sense of the word, a «grande dame». Her kindness was sharpened by her sense of duty, in respect to which she was as demanding of others as she was of herself. Her innate intelligence was sometimes imbued with the pleasant naivety of the spinster but she had a great deal of tact, the result of her worldly upbringing and of her intimacy with the Imperial Court. Her moral sense was very developed and during her whole life she never sinned. Proud and honest, she never compromized with her conscience for any intrigue whatsoever. Following her father's precepts, she was devoted to her sovereign and was a monarchist by reason and from the heart. She perfected her domestic education after she had come out into the world of society. She spoke fluently four languages—Russian, French, German and English—read a great deal and as she knew how to surround herself with enlightened and cultured people who appreciated her company, she became a very learned woman. She was greatly helped in this by her friendship with her brother André, one of the wonderful personalities of his time. One of her outstanding traits was her piety which, in her case, was a deep and intimate feeling. It manifested itself by a dislike for ceremonies which she was forced to attend and a great faith in the true understanding of Christianity.

I have lingered purposely on my aunt's personality because she played a great role in my life and I was fortunate, at an already mature age, to spend in her company many radiant and fascinating hours, the memory of which fills my heart with a feeling of gratitude towards her.

My mother's elder brother was André (1839-1912). Physically and mentally he was a typical specimen of his family. Tall, strong, with clear-cut features, a high forehead and intelligent eyes, uncle André had a shrewd mind, spoke four languages, was remarkably erudite, cultured in the European sense of the word and, with all that, also a man of the world with all the good manners that went with it. His success in society and with all the great thinkers of that time was great and well deserved. His weaknesses were the pride and the passionate character that he kept until the end of his days. His passion was applied as much to his self-esteem as to women. He was constantly having affairs and the last one ended when he died at the age of 73.

After finishing his studies very young at the faculty of mathematics with a gold medal at the written exams, he married at an early age a Muscovite lady, Strekalova, the grand-daughter of the well-known prefect of police under Alexander I, a very wealthy young girl. Entering the Ministry of the Interior as a civil servant, he was soon named Governor of Moscow and, at the age of 48, was already Minister of the National Trust. This brilliant career was suddenly cut short by the intrigues of a then well-known minister, Valuev, with whom he had quarrelled in the brusque manner that was his wont, and who saw in him a dangerous adversary. Uncle André took, as one then said, «his own retirement», that is to say he not only gave up his ministerial post but also his title of Secretary of State and Member of the State Council. He bore his disgrace badly.

At that time his first wife had been dead for a long time, leaving her fortune to their two children and to him only a small annual pension of 6,000 roubles. As for his second wife, by whom he had no children, they were separated. His children were already grown up and the son was married. He went to live alone in his small estate of «Bunakovka» near Pavlograd, in a small house with no neighbors. He lived there the whole year round, winter come summer, sitting for hours in his armchair without saying a word. Only his daughter Alexandra, who was a spinster, visited him. Winter was the hardest time when wolves howled in the park of the estate and bandits could be heard rampaging about the neighborhood. Uncle André's only solace was his large library and his studies of astronomy.

Uncle André was not a believer and even less super-stitious. All his life he had studied science and particularly astronomy and under no circumstances would he accept the possibility of supernatural phenomena such as apparitions and other similar things. However, he himself told me the story of how, one night in Bunakovka, when he was not asleep, he suddenly heard in the silence of the night the door of the corridor that passed in front of his room open and muffled steps as of someone wearing slippers come towards his door and, after a short pause, continue on. Of course my uncle would not have believed in the reality of this phenomenon if the dog who slept in this room had not started to growl and his hair to raise up on his back. The following night the same phenomenon occurred, so my uncle, on the pretext that he felt unwell, asked his valet to come and sleep in his room without naturally telling him a word of what had happened. Exactly at the same hour the sound of the door opening and the muffled steps in the corridor were heard. The dog started to growl and the valet almost died of fright. Definitely convinced that he was not the prey of hallucinations my uncle tried to explain to himself this strange phenomenon. The fourth night nothing happened, nor the following one. The answer to the enigma came a few days later when in the newspaper from St. Petersburg my uncle learned that the very night he had heard for the first time the steps in the corridor Valuev had died...

The children of my Lieven grandparents were divided in two groups. In the first group were uncle André and the three elder sisters including aunt Lina, who resembled their father physically and morally, while the four younger ones, that is uncle Nikita, aunt Ekaterina, aunt Maria and my mother were like their mother. As far as my mother is concerned this is not quite correct as, although physically she resembled her mother, morally she was very much like the Lievens. This difference between the two groups of brothers and sisters made itself felt in their relations to each other. Those who resembled my grandfather, that is who belonged to the Lieven group, were close to each other while the others were similarly so between themselves. The relations between my mother and aunt Lina were the exception, which was explained by the fact that aunt Lina had taken the place of her mother. Two of the older sisters died before I was born and of the first group only uncle André and aunt Lina remained. These two had a great affection for each other which was based on a similarity of thought both moral and intellectual.

When uncle André started going back to Moscow he often visited my aunt. Naturally we were too young to understand and appreciate this exceptional man but in me at least he awoke already then an instinctive interest. However, uncle André, because of the injustice he had suffered, did not have a very respectful sentiment for Alexander III and as, furthermore, he was not religious, my mother feared that he might have a bad influence on us and did her best to protect us from it in every possible way. It got to the point where, when uncle André arrived, we were forbidden to stay in the drawing room.

My mother's other brother, Nikita, did not always live in Moscow and we only saw him on the rare occasions when he arrived from Kiev where he was public attorney, first of the regional Tribunal, then of the law courts. He was the most brilliant member of the Pankratiev group and was particularly friendly with my mother and with aunt Ekaterina and her husband Nicholas Pavlovich Bogolepov. He was a dry man, both in the moral and in the physical sense. In his youth he had suffered a serious case of rheumatic fever that had caused a cardiac lesion and moreover he suffered from gastro-enteritis. When I knew him, he was a very tall man, very thin, with an ashen complexion and white hair. He spoke in a hollow voice, continuously clearing his throat and expressing himself, even in the most banal conversations, in a peremptory manner and in a bureaucratic language, probably the same he used in his speeches as public attorney. He judged everybody and everything in a strict manner with no possibility of appeal and it seems to me that those he prosecuted must have been terrified when they saw him seated at the prosecutor's desk. He was so afraid of catching cold that he dressed very warmly even in summer and later, when I read Tchekov's «The Man in the Case», he reminded me of him. To preserve his health he trained himself to never worry and never to regret anything. It was even said that when he visited women he took drops of valerian. Because of his concern about his health, the rooms in his apartment were never aired and the air was always foul. I never knew what his religious opinions were but as far as questions of ethics and honor were concerned he was extremely strict. As for his political ideas, I think it would have been difficult to find a more reactionary man. This explains among other things his friendship with Nicholas Pavlovich Bogolepov, the husband of aunt Ekaterina, who later became Minister of Education.

Uncle Nikita did not like young people and they did not like him. When the student disturbances started, he put all the blame on them and was in favor of applying the most drastic measures to them, supporting in every way the directives of N.P. Bogolepov. At first he was very friendly with my mother but later his attitude towards her became cooler, probably because he did not approve of the behavior, in itself totally innocent, of my elder brother who for a short while lived in St. Petersburg as a student.

Curiously enough this dry old man had been a great wit and a gay blade when he had been a student. He had even written some poetry. One of the poems he wrote in his youth has remained in my memory:

«Niet more beautiful and pleasant
In all of Europe
Than adorable Nikita
With nose, eyes and «lob» [1]
As beautiful and gothic
As a statue antique».

Aunt Ekaterina or, as we called her, aunt Katia, had a great physical resemblance to her brother Nikita. It is difficult for me to speak of her character because this woman had a tragic destiny and her character changed under the effect of the misfortunes she had to bear. I only know that she was deeply religious and that her political ideas were very reactionary, I would even say ultra-reactionary. In that respect she was even more extreme than her brother and her husband. She had married, against her father's will, N.P. Bogolepov, her tutor, who came from an ecclesiastic circle but who later made a career in public life. He was killed in a political plot and their children died on almost the same day from diphtheria. A short time later she gave birth to a girl whom she watched over like the apple of her eye, but when she was fifteen this girl also fell ill and died shortly after. The attacks of a liberal section of society against her husband's policies and the hatred he inspired in young students and finally his tragic end had made her very bitter. After her husband's death she left St. Petersburg and returned to Moscow. After that I never saw her any more but I know she became an active member of «the Union of St. Michael» or of «the Union of the Russian People», two extremist ultra-reactionary organizations. Her end was as tragic as the rest of her life had been. It was said that she had fallen from the balcony of her third-floor apartment.

---

1. Lob = forehead.

In reality she had ended her days by committing suicide because of the events of the first 1905 revolution and of an incurable illness from which she had suffered for a long time.

My mother's third sister belonged to the same Pankratiev group and was called Maria. She visited us very rarely and I cannot say much about her character. I only remember her physical appearance. She was a very thick-set woman with white hair whose features resembled my mother's. She married young, for love, and made a real misalliance. Not only her parents but also her brothers and her sisters tried in vain to dissuade her from marrying. Her husband was an obstetrician and was very comical both from a physical standpoint and from a moral one. Later he created a center for wet-nurses.

I have already said that uncle André had had two children by his marriage to the Strekalov woman, a son Alexander and a daughter Alexandra. These cousins were much older than I. Sasha Lieven was married and had three children whereas his sister Dina could already be classified as a spinster. Neither of them looked like the Lievens. Small and ugly with ashen and sickly looking faces, they were the living image of their mother. When we first lived in Moscow, Sasha was Marshal of the Nobility in the district of Bronnitsko in the province of Moscow. He rarely came to Moscow but when he did he always came to see aunt Lina. If physically he did not resemble his father, in his culture, his erudition and his moral qualities he was very much like him. Their political views differed. Uncle André disliked Emperor Alexander III but was nevertheless an orthodox monarchist, while his son was outspokenly a liberal and criticized the principles of monarchy and of court etiquette, which did not prevent him from being a chamberlain and being elected by his peers. Intelligent and talented, he was also a remarkable musician, and he not only played the piano very well but he was also a great connoisseur of music. He was married to Alexandra Petrovna Vassiltchikova who, though pretty, was very tall. The contrast between their heights was the source of many jokes. Oliossa, as she was called, had a very strict line of conduct. She was kind and devoted to her family but, in spite of these qualities, she was known for a certain odd behavior. When speaking to someone she could all of a sudden shock the person she was talking to by a sudden fiery outburst. This made one think that she was trying to be provocative or original.

Sasha and Oliossa lived in very good harmony and no family discord ever clouded their happiness. They had three children, two sons and one daughter. In their height they resembled their mother but, except for the oldest, André, their features were like their father's, that is to say they were as ugly as he. I recall these cousins not only with sadness, for two of them died young, but also with tenderness and gratitude because it is rare to meet people as attentive and kind as were Petrick and Machenka Lieven.

Dina Lieven remained a spinster but did not acquire the bad aspects of this condition, probably because she knew how to fill her life with serious activities. She was well-educated, read a great deal and being a good musician like her brother often played the piano. She spent her leisure hours working for charity organisations where she helped her grandmother Alexandra Nikolaevna Strekalova who was very well-off and well-known in Moscow.

Dina loved and had a great esteem for her father, whereas Sasha had completely drawn away from him and neither uncle André nor Oliossa could stand each other. I cannot judge whose fault this was but I think the disagreement started with Oliossa's strange and provocative manner and uncle André's strong reaction to it. Unfortunately Oliossa's lack of love for her father-in-law was transmitted by her to her children who were more than scornful with him which made him very unhappy.

I will speak later of the other members of the Lieven family when I recount our trips to the Bliden castle in Courland.

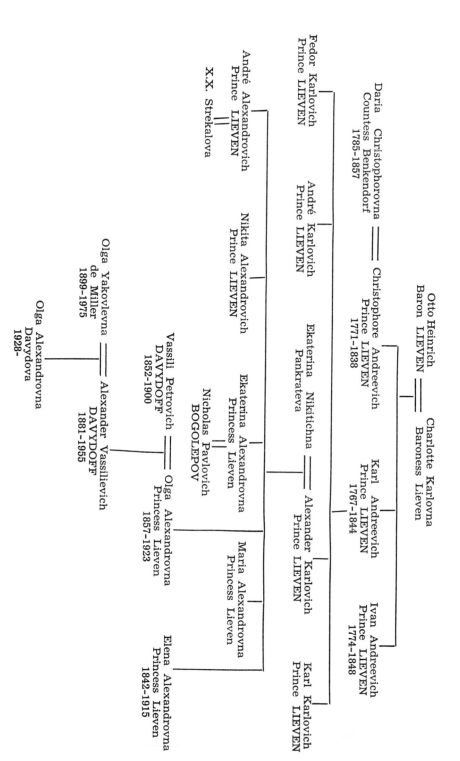

Otto Heinrich
Baron LIEVEN

Charlotte Karlovna
Baroness Lieven

Christophore Andreevich
Prince LIEVEN
1771-1838

Daria Christophorovna
Countess Benkendorf
1785-1857

Fedor Karlovich
Prince LIEVEN

André Karlovich
Prince LIEVEN

André Alexandrovich
Prince LIEVEN

X.X. Strekalova

Karl Andreevich
Prince LIEVEN
1767-1844

Ivan Andreevich
Prince LIEVEN
1774-1848

Ekaterina
Pankrateva

Alexander Karlovich
Prince LIEVEN

Karl Karlovich
Prince LIEVEN

Ekaterina Nikitichna

Maria Alexandrovna
Princess Lieven

Elena Alexandrovna
Princess Lieven
1842-1915

Nikita Alexandrovich
Prince LIEVEN

Ekaterina Alexandrovna
Princess Lieven

Nicholas Pavlovich
BOGOLEPOV

Olga Alexandrovna
Princess Lieven
1857-1923

Vassili Petrovich
DAVYDOFF
1852-1900

Olga Yakovlevna
de Miller
1899-1975

Alexander Vassilievich
DAVYDOFF
1881-1955

Olga Alexandrovna
Davydova
1928-

THE ELISABETH INSTITUTE

We did not remain long at the Razumovsky Institute. Very soon after we had arrived there, Aunt Lina was named head of the Elisabeth Institute. For her it was a promotion. In her first post she had not been independent and was under the orders of the head of the Nikolaevsky Institute of which the Razumovsky was one of the sections. In all probability nothing very striking happened during our stay there as nothing has remained in my memory of this phase of my childhood. I only remember that children of both sexes were educated there and that among the pupils there was a boy who later became famous—the clown Duroff—and also a small Turcoman girl who had been found by General Skobeleff literally on the battlefield. He took her to the Empress who handed her over to my aunt so that she could attend to her education.

The Elisabeth Institute evokes many memories in me. I was still a small child when I arrived there and when I left I was already grown up as I spent over fifteen years of my life in that Institute, that is to say part of my childhood and my adolescence. It was there that I became conscious of myself and of the outside world. It is a period of one's life that is so charged with emotions, it contains so many heartbreaks and so many joys, that at the end of one's life one only remembers the general traits with occasionally on the side a few minor events that have struck one's childish imagination. Thus there rise in one's memory distinctive faces of parents and of strangers. One hears their conversations, one

89

recalls one's education and one's studies. From these fragments one can, by reasoning, reconstruct the characteristics of an era long past but one is incapable of giving an exact and coherent description of one's past experience.

The Elisabeth Institute, like the Razumovsky, was situated at the meeting of the Yauza and the Tchetchora, the latter separating the parks of the two institutes. Its front gave onto Voznesensky street, the one that leads to the German and Lefortov streets and ends at the Hall of the Collegial Chamber. The building of the Elisabeth Institute was larger than the Razumovsky and, already in my time, it had been enlarged by additional buildings. I do not know what it was destined for originally but it was a perfect building for a school. The classrooms and the dormitories were large, high and light and there were also two magnificent halls, very vast, one of which had columns. All these rooms made up the interior of the building. The church was also large but very intimate, and incited to prayer. A big park, which included two ponds on which, in summer, swans glided and which had a row boat and a bathing place, extended right down to the river Yauza from which it was separated by a high wooden barrier.

Our apartment was in a low one-story house, the old laundry house, that was attached to the main building of the Institute next to the winter-garden. This house was very large. It had fourteen rooms with a big drawing-room and a hall. Two small gardens came with the apartment. The house gave onto Voznezensky street and right opposite our windows was the Lutheran church of St. Michael with a school of the same name. The church was surrounded by a large garden and a kitchen-garden. One would have thought that this neighborhood was quiet and pleasant but, on our side of the street against our house, were two factories, the Nevsky Stearin Factory and the Goujon Engine Factory. From the first, in summer, came a very strong and unpleasant stink and from the second the noise of hammers beating iron bars.

When we moved into the Elisabeth Institute our family was quite a large one. It included aunt Lina, my mother, us three brothers and our cousin Mitia Olsufiev, the son of my deceased aunt whose education, after the death of his father, had been taken over by aunt Lina. Apart from the family there also lived with us our niania Maria Matveevna and a French governess Mlle. Fouquet.

Mitia Olsufiev was much older than we boys and at the time when we moved to the Elisabeth Institute he was already in the fifth form at the Pokrovka. His father, who had been once upon a time very wealthy and had owned a glass factory, had been completely ruined at the end of his life and had left Mitia with no resources. He was a very nice and very well brought up boy. He studied wonderfully well both at the Gymnasium and later at the University but there was something bizarre about him which even now I have not been able to define. I have never seen on his face an expression of joy nor of sadness. He never joined in discussions and I was never able to find out his opinion on any matter whatever. At the same time he was a person quite out of the ordinary and he proved it during his long life. Much later, when I was already a civil servant working for the government and living on my own in St. Petersburg he would arrive from the country and stay at my place and we became very close, but even then he remained very uncommunicative.

The niania Maria Matveevna or, as we used to call her, Matosha, like many other Russian nannies had brought up several generations of the Lieven family, among others my mother and my first cousin Dina. All her interests in life were centered in that family and she was wholly devoted to its members. She loved all three of us as if we were her own children. In spite of her kindness she had a nasty character and used to have incomprehensible whims. When she got furious with someone she would raise her right eyebrow and her face would take on a tragic expression. Having thus manifested her displeasure she would not utter another word and would sometimes sulk for two or three weeks. She was particularly difficult to please in the cooking line. Although we had a good cook, because my mother liked good food, for nothing on earth would Matosha eat at our table and she used to prepare her own food in her room on a Dutch stove. I do not remember what these dishes were. I only know that they included a lot of mushrooms and onions and, because of that, a strong smell would pervade the adjoining rooms. As she never finished a dish in one go, she would keep them not only in the stove in her room but also in the stoves of other rooms. Everyone had a great deal of consideration and affection for Matosha, especially my mother, although her caprices and her sulks ended by being insupportable. She had a separate room in our apartment which remained her own even when, after a fit of sulks, she would leave for a long period of time to visit some friends. Finally, when we reached adulthood and did not require her services any more, we had to accede to her wishes and get her a bed in one of the Muscovite homes for old people, and when, after my father's death, my mother went to live permanently in the country and offered her a room in our house with the understanding that she would have a servant at her disposal and that on Saturdays and Sundays she would be driven to church, she indignantly refused this offer and stayed in her old people's home. When I was a student and lived in St. Petersburg, I would occasionally go and visit her whenever I found myself in Moscow. It is quite impossible to describe how proud she was in front of her companions. I remember arriving one day in a luxury coach which waited for me in the courtyard. The little old ladies clustered close to the window and admired the smart coach. I can imagine all they had to say to each other after I left. In one sense she had a good influence on us. Being very religious she taught us how to pray and to respect the rites of the orthodox church.

Of Mlle. Fouquet I can remember almost nothing. She was the most ordinary of French governesses. She did her duty honestly towards us, that is to say she taught us very quickly to speak French and to behave properly at the table. I think that, like Onegin's Mr. l'Abbé, «she did not bore us with strict morals» and hardly chided us for our pranks. In a word we did nothing disagreeable to each other and no unpleasant memory is linked to her. She never got used to our family and when she left we all forgot her very quickly and she never came to visit us. She was probably a lonely soul and an unhappy one, and now I would like to think that she ended her days in peace somewhere in her home in her own country.

I must not forget to mention the servants who were very numerous in those times. Our staff included a butler and his assistant, a footman, a kitchen-maid, two chambermaids and a coachman. The chambermaids and the footman lived in the house with us. The others were lodged in rooms which had been put at their disposal in small houses in the courtyard of the Institute. The reason for having so many servants was that they cost almost nothing at that time. Our excellent chef, Vassili Baranoff, was paid the highest wages—25 silver roubles per month. The butler received 15 roubles, each chambermaid 10 roubles, and the lower ranks like the coachman, the butler's help and the kitchen-maid even less. Other expenses were not greater and life in general was cheap. I remember how my mother would get angry when the cook's daily expenses would exceed 5 roubles although 14 people had to be fed. My father gave my mother 10,000 roubles a year and my aunt's salary amounted to approximately 2,500 roubles. This amount of money enabled us not only to eat, dress and have tutors and teachers at home, but also to go out and, in summer, if someone's health required it, spend two months abroad.

As in all public schools, many people lived in an establishment such as ours. In addition to the teachers and mistresses, the whole staff of the Institute lived in rooms that were provided for them. Apart from the teaching staff and the pupils, The Institute also included women assistant-teachers, needle-workers, a woman in charge of clothes, a charwoman, a crowd of chambermaids and sewing-maids, a watchman, a treasurer, a doctor, a priest, a deacon and many underlings like the porter, the carpenter, the gardener and the stokers. All these people were lodged either in separate buildings or in the small houses in the courtyard. Some had large families and the daughters worked as charwomen at the Institute while the boys attended the same classes as we did.

I remember that during the fifteen years I lived at the Elisabeth Institute the number of its occupants hardly varied. It seems to me that those who were already there when I arrived were still there when I left. I remember them all very well but few of them had any distinctive characteristics. I will only talk about the priest, Father Dimitri Nikolaevich Beliaev and two of the teachers.

Father Dimitri, who had gone through the Theological Academy, was a very erudite man and also deeply religious. His masses were particularly moving and sincere. This was especially true during Holy Week which Father Dimitri lived through as if the Christ's passion were his own. I remember his tears at the moment of the burial of Christ. Later on I could never get used to the solemn tone of voice, so full of pathos, of the other priests' masses, so alive in me was the memory of the simple and moving masses of Father Dimitri.

Two of the teachers who have remained in my memory were Serge Alexeevich Sokoloff who, for a time, taught me Russian grammar, and Serge Vassilievich Zentchenko, though they were completely different from one another. The first tall, thin, with deeply sunken eyes and wearing spectacles, taught Russian in the lower forms of the Institute. He was considered to be very strict but in reality he was very kind and honest. He simply did not like slackers and without pity gave them bad marks. He had a passion for Russian grammar and could not abide misspellings in his pupils' exercises. However, I think that if he had had to teach Russian literature, his courses would not have been interesting. He was my second Russian teacher before I entered the Gymnasium. I do not know how he did it but, without being particularly strict and without getting annoyed, he taught me very quickly how to write without making mistakes and, thanks to him, the letter «iat» never caused me any trouble. Pleased with this result, he used to say to my mother: «Sasha is a good boy of good morals. He writes Russian without a mistake».

Serge Vassilievich Zentchenko was a totally different man and teacher. Small, blond, wearing a pince-nez over intelligent eyes, he attracted by his culture and by his interesting conversation. At the Institute he was considered to be «red», an epithet then given to the most innocent liberals who never thought of changing the existing regime. It would have been more correct to call them «progressives» because, by their culture, they were far ahead of other people. S.V. Zentchenko taught history but I was too young to be taught by him.

I only knew him because he often visited us. In my memory his name is linked to an amusing incident. One day, much later, when we were already at the Gymnasium, my mother asked Serge Vassilievich what books he suggested for us for the summer holidays. He mentioned the author Mamin Sibiriak and my mother bought some of his books. In the country one day my father came into our room and started to leaf through a volume of Mamin Sibiriak's which happened to be there. Suddenly his face expressed the deepest indignation and, taking the book, he hurried out of the room. Later we heard that he had made a terrible scene to my mother about this harmless author. To this day I do not know what my father had against him. Was he guilty in his eyes of being against the laws of morality or against his political views? In any case that very day the books were taken away.

It is with a feeling of gratitude that I remember the wife of S.V. Zentchenko, Maria Mikhailovna, who gave private lessons to the very small children. As cultured and as «progressive» as her husband, she had a great pedagogic talent. I was fortunate enough to have her as my first teacher. Quiet, gentle, always smiling, she was responsible for the fact that at the age of seven I knew how to read and write and had mastered the basic elements of arithmetic without even realizing it.

The Institutes that were under the patronage of Empress Marie were headed by counselors. These included the head-mistress who lived in the Institute and two honorable tutors, members of the board of directors of the Opekunsky Council, the seat of which was in St. Petersburg. The headmistress was the most important figure among the directors of the Institute and she bore the largest responsibility for running it. It was she who made the decisions at the meetings of the Council. The tutors, one of whom handled the teaching side and the other the administrative, although they had a certain influence in their own sphere, acted more as consultants. They assisted the headmistress and represented the interests of the Institute at the Opekunsky Council. It may seem strange, but the tutor responsible for the teaching section of the Elisabeth Institute was a retired General of the Cavalry, Count Alexis Vassilievich Olsufiev. He was a small man, completely bald, who always wore the uniform of the Grodnensky Regiment of Hussars. The surprising thing was that this man, who seemed to be the archetype of the soldier, was in reality a great erudite, a specialist in Roman poetry and literature. At the time I knew him he had just written an admirable book on Martial and he gave us one as a present with a very nice dedication. He was also a bon vivant and loved to tease aunt Lina, with whom he was very friendly. His wife, Alex as she was called in the world of society, née Miklachewsky, who had probably been very pretty in her youth, retained until the end of her days a great gracefulness but also a certain preciosity. She feared her husband's teasings as he, in her presence, often took on a rather too frivolous tone of voice. We liked Count Olsufiev very much as he chatted with us and teased us very nicely.

The tutor responsible for administrative affairs was Prince Nicholas Petrovich Trubetskoy. There had been a time when he had been a very alert and educated man who had been a well-known member of the intellectual set in Moscow (B.N. Tchitcherin mentions him in his memoirs). When I knew him he was quite senile, an amnesic old man who, by his strange remarks, often provoked the indignation or the laughter of others. His absent-mindedness was legendary. For instance, having been named when he was forty or so Governor of a certain town, he was making rounds and as he was leaving one of the houses he put on by mistake the coat of the chief of police who was on bad terms with most of the citizens of that town. He continued to make his rounds and left the chief of police's cards instead of his own, which put the chief of police back on good terms with everyone. One of his charateristics was his illegible writing which made people say that one should give it to decipher to the pharmacist. One day when he was away on business in St. Petersburg, he wrote to aunt Lina letters that she was unable to read. Finally, she could stand it no longer and she sent back one of the letters asking him to dictate it to someone. One week later she received a letter written very legibly and without a mistake.

He himself had only added a few words to say that it was his butler who had written the letter!

A last person who, although he did not take part in the running of the Institute, held a position of some importance, was the church-warden. In the schools of ancient Russia this function was usually held by rich merchants. They received no salary and, indeed, gave yearly donations to the church and presents of money to the clergy. Because of this they were decorated with medals and ribbons of merit. At the Elisabeth Institute the church-warden was a certain Juravliev who owned the Grand Hotel Continental on the market square. He was the representative of the new corporation of merchants of Moscow, which meant that he had received a certain education and spoke French. Aunt Lina rather intimidated him and when after mass she would invite him for a cup of tea, to show how well educated he was he would converse with her on the latest subjects of French literature, particularly Paul Bourget who was then in fashion.

Aunt Lina spent a great deal of time on the musical education of her pupils. She was well seconded in this task by the musical inspector of the departmental establishments of Empress Marie, the famous orchestra leader and head of the Conservatory Vassili Ilyich Safonov. The piano teacher at the Institute, David Solomonovich Chor, had organised a quartet that gave chamber music concerts in Moscow that we attended assiduously. V.I. Safonov, in accordance with aunt Lina's wishes, brought to the Institute all the best known artists. I remember the marvelous concerts of Hoffman, Gabrilovich and others in the admirable two-colored hall of the Institute.

I will not speak of the balls of the Institute which bored us to death and where the pupils stared at us, the nephews of the headmistress, as if we were wild beasts, which both annoyed and vexed us.

EDUCATION

In olden days, in Russia, noble families had adopted a system of education of their children which the intelligentsia and the progressives called «education in the fear of God». The characteristics of this system were that it taught children two basic things: religious piety and an ethics based exclusively on this piety. Religious piety should express itself inwardly by faith in God and fear of Him, and outwardly by respect for liturgical rites. All debate on religion was forbidden because it might shake a child's faith. A child had to accept both the moral and intellectual aspects of religion in the same way as did his parents. Ethics based on religious piety was to be the only guide to his conduct. It was part of a person's duty whatever it was applied to, whether diligence in studies or the unconditional respect of parents and teachers. The authority of parents had to be accepted as sacred even if their views were old fashioned and wrong. Any manifestation of independence of thought in children that went against the ideas of their parents was considered immoral and unhealthy and, depending on the character of the parents, was judged by them with more or less severity. Some of them reacted to the ideas of which they did not approve with words such as «stupid» or «absurd». Parents gave orders to their children and these orders had to be executed to the letter. With that sort of system, parents paid little attention to a child's personal traits, his intelligence, his talents, his aptitudes. The «rules» they adopted, which naturally in their eyes corresponded to the absolute truth, had to be applied to all children in the same manner and accepted by them without a murmur. Even when, in a family, there were several children with different talents and characters, they were expected to have the same reactions and they were fed the same religious and moral nourishment.

The most acute and dangerous problem of this educational system «in the fear of God» was the sexual one. To go against nature or to deny its needs was impossible but as ideas and especially conversation on this matter were considered to be sinful, a way out of this situation had to be found. This way out was found in the secrecy which surrounded this whole question and in the admission that it was shameful. At the time of the sexual maturity of young people and of the great psychological upheavals that accompanied it, parents simply paid no attention. The reactions in which these upheavals manifested themselves were considered to be signs of the immoral conduct of the adolescent whose vicious nature upset the rules firmly established by parents and teachers.

It is obvious that with this system all attempts at a psychological approach to a child was impossible. Nobody ever asked what impression these rules made on a child. As they were the basis of all truth, their consequences for the children were inevitably good and pleasant for them, and if this was not the case then the fault was the child's who was vicious by nature. In view of this, it was impossible to accept the idea that an injustice could be done to a child. Parents did not realize that their children resented in an acute way any unfair action against them and that each humiliation left deep traces, partially indelible for the rest of their lives.

The absence of any psychological approach to a child manifested itself also by the impossibility for parents to try and develop in him any serious interests. One was even suspicious of such a development, probably because both parents and teachers were afraid that the child might do better than they and thus find a way of escaping their authority, or else might subject the rules of the educational system to the test of criticism. They forgot that the ethics «in the fear of God» imposed by the persons in authority were, by the mere fact that they were imposed, considered by the child

100

to be a boring discipline, any infraction of which was a forbidden and therefore a pleasant fruit, while the fact of developing in a child, and especially in an adolescent, any serious interest would have occupied his mind and prevented him from having futile thoughts and desires.

All this does not mean that parents did not love their children. On the contrary, the more they loved them the more they applied this system of education with rigor and strictness, thinking that in this way they were doing him the maximum amount of good. They did not realize that a child, and later an adolescent, had to be not only loved but also pitied and helped in the difficult moments he went through because of his sometimes painful emotions. They did not know that the best and most precious stock of knowledge that a child could take with him for his whole life was the memory of a happy childhood. It is this memory that softens and sets aside wickedness, that makes a human being optimistic and pleasant to the people around him and helps thereby to surmount the difficult moments and the vicissitudes of life.

As the system «in the fear of God» was strictly applied to me and my brothers, I can speak about it from personal experience. God save me from having any ill-will against my mother because of that. This system of education was the accepted one in her social sphere and she had no choice. She loved us passionately and after the marital troubles she suffered we were for her her only joy and her only object in life. In us, her sons, she hoped to find the satisfaction of her pride. By nature she had a great deal of pride and the misfortune she suffered turned her, as I have already said, into a resolute and authoritarian woman. These traits of my mother aggravated the unpleasant side of our education. Many times she inflicted corporal punishments on me and the last time when I was already 8 years old.

I will speak very little about the consequences of this system of education on my brothers. I will only say a few words about them as it is difficult for me to judge the way they reacted inwardly. I must take time to reflect on my personal case, not that it was in any way special but on the contrary because it was an example of what happened to many young people. My tale will show how the best intentions of a mother as wonderful as mine caused me a great deal of suffering which had its influence on the course of my whole life.

Neither of my elder brothers possessed great will power and my mother's iron hand destroyed in them all trace of the little that existed. If for the eldest this manifested itself by the fact that he became uncertain of himself for the rest of his life, for the second one the results were catastrophic. Weak and prone by nature to enjoy the pleasures of life he lost all control over himself and died young.

For me things were very different. I can characterize my education by saying that it was a fight that went on for several years between two wills, one of which fought for its authority and the other for its independence. From the age of 13 until my adulthood I lived in a permanent state of revolt against my mother until I finally emerged the sole winner. I realize now that this opposition was not directed so much against my mother, whom I could not help but love, as against the system of education she subjected me to. I remember that it was only after my total victory, when I had already succeeded in life not so much thanks to my mother's advice as against it, that I told her about my life not as she had seen it but as it had really been. She understood me and cried bitterly. But it was not possible to go back. How much painful suffering I had to bear and how much moral strength and precious time I had to expend in my fight with the person closest to me, whom I loved most of all and who loved me also, my mother. And all this because of this system of education based on the best intentions in the world...

Until I was ten years old I was under the direct care of Mlle. Fouquet of whom, as I have already said, I have kept very little memory. She only taught me French and good manners. My mother took care of my moral education herself. When I reached my ninth year Mlle. Fouquet stopped looking after my elder brothers and a tutor, a German from the Baltic provinces, was called upon to look after them, and a year later I also came under his care. In choosing the tutor's nationality my mother acted for two reasons. Firstly because she thought it was essential for us to learn German. Secondly because it had been decided that the time had come when we boys should be given some notion of duty. The first of these reasons cannot be argued against. The second one is questionable. My mother herself had no doubt whatever about it. One must not forget that she came from a Courlandian noble family that had kept the traditions of the Teutonic Knights and that, in spite of the fact that she lived in Moscow, she kept close ties with Courland where many of her relatives lived. It was they who conveyed the idea to her that it was only among the Baltic Germans that the true traditions of the Teutonic Knights were still kept and that there could be no better tutors for young boys than the old students of Dorpat university who had been members of the student corporations known as «burchi». These «burchi», as well as life in them, are well known and are described both in German and in Russian literature. It suffices to remember the German student corporation described in Turgenev's novel «Acia» and in the play «Old Heidelberg».

Through our Courlandian tutors we got to know all about the mores of the «burchi», especially I who had six of these tutors. We learnt very quickly that every student should despise the «petit bourgeois», that is an adult man who worked and had serious interests in his life. We got to know the drunken brawls and the pleasures that were part of their life. We learnt mockery and the appeal of rather flat jokes of poor taste directed against those who did not have the honor to belong to student corporations and more particularly the Jews whose only reason for existing was to lend money to students. With our tutors we sang German student songs in which were celebrated «Wein, Weib und Gesang» and the gay life. As far as honor was concerned, our tutors taught us the rules of duels with sword, espadon or pistol, and explained to us that the place occupied by a student in a corporation was directly proportionate to the number of duels he had fought. The slightest sign of disrespect towards the corporation or the person of a student, often even without in any way attainting his honor, was a pretext to a duel. Furthermore this sort of offense was usually made in a state of drunkenness.

103

All our tutors were obvious drunks and dissipated men and not cultured people, even in the German sense of the word, and as none of them spoke a word of Russian and therefore never read a Russian book, they had no notion of Russian culture. Notwithstanding, they were good fellows and the first of them, F.F. Tchernai, was a very kind and honest man. He was a great lover of forests and of hunting and later became forester on our Kiev estate, learnt the profession in German books and was very good at his job. When we grew up and became friends with him, he became an integral part of the family. There is no need for me to say anything about the five other tutors. They influenced mainly my elder brother. They were quite indifferent to my other brother and as for me I treated them with a good deal of irony.

I do not know if my mother realized how useless all these tutors were and even the harm they caused us, but the mere fact that she changed them so often during the six years we had them at home shows that they did not satisfy her. That may be the reason why she continued to keep a close eye on our education. Thus all the ethical and religious measures came directly from her. This was perfectly understandable as far as the religious measures were concerned because our tutors were Lutherans and furthermore showed little interest in religious matters. Although my mother had come from a Lutheran family she had been baptised in the Orthodox faith because, according to the laws of that time, in mixed marriages children had to take their mother's religion. However, atavistically she was in favor of Lutheranism and liked to go to Protestant churches and listen to the sermons of Protestant ministers, but as she considered it her duty to confirm us in the rules of orthodoxy she went regularly to the Orthodox church and kept a close check on our doing the same. She perceived the church in an emotional way and the fundamentals of the teachings of Orthodox Christian religion escaped her completely. That was why she could not help us in that domain. Because of that she insisted that we obey to the letter every rite, the respect of fasting days (not all, by far), our regular presence at mass, confessions and communions. As she was incapable of giving us respect for religion by explaining to us the fundamentals of Christian teachings and the meaning of religious rites, she had recourse to the fear with which she inspired us to create in us the beginnings of a religious sentiment. When we were very small, we were literally terrified at the thought that lightning was going to strike us immediately and unerringly as a sign of God's wrath if we did not believe in Him and if we were careless in observing religious rites. For instance when we were taken to church we had to remain standing at attention until the end of the service. If we did not feel well we were given smelling salts to breathe and were allowed to sit down on a chair for a few minutes. Going to church became a torture for us and once there the meaning of prayer escaped us and we had only one thought in mind—when was the service going to end? To refuse to go to church for any reason was impossible because then God's wrath would be revealed to us in the most materialistic fashion, that is to say by an illness or a physical abnormality. Even more horrible were the possible punishments for sins during confession or communion. We were told that if, during confession, we did not tell the priest the slightest little sin, or if, at the very moment of communion, we thought of something other than communion or of something sinful, then the devil would appear forthwith on the ambo in front of the chalice and ravish our soul, and this would result in our immediate death.

The results of this sort of religious education are obvious. At first when we were very small, religion and the church scared us and God seemed to us to be a punishing and avenging Jewish Jehovah. We could not conceive of a clement and loving Christ. Later as we grew up, our fears were dispelled and, although we respected religion, we considered it to be a formality and never looked to it for any support or appeasement in the difficult moments of moral dissatisfaction.

I presume that, at the time of my childhood, parents did not read a certain stanza of Eugene Onegin, and if they did read it they did not ponder over its meaning and maybe even found it immoral. And yet it says certain things the comprehension of which might have eased enormously certain difficult moments of young people. Here is this stanza:

The fires of our heart soon inflame us
And love's bewitching lies to us
Will not be taught by nature
But by de Stael or by Chateaubriand.
In dirty novels in haste we seek
The knowledge that we crave for
And yet no pleasure do enjoy.
Postponing love will only harm
Young people's future happiness...

When I remember the mystery that surrounded the question of childbirth, a perfectly simple and normal subject as is that of the sexual act which people were ashamed to talk about and allusion to which seemed to be a sin, then I envy the young generations of to-day who learn about love from nature and who, from their early age, are used to consider the relations between man and woman as a simple and natural thing. How much purer is their imagination and how much more peaceful their nights. The mystery that surrounded the sexual problem only exacerbated one's sensitivity. Under those conditions, the first love lost its idyllic character and became a simple animal passion which, if jealousy set in, was a source of terrible and quite unnecessary suffering. One would have thought that it was here that the helpful role of tutors and parents, with whom the adolescent could share his sorrow, would have manifested itself. But on the contrary, such a notion was shameful especially for a young man who had some pride, who feared that after confessing his woes he would be teased or treated matter-of-factly, and who, because of this, preferred to suffer in silence. Furthermore discussions and conversations on these matters were considered to be sinful and if the parents and tutors did not mock the young man, in any case they would judge him to be sinful and depraved, with no moral sense, and would take strong measures to put him back on the right track. Once the adolescent had taken refuge in silence, his internal sufferings would reflect themselves in his conduct and even sometimes in his health. At first he would become pensive, distracted and lazy, which, was reflected in his studies. Then his parents, without trying to find the cause of this state, would pounce on the culprit with all their authority, flood him with

106

reproaches and punish him for his bad marks. This would alienate people who loved each other and who should have been called upon to help each other.

For me «the time of hope and tender sadness» or, to speak more simply, sexual maturity, occurred very early, at thirteen, and manifested itself in a sudden and «violent» manner. The psychological shock was so strong that my character changed completely. From a nice and studious boy, I became in no time distracted and irritable and above all lazy. I simply could not study and the simplest of homework became incomprehensible. I must say that what my mother and my tutors were trying so carefully to hide from me, I had learned from my schoolmates the first month after I started school and the naughty novel that enlightened me completely was Zola's «Nana» in its Russian translation. I read it at night when the whole house was asleep. The results of all this are fairly obvious. I lost all the prestige I had enjoyed until then at home and only got it back gradually later and not without a fight. My mother's attitude towards me changed completely and suddenly. She was no longer proud of me and scolded me for being so depraved. It is about that time that my revolt against my mother's authority started, which caused me so many moral trials.

As I have already said, my mother was of German origin, understood nothing about Russia and was closed to Russian culture. All she learned about it seemed to her to be filled with free and immoral thoughts from which we had to be preserved at all costs. This could be done quite easily as visitors to our house were all «right thinking» people except for uncle André and when he arrived we were sent to our room or later to our class. What we read was closely supervised (although I read Zola very early) and, except for the slip-up of Mamin Sibiriak, this control was applied to literature that was considered to be unhealthy from a moral and a religious point of view. Even Tolstoy was forbidden to us, except for «War and Peace», because he had just written a novel as dangerous as «the Kreutzer Sonata». I have already spoken about my German tutors. It is therefore unnecessary to think that they could have had the slightest cultural influence on us.

One may wonder if we really needed serious interests. Wouldn't we have found boring our elders' conversations on subjects that were beyond our comprehension? Wouldn't we have shied away from them of our own free will, so occupied were we by our materialistic thoughts and pleasures? I cannot answer these questions for my brothers but for myself I must say that it would have been a joy for me to have known at a younger age the charm and the pleasure of prolonged and profound reflection.

In the difficult moments of doubt and painful conflicts I was alone and my only weapon was the fear of God and the ethics derived from it. These weapons could in no way satisfy my spirit and warm my heart. Why did no one give me what could have driven away futile pleasures, nourished my mind and filled the loneliness of my soul?

What happened to me during those young years was also the fate of many others, but I had something special that I could not perceive at that time. This something, so I understood later, aggravated subconsciously the difficulties of my internal conflicts. I know now that deep inside me, in my subconscience, fought two atavisms. On the one side was the long list of ancient German knights hostile to all that was Russian. On the other side were my Tatar ancestors, completely russianized through the centuries. In me were united the traditions of German knights and the spiritual heritage of the Decembrists. These elements could not melt into one whole and in this conflict the second one emerged the winner. All that was linked to Russian history and to the name Davydoff became dear and close to me. The illustrious origins of my mother's family never flattered my ego but the place taken by the name Davydoff in the history of Russian culture always awoke in me a great feeling of pride.

TRAVELS ABROAD IN CHILDHOOD

When I was nine, my mother's health became a cause for concern. The doctors were worried about her lungs. They had forbidden her to go outdoors in winter and she was only allowed to take a walk for not more than half an hour and then only on the sunny side of the street with her breathing apparatus. In summer she was sent to Switzerland.

This trip was my first one abroad. We stayed at Territet on the lake of Geneva not far from the castle of Chillon. The view from the window of our pension, which I later saw over a thousand times reproduced on color post-cards, on boxes and on other useless souvenirs, ended up boring me intensely, but at first the lake of Geneva, the castle of Chillon and the surrounding mountains formed such a contrast from Moscow and our Ascension street that I was thrilled. As was the custom with tourists, we took a boat ride on the lake, visited the castle of Chillon and gazed fearfully at the place where poor Bonivard had been locked up. We also climbed the mountains that rose above Territet and admired the view of the lake. Nevertheless in spite of my initial enthusiasm for the beauty of this nature, neither then nor later, when I used to travel frequently to Switzerland, could I ever really get to like it, without being able to say exactly why. Maybe mountains oppress a person like me who is used to living on steppes, and maybe also Switzerland seems to me a little bourgeois and provincial. My attitude towards it is probably unfair. One feels free there and its history shows that it is the birthplace of many great thinkers and patriots.

109

The following year we returned to Switzerland but this time to a small village, Aigle-les-Bains, at the top of the Rhone valley, almost facing the Dent du Midi. Nowadays Aigle has become a big spa but in those times there was only one hotel which was frequented solely by English people. It was a very boring place and had there not been the walks in the mountains one could easily have fallen prey to melancholy. Every day for breakfast, lunch, tea and dinner, we were served rhubarb, in every conceivable form, in salad, in jam, in sweet cakes and in other preparations; everything was made with rhubarb.

Our later trips to Switzerland were much more interesting. Again for health reasons we went to a small town, the name of which escapes me, near lake Konstanz, and twice to St. Moritz in the Engadine. At Konstanz I remember very distinctly an abbey that had been turned into a hotel. In the dining-room well-preserved frescoes covered the curtained walls. It was probably in this place that the conclave convened in 1417. Naturally we made an excursion to the place called the «Drei Länder Blick» (the view of the three countries) where one can see at the same time Germany, Austria and Switzerland. We admired a picturesque islet in the middle of the lake where there was at that time a famous clinic for alcoholics.

In those times there did not exist what is so fashionable nowadays, winter sports. In winter people dreamed of warm countries and of the Mediterranean, and went to spend the winter months on the French Riviera or in Egypt. That is why St. Moritz was almost empty in winter. One only went there in summer. It seems to me that the winter tourists were very fortunate as they could admire the magnificent panorama covered in a white shroud. The other advantage of travelling in the Engadine in those days was the absence of any railway linking it to the rest of Switzerland. Nowadays tunnels have been bored under the two great passes that lead to the Engadine—the Julierpass and the Albulapass—and travellers take about twenty minutes to cover the distance that it used to take them all of a day and a half to travel by post-chaise on the excellent Swiss roads, stopping for the night on the way. Today's tourists cannot enjoy, as they come down from the Julierpass, the splendid panorama of the Engadine valley with its chain of lakes which, on a sunny day, take on an emerald color as they reflect the pine forests that cover the mountain slopes. The view as one crosses the barren pass is a striking one. At the top stands a stone column which commemorates the passage of Julius Caesar, and on the right one can see the Piz Julier with its eternal snow.

We arrived by rail at the station of Chur and there took what was called the «Extrapost», a large coach with two seats at the back, drawn by four splendid horses. The coach, the harness, the horses and the coachman's picturesque costume, were spick and span and spotlessly shiny. The first day, after riding through open country at a moderate altitude, we arrived in the evening at Tiefencastel. There we spent the night in a very clean small hotel where we were served a simple but good meal with a light local white wine. The next morning, after a breakfast with delicious cream and excellent butter, we started off. The climb up to the pass began at Tiefencastel and took several hours. There was no village on the road nor any posthouse and we fed on provisions taken from Tiefencastel. It was only in the evening that we arrived in St. Moritz.

We had a very gay time in St. Moritz because on both occasions we went there with aunt Lina and members of the family from Courland including two young cousins of Countess Kaiserling. We made long excursions, climbed glaciers and picked edelweiss on the high rocks. We sometimes went by coach, driven by Italian coachmen and drawn by bedecked horses along the Engadine lakes on the road to Chiavenna up to Maloja where the Inn forms a small waterfall that drops down to the valley before becoming a large river far away in Austria and mingling its waters with those of the Danube.

Our most picturesque journey was the one we made after our second stay in St. Moritz. I cannot remember why, that time we had to go through Vienna and my mother decided we would take the train in Austria after going by road through the Arlberg to Innsbruck. Once again in an «extrapost», we crossed this time the Albulapass and continued along the Inn to enter the Tyrol at Landeck. The road to Innsbruck, both in Switzerland and in Austria, was beautiful but I remember particularly well the bridge over the Inn in the middle of which runs the frontier between Switzerland and Austria. After spending the night in Innsbruck we boarded the train and, after passing through the Arlberg tunnel, arrived in Vienna.

One year my brother's health required a stay in Bad Kreuznach. There we stopped at the largest hotel, the Oranienhof, where during the First World War the general staff of Emperor Wilhelm had stayed. We did not stay in the hotel itself but in an annex, the other half of which was occupied by an American family who liked to drink. On their national holiday they became drunker than usual and fired rockets and crackers until late in the night. It was my first contact with Americans and they created a strange impression on me.

I liked Bad Kreuznach and its environs very much. Situated on the river Nahe, an affluent of the Rhine, it is surrounded by rather low picturesque mountains on which stand medieval castles which were still lived in at that time. The beauty of Schloss Rheingrafenstein greatly appealed to me. One could not visit it as its owners lived there. Naturally we went with our tutor to Bingen on the Rhine, 30 kms by rail from Kreuznach. There, we visited the famous tower on an island named Mäuseturm where the miserly bishop Hatto after amassing, a long time ago, a large quantity of wheat, refused to share it with the people during a famine and was devoured by mice that swam across the Rhine. After crossing the Rhine by boat we sat in a tavern at Rüdesheim renowned for its wine. Having climbed the mountain up to the statue of Germania at Niederwald erected in memory of the Franco-German war of 1870, and gone up to the room situated in the head of the statue, we were able to admire through its eyes the panorama over the Rheingau with Assmannshausen and Schloss Johannisberg, property of Prince Metternich, famous for its wine, said to be the best of the Rhine valley. Later when I read «Acia» by Turgenev in which the author describes these landscapes and the character of its inhabitants, it all sounded very familiar to me, the only difference being that he did it all on foot with a rucksack on his back whereas I was on bicycle.

At that time our impression of Germany was of a pleasant and cosy country. The cleanliness, the tidiness, the honesty and the hospitality of its inhabitants in such tender and beautiful surroundings inspired peacefulness and confidence in the future. Who would have thought then that, first under the leadership of Prussia, then under that of the Austrian corporal Hitler, this nation so pleasant and sentimental would try and bring into subjection the whole of Europe and commit unheard of atrocities.

My mother had to consult a well-known professor who lived in Heidelberg and who gave conferences at its famous university, so we went there after leaving Bad Kreuznach. For us young boys it was a great joy to find ourselves in this sanctuary of German science and to see an example of the German student mores we had heard so much about from the tutor who accompanied us, F.F. Tchernai. Brimming over with enthusiasm, he had never dreamed that such a thing could have happened to him. It is then that he taught me a charming poem dedicated to Heidelberg by an author whose name unfortunately escapes me:

> Old Heidelberg, so beautiful,
> City rich with honors
> Twixt Neckar and Main
> None other equals you
>
> City of gay lads
> Rich with wisdom and wine.
> Clear are the waves of your river
> In which sparkle blue eyes.
>
> And when from the South
> Arrives gentle spring fom the country
> Petals fall from blossoming trees
> To make you a shimmering dress.

We only spent two days in Heidelberg but while my mother saw the doctor we and the tutor had time to see the interesting parts of the town: the castle, the university and the famous Hirschgasse where stood the house of the first student corporation «Sachso Borüsen». We saw its Kneipe, a bistro, and the room where the duels were fought. On the walls of the room were hung espadons, ribbons of the color of the corporations and photos of glorious contests and the floor was covered with red stains, bloodstains from the duels.

You should have seen the fire that lit up the eyes of our tutor as he gazed at these sights. I can imagine what letters he wrote to his colleagues in Courland and what he told them when he saw them later.

COURLAND

Before my eldest brother started going to the Gymnasium, we would leave Moscow every year in May for the summer months. At first we would go either to the palace of Bliden in Courland, main seat of the Lievens on the Riga coast, or to Kamenka, the estate of the Davydoffs in the Tchigirin district of the Kiev province. Later on, when the health of my mother or of another relative required treatment in a spa, we often went abroad. Finally, much later, we used to go and visit our Davydoff grandparents in their Crimean estate of Sably. I have already written in detail about Kamenka and Sably as these places are linked to the history of my father's family and have their own historical past. I will now describe the life of my Courland family in their palace of Bliden.

Before doing this I must open a slight parenthesis. I cannot limit my impressions of Courland to the period of my childhood and of my youth. They would not be complete and would not give a true picture of the milieu of that time that played a leading role in the history of the Empire. I also went to Courland when I was a student and when I was an adult. Besides my family, I knew many Balts who lived in St. Petersburg and because of this I was able to acquire a thorough knowledge of them.

My Courlandian family was very large and very well off. They owned large estates in Courland with beautiful palaces and 44,000 dessiatines of land on the southern banks of the Volga. The main seat of the family was the palace of Bliden. This

115

estate was situated 45 versts from the station of Aoutze on the railway line that linked Mitau to Libau. The palace itself, built in monumental Russian Empire style, stood in the center of a large park that merged gradually into a dense forest. The main entrance, adorned with heavy columns, gave on to a very large circular courtyard divided in two by a central alley. The part close to the house formed a lawn with bushes and flower beds. The other half included a pond where birds swam. Just in front of the entrance, behind the pond, were the stables and the hangars for carriages, also built in Russian Empire style. The other facade of the palace gave on to the park. On that side ran a large terrace also adorned with columns. From this terrace one looked out on to a big lawn with, on one side, a small lake and a picturesque islet which could be reached by boat, and on the other side a forest. The pathway that led up to the house was large and shaded and two versts long. The interior of the palace consisted of a large hall painted in two colors which on two of its sides gave on to a suite of drawing-rooms and cabinets. On the right these led to a dining-room that could easily seat fifty people. In the left wing were the private apartments of the old Princess Charlotte Karlovna Lieven and of her unmarried youngest daughter Marie. On the second floor of the palace were the guest-rooms and those of the governesses and of the housekeeper.

At the end of the pathway that led to the house stood the doctorate or doctor's pavilion, a building also built in a good style. The servants' quarters were not near the house but 6 versts away in the «Gross Bliden» where lived the manager, the head-forester and the pastor. The «kirk» was also there.

Long before the general liberation of the serfs in 1861, the Balt nobles, of their own initiative, had proposed to free the Lett serfs without giving them any land. The Russian government accepted this proposal and agriculture in these regions took on the character of English farms. The owners themselves only farmed a small part of their land and, for this reason, did not require a great deal of equipment, nor many buildings for their farming.

116

A large part of the Bliden estate was made up of forest which was remarkably well kept and exploited according to a rigorous plan. Hunting was protected and game abounded. The head-forester, Buch, a fervent hunter like all German Balts, was said to have drawn a map of the forest on which were marked the spots where such and such game could be found, the animals being drawn figuratively.

As in the whole Baltic region, the farmers were Lett peasants, ex-serfs, while the owners who managed their estates, the doctors and the pastor were all German. The Letts spoke no other language but their own and the German Balts were forced to learn their language, which was not really difficult as the nannies and the servants were all Letts.

In the palace of Bliden lived the year round, winter come summer, the oldest representative of the Lieven family, the «matriarch», as one might call her, Princess Charlotte Karlovna Lieven, who was a widow. When I saw her for the first time, she was a small plump old lady whose face still showed signs of a past beauty, her hair parted in the middle and combed over her ears. As was the custom at that time she wore a lace bonnet. Aunt Charlotte, as we called her, was a charming, exquisite, old lady, the kindest that could be. She was especially kind to children and spoiled them terribly. We all loved her. The other relatives who lived in the palace were aunt Marie, a spinster, and her brother Leon, a widower, and his small daughter.

In the summer and at Christmas time arrived in Bliden all the offspring of aunt Charlotte, her sons, her married daughters with their husbands, her grandsons and granddaughters, and her great-grandchildren with their tutors and governesses. The house was bursting with people and 40 or 50 people sat at table. I liked to visit Bliden at those times because, in spite of the fact that these relatives were of little interest, at least one could get lost in the crowd and not be obliged to sit with the old people and entertain them with boring conversation. One could go for walks, ride horseback and especially hunt. When I was there beats were organized almost every day and what was pleasant was that they were not done especially for me.

There were also family celebrations, for instance the birthdays of those who lived the year round in the palace as well as of guests. These celebrations followed a ritual that was set once and for all, very intimidating and tiring for the one in whose honor they took place. At 8 a.m. a visiting orchestra hired especially for the occasion would wake up the person whose birthday it was with a serenade that included a few German airs of which I only remember one, in fact only one verse:

> «My heart is like a beehive,
> Young girls are inside
> Who fly in, who fly out,
> Exactly as in a beehive,
> In my heart that is a cell!»

When he came down to the dining-room for his breakfast he would find his place at the table all decorated with garlands of flowers. Before eating he had to receive the good wishes not only of all his relatives but also of the oldest servants of the palace and all these people offered him presents as modest as they were useless. In addition to presents the young cousins gave poems in German that they had composed. That entire day he was the object of special attentions. At lunch and at dinner his place at table remained decorated with flowers and toasts to his health were drunk with very sweet champagne.

As I have already said all this was rather embarassing and tedious so when I went to Bliden I would avoid at all costs, even by a chance remark, reminding anyone of the date of my birthday. You can imagine how pleased I was when during one of my visits, aunt Marie said she had forgotten the date of my birthday (I was born in September) and asked me to remind her of it. Without hesitating I answered that I was born in October and I thought I had got away with it. Imagine my chagrin when on the morning of September 29 I was woken up by the «Ständchen»!! Aunt Marie had found her birthday agenda and had punished me by doubling the celebrations. Even the little old woman who lived retired in one of the pavilions in the park offered me a cake with marzipan that she had made. I had to eat it and God knows how I hate marzipan!

Needless to say my whole Courlandian family was Lutheran and very religious. On Sundays almost the entire family went to the kirk in «Gross Bliden». Every morning before breakfast aunt Charlotte would sit at the big harmonium that stood in a corner of the big hall and play a choral while we all sang in unison standing along the wall. The same thing happened in the evening not once but twice, the first time when the children went to bed, the second time when the older people retired for the night. In spite of the fact that it was always the same choral that was sung the year round, the majority of singers sang completely off key, probably because they had no ear. I remember the high strident voice of the Russian housekeeper, Anisia Stepanovna, who sang so false that it set my teeth on edge just listening to her. Only Aunt Marie had a good accurate voice which made a pleasant exception.

When I think nowadays of my Courlandian family I realize that its unity and its solidarity were only held together by the «matriarch», aunt Charlotte. Even during her lifetime it was obvious that brothers and sisters did not get on. For instance, though they lived under the same roof, uncle Leon and aunt Marie never spoke to each other and when they met they would stick out a hand while looking the other way. One day as I was passing my uncle's study where a stormy talk was in progress, I heard uncle Leon shout at aunt Marie that she was nothing but «ein blödsinniges kahlhuhn!» which means a stupid old hen. I do not know for what reason there was this animosity between my relatives but I do remember that a short time after aunt Charlotte died the family split up, and when uncle Leon also died and his daughter had created a great scandal by marrying a Lettish nobleman, the windows of the Bliden palace were boarded up and the palace was sold.

One of the special traits not only of my Courlandian relatives but also of many Balt nobles was their physical ugliness and their degenerate looks. The reason for this may have been that they intermarried because they were in small numbers and refused to marry Russians. The Lutheran religion allowed marriages even between close relatives and these incestuous marriages caused a weakening of the race. Thus aunt Charlotte was the first cousin of her deceased husband Prince André Karlovich, and their son Leon used to say jokingly: «Ich bin mein eigener Grossonkel» which means «I am my own great uncle».

By their national and political opinions, which they naturally kept to themselves, all these nobles were and remained true Germans, their only Russian loyalty being to the Tsar. These descendants of the Teutonic Knights did not feel Russian at all in spite of their allegiance to the Emperor. Germany and the German Imperial family were much closer to them than the Russian. To tell the truth they felt themselves strangers in Russia. Their real mother country, deep in their hearts, was Germany. As I have already said this was never expressed openly nor specifically but one could feel it. I can recall several examples of this. One day one of my cousins went to Germany with her parents and when they returned told about their trip in my presence. It was incredible to hear with what enthusiasm she spoke of the great honor that had been bestowed upon them by allowing them to meet the sons of Wilhelm II. She was in raptures when she described the physique and the mannerisms of the Kronprinz Wilhelm and of Prince Eitel-Friedrich. When I asked her how many daughters our Tsar had and what were their names she was unable to answer. Another time during a talk with uncle Leon's daughter I spoke about Kazan and she had to admit she did not know what it was. Finally one day I happened to be in Bliden for the New Year and I perceived quite clearly how little my Courlandian family was Russian. According to the fixed ritual, five minutes before midnight aunt Charlotte sat down at the harmonium in the big hall and we all sang together, then the doors opened and the butlers brought in some champagne already served in glasses. When the clocks struck midnight the eldest of my uncles came up to me the youngest person there and also the only Russian male and, touching glasses, said: «Auf Wohl unseren Kaisers!» (to the health of our Emperors!). It must be remembered that all German Balts studied in gymnasiums where all the teaching was in German and where Russian was not taught, then at the

University of Dorpat (later George University) where all the professors were German. None of the Balts, be they men or women, spoke Russian and apart from German knew only a little Lettish and a little French.

Following German tradition they despised the Russians and all that was Russian and were very full of themselves. Everything was better in their country, especially everything that had to do with agriculture. One day I dared to say that in the Ukraine the yield of agriculture was very high, higher than theirs, and my statement provoked an indignant uproar. Finally when a young man was sent to study in St. Petersburg, which went against all tradition, he was said to be «ganz verrückt» which meant russianized, and this was said with regret and disapproval.

Being part of the nobility they were naturally monarchists and because of their Teutonic ancestors they were fervent feudalists. They looked down on simple people and despised them. The tradition of kissing a lord's hand by men and women alike persisted in the Baltic provinces until the revolution of 1905.

However when much later some of these families realized their mistake in adopting such an attitude and started to send their sons to the universities of St. Petersburg and Moscow these sons quickly grasped the advantages of Russian culture and of the Russian mode of life, learned to speak Russian and became assimilated. These young men returned unwillingly to their palaces and only wished to settle in St. Petersburg in some government job. I had many relatives and friends among them. Most of them were good and honest people and excellent friends. Having lived in Russia they got to like it and became loyal subjects. They served in regiments of the Guard and in government posts and their qualities enabled them often to make good careers. However in spite of everything one could always sense their origin and they could never completely understand Russia and the Russians. Those who were close to the throne did not exert a good influence.

THE GYMNASIUM

«We learned of everything a little
What there was and as best we could».

A.S. Pushkin

«The young learn nothing in particular
Just a little of everything».

Heinrich Heine

In September 1892 I passed the entrance exam into the second form of Moscow's second gymnasium. As I was an excellent pupil and had been well prepared by good teachers, this exam presented no difficulty for me.

The second gymnasium was situated at the intersection of Elohovsk and Razgul streets, in Bruce's old palace, the collaborator of Peter the Great, a ten minute walk from the Elisabeth Institute. Though old, this establishment was large and spacious. Of Bruce's time the only thing that remained was a sundial on the outside wall that gave on to Razgul street. On its three floors were spaciously installed large and light classrooms and halls, the library entrance hall, the medical dispensary, the dormitories for boarders, their dining room and the church. One could not complain about any lack of hygiene. Everything was clean and as my boarder schoolmates said to me they were fed simply but well. Giving on to the

123

courtyard were the annexes where the heads, the inspector and the servants lived and where the administration office was located. Behind the courtyard there was a garden where in summer we used to spend the «long interval». The «staircase of honor», which only the teachers and the visitors could use, and by special privilege, the pupils of the upper eighth form, led directly to the cloakroom. It gave on to the library entrance hall, one of the best libraries in Moscow as I was told by my uncle André who had been Governor of Moscow and who used it for his scientific studies. We pupils did not have access to it. From the library one passed into the festival hall and into the eighth form. This upper form had another privilege, that of being allowed to remain in its classroom during the «long interval» and to use a piano that stood there. The library gave onto a corridor onto which gave the classrooms. On the third floor were the boarder's dormitories, four studies and the church. During the eight years that I spent at the gymnasium I sat in almost all the classes.

When I started school the term had already begun. I was taken to my class by the inspector and presented to the teacher and to my classmates. My place and my desk had been fixed beforehand. My mother had asked the head to sit me next to a good student. Kolokolov, a nephew of Boldyrev, a temporary tutor at the Elisabeth Institute, was just that, an excellent student and a nice boy, timid and clean, but he had a silent passive look that did not go with his age. We never really became friends because of his uncommunicative character but at least he did not try to dissipate me and taught me no evil things. Other classmates took care of that. For that it was not necessary to be seated by my side on the same bench.

As was the custom at the first interval the class proceeded with the «baptism» of the «novice» which consisted of beating him up. He was given «a citizen's right» if he stood up to the beating in a manly way, did not cry and did not complain to the headmaster. I was very fortunate in having a brother who had studied in the same school for two years and who had warned me about what was going to happen. Also I was much taller and much stronger than my schoolmates. As soon as I realized that the attack was about to take place

I quickly backed into a corner of the classroom so as to protect my rear. When the most dangerous «leaders» got close to me and tried to trip me up and make me fall, without waiting for this manoeuver I immediately attacked and with my fists knocked down those who were in front. At that moment, attracted by the noise, the class supervisor arrived and stopped the fight. To my surprise at the next interval the attack was not repeated and I discovered that not only had I been accepted as a member of the class but also I was to be respected because of my physical superiority and my manly resistance. My classmates did not know that at the time I entered school I already had a good experience of fighting. It was not for nothing that we were three brothers at home and that we trained by fighting with our friends the sons of the servants of the Institute. This incident gave me a special prestige that I kept until the end of my stay in the gymnasium.

The teachers of the second form had no particular characteristic and I don't remember much about them. Only three of them remain in my memory for different reasons. The first was our headmaster Serge Vikentievich Gulevich. He taught us Latin. Later I understood that he was a cultured and erudite man but at first I only respected him for his strict fairness, his calm and the nice gentleness with which he treated us, the children of the second form. He was an excellent teacher and he knew how to arouse our interest even for subjects as boring as the first notions of Latin grammar. In the upper classes he sometimes replaced a teacher who was ill and it was interesting to translate the Roman classics under his supervision.

One of the two other masters whom I remember was the drawing teacher who could in no way understand that his subject was not a normal one but an art that, independently from any effort of concentration, requires talent. As I never had any for drawing I was often given a «2» which made my mother very unhappy.

The third master who has remained in my memory was a very special case which fortunately was not encountered frequently even in those distant times. I cannot remember his name but his features are ever present in my memory

125

up to this day. A very old man, thin and tall, with a gruff voice, he terrified the pupils. He taught orthography and if one of us made a mistake not only would he beat the culprit's fingers with his ruler, he would also insult him with well-known Russian expressions that I can in no way reproduce in these pages. One day he became furious with me and started to insult me in the way I have just described and took his ruler in his hand, and I, a boy of 12, found in myself enough strength of character to say to him that I did not accept his methods and that if he did not agree I would go and ask the headmaster if he did not think I was right. The old man naturally understood that he was running the risk of losing his job, did not say another word and gave up using his teaching methods, at least in our class. When I was already in the seventh form, I was travelling with my brother and his tutor on the south coast of the Crimea. On the boat that was taking us from Yalta to Gurzuf we met a priest in whom I recognized a bishop. During our conversation we very soon understood that this bishop had studied in the same second form of the Moscow gymnasium as my brother and I. We started talking about old memories and to my great surprise I learned that the bishop's orthography teacher had been the same cantankerous old teacher we had had.

My year in the second form was marked by two events, the first of which was tragic. One Sunday morning in one of the empty classrooms on the top floor, in a corner under the icon, the classmate who sat at my desk, Kolokolov was found dead. Next to him was a half-empty bottle of ammonia. He was a boarder and no doubt while the others were at mass, without being seen he had gone to the empty classroom and had committed suicide. We never found out what had driven him to this act.

The second event was that during Holy week, I caught a very severe case of pneumonia and had three relapses. It was our family physician, Gabrichewsky, who saved my life although when I had my third relapse on Easter day he had warned my mother that I had very little chance of pulling through. Nevertheless I recovered and my mother insisted that I go in for the entrance exam into the third form. The head of the school was totally opposed to this idea, invoking a ridiculous excuse that by doing the second form over again I would be able to perfect my French. I must say that in my class I was the only boy who knew how to speak and read French fluently. My mother took me out of the school and in the autumn of that same year I went back there—in the third form.

It seemed that all was going well and that I would continue my courses sucessfully at the gymnasium, but it was then that the first failure of my life occurred. I was just thirteen and for me the «hour of love and of tender melancholy» had arrived. As I have already said this phase was associated for me with a tremendous psychological shock. I changed completely and from a child I became an adolescent with a fiery temperament and a bad temper. I studied very badly and life for me at home became hell. Every day reproaches fell on me and I never heard a kind word any more. I closed up and learned to hide my thoughts and my feelings. If before I had adored my mother, I now began to avoid her. As I was incapable of learning I started to study the techniques of successful scholarship, that is to say, the methods by which one could pass from one form to the next and finish one's courses with the least possible effort. It must not be supposed that it was easy for me to accept my first failure. Deep inside me I realized perfectly well the irregularity of my position but I could not find the moral equilibrium necessary to get me out of this situation. The worst of all was that my mother had said when she sent me to school: «You must finish the gymnasium. The way in which you do it is none of my business—it is yours. I will not interfere, neither will I help you». I had been very proud of these words and my pride suffered all the more at my first failure. It is precisely there that the inadequacy of the educational system «in the fear of God» became evident. In that difficult phase of my life nobody stretched out a hand to help me nor did anyone try and read in my soul where at that time darkness reigned. Needless to say I stayed in the third form another year.

What saved me was my good health. The first storms of «love and tender melancholy» having passed, my moral strength enabled me to recover a normal equilibrium and my perfect knowledge of the school techniques of learning enabled me to pass the exams easily. Three years hadn't passed before I was able to answer my mother's question as to why during one of the trimesters I had slumped from first to sixth place in my class: «You promised that you would not interfere with my studies so why should you care?» And when a tutor was engaged for my brother, who studied badly and with difficulty, and my mother wanted him to make me work also, I protested and reminded her that she had promised not to help me with my studies.

The teaching methods at school consisted of the following. First of all one must keep in mind the fact that in the school there were two enemy camps: on the one side the heads, that is to say the school administration, the teachers and the supervisors, on the other side the pupils. The first camp had one incomparable advantage over the other. It had for itself total authority, the possibility of doing what it pleased, of judging a student without any possibility of appeal, of causing him all sorts of difficulties and at the extreme of destroying him by dismissing him from the school. The position of the first camp was reinforced by the fact that it was presumed to be always right and fair. It also had a faithful ally in the person of the parents. The educational system «in the fear of God», which was particularly powerful, had entrenched solidly the rules whereby adults were always right and could not be unfair.

What could the second camp do to oppose this force? First of all there was the solidarity of the pupils among themselves. Each pupil who supported this solidarity knew that in a difficult moment his schoolmates not only would not denounce him but would even do all in their power to help him. Conversely the pupil who put himself on the side of the administration, who tried to help it even by taking the path of denunciation, was doomed to a sad fate in spite of the privileged appearance of his friendship with the people in power. The administration itself despised him and his schoolmates missed no opportunity to punish him by applying their own justice. In a difficult moment, which could happen to anyone, he found himself alone, for although his schoolmates would not go so far as to denounce him to the administration, they did nothing at all to help him out of it. Knowing he could count on this solidarity each student could be certain that every expedient and every trick he would use for his defence would be supported by his schoolmates even without asking them.

In my time there existed a special system by which one need not complicate one's life at exams. Exams to pass from one form to the next were only compulsory for those forms that gave special rights for military service, as for example the sixth form. In the other forms the pupils passed according to their average marks during the year. To pass an average of «4» was required in the main subjects. It is obvious that for these last forms one had to work all through the year whereas for the others it was only necessary to work before the exams. As for the exams themselves, it was sufficient to study the oral part because at the written part one could always «borrow» from a more knowledgeable neighbor!

For a long time the camp of the pupils used only the method described above, but when the active Russian youth started to take an interest in politics, to have recourse to strikes and to use violence against the administration, a new strategy originating from the universities gained the gymnasium. It was not that the gymnasiums had become revolutionary centers. Politics continued to be unknown to the pupils but they understood that if they formed an organized group they could not only defend themselves by trickery but they could also organize demonstrations. These demonstrations were of two sorts: strikes and direct demonstrations against the teachers who were considered to be undesirable. The first method consisted as a rule in the whole class refusing, from a certain date on, to answer the aforesaid teacher or refusing to write their homework or their compositions. This method was the least dangerous for the pupils because it was not possible, practically speaking, to expel a whole class. In such an event the council of teachers would inflict a general punishment which by the same token had no individual effect. For the teacher, on the other hand, the strike of the pupils had a fatal result: he lost his job. The result was that the pupils achieved their objective without too much difficulty, for the collective punishment was easily borne and quickly forgotten. There only remained the halo of what they had suffered for the truth. The second method was catastrophic both for the teacher and for the pupil who had offended him. Both had to leave the school. Later on it became easier for the pupil than for the teacher because the chosen pupil was in any case going to be dismissed from the school either because of all the faults he had committed or because of the age limit he had reached, which prevented him from continuing to frequent the gymnasium. There were several pupils of this type in each class, especially among the boarders. Those who were punished by being given «the wolf's passport», which was a certificate according to which after being dismissed they could not enter any other state school, were a pitiful sight. Unkempt, dirty, badly dressed, smoking and drinking vodka even during the courses, they were the candidates of the «bottom» of the class. It was one of these that was picked to execute the demonstration, which took place in the following manner. The pupil waited until the condemned teacher questioned him. Naturally he did not know his lesson and when the teacher rebuked him because of this he reacted with brutality and provocation. The teacher would lose control over himself and try to interrupt him in an insolent manner. Then the pupil would slap the teacher's face. No one in the class would come to the teacher's aid and all that was left for him to do was to go and complain to the administration. The inspector would arrive accompanied by the supervisor and the culprit was sent to the «cell», from which he only emerged to leave the school permanently. The heads knew very well that this whole affair had been staged by the entire class but as they had no proof they could not apply any disciplinary measures to the class itself. As in the first method we would never see the teacher again.

I remember three active demonstrations of the students in our school and I must say that in all three cases the students were right. Two of these incidents took place in my class and I took part in them.

When one of the regular teachers suffered a long illness, a replacement was sent to take over. These replacements were usually young men with no teaching experience but who considered themselves nevertheless to be great experts in their field. Our form had to put up with two novices of this sort. The first one was simply abnormal. While conducting his courses he would gesticulate in a way that would make us burst out laughing and when he would ask us to translate Russian sentences into Latin they would be devoid of all meaning. I still remember one of them: «When the enemy soldiers saw that they were dead the general occupied the town». I don't know in what way we got rid of this phenomenon but I don't think it was anything very serious because we were not punished. Maybe the administration was in agreement with us on our evaluation of this teacher and it decided to keep the incident quiet. The other case was more serious. The young teacher had decided he had to be strict with us, forgetting that strictness must be accompanied by fairness. I think that if he had been an old and experienced teacher we would not have decided to take any strong action but we had no respect for this novice. It was decided to go on strike by refusing to do our homework. A few minutes before the class started, at an extraordinary meeting we, the five top pupils of the class, agreed to take part in the strike. I underlined the fact that our taking part in this demonstration gave it a special strength. All went according to plan. No one defected. We never saw the teacher again but the teaching council decided to take the following measures against us: 1) Give everyone a «O» for the homework. 2) Have the whole class come on a Sunday for another written composition. 3) Give everyone a «1» for conduct. Of these three punishments the third was the most unpleasant. The reason for this was that these incidents took place when we were in the seventh form and students who at the end of their studies at the gymnasium did not have good conduct marks came under the surveillance of the police and ran the risk of not being admitted into the university. Naturally this affair fizzled out. We did the Sunday work for which I was given a «4». The regular teacher, when he recovered from his illness, did not give the «0» that had been ordered but an average mark of «4», and the conduct marks were corrected before the end of the school year. The heads played a great role in this clemency because they were very liberal-minded and admitted that we might be right. I drew this conclusion from a conversation I had with Professor S.A. Ivantsov whom my mother and I knew very well. He called me to the parlor and asked me how I, a young man from a good family, could have taken part in this strike. I answered him by asking him how he would have reacted if he had been in my place. He turned round without a word and left.

The third incident, which did not take place in my class, was an example of the second type of demonstration where violent action was taken. In our gymnasium physics were taught by Fedor Fedorovich Handrikoff. He was a middle-aged man who was known to have a bad temper, be quibbling, heartless and unfair. His lessons consisted in making us learn by heart the famous school book by Kraevich, the one of which a university professor said to his students: «In school you certainly studied Kraevich, so here is my first advice: forget all you have learned from him and let us start again from scratch». The whole school hated Handrikoff but for I don't know what reason the administration could not decide to dismiss him. Finally the students lost patience and could not stand him any longer. One of the forms decided to take action. In that particular class there was a student aged 20 who could not spend another year in the same form and had no hope of passing his exam successfully. He was chosen to be the executioner. During one of the courses this student was called by Handrikoff and naturally did not know his lesson. Handrikoff started to make fun of him in an insulting manner. The student sprang forward and slapped him in the face. What happened next is obvious.

My position in school was a special one. When I was in the fourth form my aunt Katia's husband, Nicholas Pavlovich Bogolepov, was named head of the board of trustees of the schools of the Moscow district and when I was finishing school he had been named Minister of Education. The heads of the school knew that N.P. Bogolepov was a relative of mine and naturally were very wary of me. My position was all the more delicate as my schoolmates also knew about the uncle-minister and might think that I was taking advantage of this connection.

I had to act with a great deal of tact and convince my school-mates that if ever I did seek to do this it would only be in the interest of the class and not my own. Just such an occasion presented itself when I was in fifth form and Bogolepov was head of the district. This happened before Shrovetide which meant three days holiday. We learned that there was an epidemic of diphtheria among the boarders. I did not delay in telling my aunt, who was head of the Elisabeth Institute, and she was obliged to take measures to prevent the epidemic from gaining the Institute. She therefore immediately called Bogolepov who told her that the schoolboys would be sent home the following day at noon, that is to say three days before the normal date. When I arrived at school the following day I told my classmates about this and they in turn, without naming the source of their information, told the supervisor who told the administration. As the latter knew nothing about it we were told that we had invented this stupid thing, but at noon the inspector entered the classroom and announced that we could go home and only return after the holidays. Naturally the management guessed who was at the origin of the affair and my classmates thanked me for my cleverness. My special position did not entail any favors from the heads, but I could be certain that I would finish school in the prescribed time, if only because the management wanted to get rid of me.

Among the teachers there were good ones and bad ones. The mediocre ones were the majority and this is under-standable, the reason being that in those times the Depart-ment of Education was in very poor condition and cultured and able people were the exception. To make a career was difficult. In the best of cases the teacher could become inspector and later headmaster, but there were many teachers and the posts were scarce. Furthermore, to get an advancement one had to have not only good professional reports but also political ones. It was not easy to handle 25 to 40 scamps who only tried to mock and play tricks. To prove one's talent and gain the respect and love of the pupils was not easy either. The main obstacle was the system applied at that time in Russian schools. In spite of Heine's opinion, we did learn something, but nothing was done to develop our interest in study. The teachers had to follow to the letter the school program and were not allowed to do anything for our general culture. The result was that a good student was good in Latin grammar, wrote his homework without making a mistake, translated correctly Ovid and Horace, but had no notion of the culture of ancient Rome of which these poets were the representatives and understood nothing of the value of their literature and the beauty of their works. The teachers could not help a student either in the study of history because this was learnt in the manual of Ilovaisky, the only manual authorized by the Ministry and renowned for its worthlessness. Even now, after so many years, I can remember a few isolated sentences from this book: «The history of the Medes is dark and incomprehensible», or else «Alcibiades was wealthy and famous, nature had spoiled him, but when the Germans [1] (!!) that stood at street corners in Athens were smashed the citizens of one accord condemned him». There were many of these pearls. In the modern history of Russia the arm of the censor was particularly evident. According to Ilovaisk, Paul I and Alexander I had died natural deaths. There was no mention of «the wonderful beginning of Alexander's days». Our adorable history teacher Mikhail Ivanovich Vladislavlev had perhaps been greatly interested in this subject when he was a young student but when I knew him and was studying under him he had accepted the official version and recited listlessly what was written in the Ilovaisk. He interrogated us every trimester and although we knew nothing gave us a «5». We, on the other hand, never did anything against him and we lived in good harmony. Even his unattractive looks did not make him a target for our mockery. He was small with short legs, a bloated stoutness, a mass of hair on his head, a big nose and was short-sighted.

Another monster from a physical standpoint was the Latin teacher, Alexander Nikolaevich Bykoff. Even smaller than Vladislavlev, thin with a red beard and hair combed straight back, an enormous nose topped by a pair of glasses, he gave the impression of a small Mephistopheles. The students thought he was a «beast» and indeed he was without pity but, in my

---

1. Instead of «Hermae».

opinion, fair. He had confidence in me and as I was a good pupil he gave me good marks although he seldom interrogated me. One day, probably to check, he interrogated me without warning when I did not know my lesson. Without a word he gave me a «0» and for a month he interrogated me every day. At the end of the month he crossed off the «0». Suddenly this «beast» changed completely. All his strictness disappeared, he became tenderly sentimental with his pupils and started to give «5» to everyone both for the oral and the written homework. At first we could not understand what had happened but we soon did. One day, while listening to a boy's answer, he covered his face with his hands and said with a painful expression on his face «Wait, I don't understand a thing». When he had recovered his wits he got up and quickly walked out of the class. When one day he arrived in class and took out a pack of advertising cards of some firm or other and, walking between the desks, started to distribute them to us, we realised that our «beast» Bykoff had gone completely insane. I must say that the whole class then showed a great deal of humanity and we did everything we could to protect our sick teacher. During his lectures one could have heard a pin drop and no one reacted to his strange actions, and there were many. We all learned our lessons and deserved our «5». This situation lasted two months and we were surprised that the administration had not noticed anything. Finally one day Alexander Nikolaevitch did not appear. He had been taken to an insane asylum.

I have never liked mathematics but those that were taught us at school were not difficult to assimilate. In addition to arithmetic we studied algebra and trigonometry. Our math teacher was Nicholas Kazimirovitch Kviatovsky, a small, neat and clean old man. He, without doubt, knew his subject very well and taught it to us perfectly. I always admired the mastery with which he drew geometrical figures on the blackboard. He liked me, I don't know why, because I studied very badly under him. In those times, in gymnasiums, there were tutors whose function, among others, was to help the students but in practice their work limited itself to writing down the marks on the notebooks that the students had to have signed by their parents each week. In these notebooks were also written their trimestrial results. The pupils could complain to the tutors about the injustices they felt had been done to them and ask them to explain all the questions that they had not understood. Our tutor was N.K. Kviatovsky. As he liked to talk we found a way of not being interrogated. The first half of study time was spent explaining the following lesson and the second half interrogating students. When nobody wanted to answer, it was up to me, his favorite pupil, to ask him to explain something or other, for instance our situation as students of the upper forms and the rights that went with it. His answer would fill the whole second half of the course.

Catechism was taught us by Father Rogdestvensky whom we nicknamed Judas Iscariot. He was tall, had red hair and was sly. I knew a secret about him but never told anyone. He had been a priest at the Elisabeth Institute and while there had embezzled church funds and had been dismissed. Aunt Lina took pity on him and found a post for him at the second gymnasium as tutor. He was involved in an amusing incident in my elder brother's class. One of the pupils he was interrogating said to him, I don't know what about, that he did not believe in God. He gave him a zero.

I have only kept warm memories of two teachers. One was Serge Alexandrovich Ivantsov who had taught me Latin at home before I entered school, and then again later in school. The other was Serge Nikolaevich Smirnoff who taught literature in the top classes of the school. Both of them by their intelligence, their erudition and their talent as pedagogues were exceptional men. It was perhaps because of them and of the headmaster S.V. Gulevich that our school had the reputation of being liberal and even «red». They were certainly liberals but they did not take advantage of their classes to make any propaganda. Their liberalism manifested itself mainly as far as we were concerned by their attitude towards us and if they never said «tu» to us neither did they use any insults, shouts or invectives. They respected us as one respects human beings and because of that not only did we respect them deeply in return but we even loved them. The «official» teaching line did not allow them to expound the whole beauty of a subject but they did manage to stimulate our interest in it and in that way justify what Heine had said. At that time Russian literature had stopped at Turgenev. Tolstoy and Dostoievsky seemed not to have existed, probably because even these authors were considered by the administration to be subversive. Of course it was forbidden to speak about Belinsky. However S.N. Smirnoff managed to get around this obstacle. He spoke about Tolstoy and Dostoievsky as if by chance, and quoted Belinsky without specifying his name. It is interesting to know Smirnoff's opinion about how to write a narration. He tried by every possible means to root out of us all emphasis, all pathos and all awkwardness of thought. For him simplicity and veracity in art were the major qualities. That is why for us, at least for those of us who understood him, writing was such a pleasure and came to us so naturally. I remember how in 8th form he gave us a composition on the subject of «What games did I play in my childhood?» I did not spend more than two hours on this work and described my childhood games as they had really occurred. I did it so easily that I thought it would be the subject of mockery and that I would be reproached for my naivety, especially as my classmates boasted of the fantastic things they had invented. When S.N. Smirnoff gave us back our exercise books he put one aside and after having distributed the others said to us: «And now I am going to read to you the essay which will show you how you should have tackled the subject», and he read my essay. It turned out that the naivety that had worried me was exactly the artistic truth he was expecting from us.

Serge Alexandrovich Ivantsov was the son of the famous Moscow scholar, Dean Ivantsov Platonov. The second name attached to his family name showed that when he had been a student at the Religious Academy he had merited by his work a special prize that was given by the metropolitan Platonov. All the sons of this dean, of whom I knew two, Serge and Nicholas, were very able men but Serge was the most remarkable one. Up to this day I cannot understand why he did not make a career in the civil service. Intelligent, cultured, erudite and honest, he occupied a choice place in the progressive circles of Moscow and had a great reputation. What was very pleasant about him was that he did not take himself seriously and was not pedantic. On the contrary, in his moments of leisure he liked to drink a glass of vodka, play whist and go hunting. He was «human» and we all loved him. I remember with what interest we translated under him Ovid and Horace and how, thanks to him, we learned how to appreciate the beauty of these poets. He was an admirer of Ovid and I preferred Horace and sometimes, even during classes, we used to discuss the merits of one or the other.

When the parents who applied the system «in the fear of God» put their children in school they were afraid of the bad influence that school circles might have on their children, especially if these had a «democratic» upbringing. This was a great mistake. Whatever its composition the pupils were still the best educators. At least this was the case in Russia during my childhood and in my youth. As I said earlier speaking about my education, for children and adolescents the sentiments of justice and honesty are innate and these sentiments are even exalted when the child is part of a group. In the eyes of all children and adolescents collective friendship is the final arbiter of honesty and justice. It was only in rare cases that it did not justify its reputation. The more democratic the circle, the stronger were these sentiments and the more severe the judgment. This last fact was understandable and logical because children who belonged to families who suffered social pressures and injustice reacted to them in a morbid fashion. The judgment of their schoolmates was accepted as something sacred because it was the judgment of their peers and not of the administration and was founded not on prejudices and principles but on convictions and general views. Furthermore this tribunal was clement and if the culprit corrected himself his fault was quickly forgotten and he got back his equal rights.

For me my eight years in the gymnasium among young people of my age were very precious and useful. I must say I was fortunate for the elite of my class was composed of good elements. I came from a circle that was unknown to them that of high society where my mother held an influential position. In the eyes of my schoolmates this was not an

138

element in my favor and I had to be very careful. Fortunately I never had any problems, maybe because I never took advantage of this position except to do something for the benefit of the class. I still think with gratitude of the positive influence of my schoolmates who gave me what I had been unable to get from my German tutors.

The peace of the era of Alexander's reign also exerted an influence on schoolboys. Not only did no one speak about politics in our school, no one even thought about them. Thus all possibilities of friction were eliminated. Neither did anti-semitism exist. We had two Jews in our class. One, Schwartz-mann, was the son of a private commissioner. The other was my desk mate, Golman. During the seven years I spent next to him on the same bench it never entered my mind to ask him where he came from nor what his father did.

The stock of knowledge I took away from school was not very heavy. We really learned «a little of everything and a little anyhow» but personally I took away my first experience of life and my first meeting with a circle that was unknown to me and this made life much easier at the time of the great upheavals and of the re-estimation of all values.

THE KHAMOVNIKI

I am 16, my older brother one and a half years older. We live in Moscow on the «Field of Peas» and we are students at the second gymnasium of Moscow, I in the sixth form, my brother in the seventh. All our schoolmates live at the other end of town near Pretchistenky or in the small streets of the Arbat. To get to them is not easy. If our mother does not lend us her carriage we must either drag along for more than an hour in a cheap cariole, which means being frozen in the icy cold air of Moscow winters, or be shaken up in a noisy droshky on the badly paved streets, but our longing to spend a few hours with our friends makes us overcome with ease these minor obstacles. We do not dance yet at children's balls. As one used to say we do not «go out». This pleasure awaits us next year but we already know our future «ladies», charming young girls a little younger than us. However, we get a special pleasure out of our stag parties, but we can only get together in this way when the parents of one of our friends are away.

On a splendid day of an early Moscow spring there is still some snow in the gardens and the squares but the janitors are already removing it from the streets when my brother and I take a droshky one evening to go and visit the Danilevsky brothers. The day before they had told us that they would be alone in their small house situated on one of the streets of the Arbat and that our group would be meeting there. Petia Glebov, Mika Latchinov, Dmitri Kapnist and Cegui Chuvaloff and many others are already there but new acquaintances await us. This is our first meeting with the

Tolstoy brothers, Andriusha and Misha. The first one is much older than we—he is already a student officer at the Tversky Cavalry school—but the second one is our age and goes to school at the Katkoff gymnasium. There is no food but on the table stand several bottles of wine and very soon we are drinking to saying «tu» to our new acquaintances. Andriusha has brought his guitar and we sing as best we can gypsy romances and other songs. The evening goes by very quickly and is very gay. We leave for home reluctantly.

The month of May is here and with it the boring time of exams. Then summer arrives when as usual we leave for the country, for Kamenka. None of our friends live in that region. Their parents' estates are either near Moscow or in central Russia. Summer ends and in August we must resume our studies. This unhappy thought is compensated by the fact that we are going to see our friends again and this year a great joy awaits us—we shall start going to evening parties and dance. At one of these parties Misha Tolstoy introduces us to his mother Countess Sophie Andreevna. Though she does not have any daughters of our age she sometimes appears at our parties. Her youngest daughter Sasha is still a very small girl.

Winter comes and with it another great joy—skating on the Patriarch ponds where our group meets. One day after skating Misha convinces us to go to his home on Khamovnitcheski street where his mother will give us tea. We all accept with pleasure and our joyous group leaves for the Tolstoy home.

A thought suddenly crosses my mind. Now, right away, in a few minutes, I am going to see Tolstoy. I immediately chase away this idea as an impossible dream. Naturally I have already read twice over «War and Peace» and «Anna Karenina» and even, unbeknownst to my mother, «the Kreutzer Sonata», without mentioning «the Cossacks» and other stories by him.

At home when the grown-ups forget my presence I have listened to many discussions on the Kreutzer Sonata and Tolstoy's teachings, and in my imagination he has become a person who lives in a world of his own that I cannot reach. It seems to me that there are two worlds, in one of which live my parents, their friends and we small boys, and another

142

world, the world of Tolstoy and his fellow men. It seems to me that from this lofty world he cannot see us, for him we do not exist.

But here is Khamovnitcheski street with the enormous brick building of a brewery and next to it a two-story wooden house separated from the street by a railing with a garden at the back of a courtyard on which gives the porch. From the hallway we go into a small room on the right that leads to the drawing room.

I stop at the entrance and look around for our hostess but instead of her I see, a few feet away from me, standing in the middle of the drawing room and talking to a stranger, him, Tolstoy.

Needless to say I recognize him at once. Before me, here is Lev Nikolaevich whom I have only seen pictures of. Involuntarily I think «what will come next?». Turning round I see in a room behind the drawing room Countess Sophie Andreevna. I try and sneak out along the wall but Misha comes up to me and leads me to his father. With an air of great respect he says to him: «Papa, allow me to introduce Davydoff». Lev Nikolaevich turns towards me, holds out his hand and, without saying a word, smiles. During the few seconds that Tolstoy looks at me and gives me the present of a smile, it becomes clear to me that he is a man like all other men, that not only does he not live in another world but he even accepts us little people with our daily routine as worthy of his attention. I understand that this man of genius does not look down upon us ordinary people and that everything on this earth is close to him.

One evening Countess Sophie Andreevna invites me to a dance at her home. I accept this invitation with pleasure and on the appointed day my brother and I go to «the Khamovniki». On the way, I wonder if I will see Tolstoy again. I still cannot get used to my new impression of him and it seems to me that his «peasant» disguise does not fit in with the social gathering and the evening dresses of the ladies and the young girls. I think that, having agreed to have this party in his home, he will not want to show by his presence that he approves of it.

When we enter the ballroom guests have already started to dance. Apart from our usual «ladies» we see several unknown young women and girls dressed in gorgeous evening dresses and wearing beautiful diamonds. This makes the party seem even more brilliant.

Misha leads me to a small plump girl and says «This is my sister Sasha». I am caught up by the glitter of the party and forget in whose house I am where I am having such a good time. By chance my eyes fall on the door and I cannot believe it. At the entrance in his usual costume stands Lev Nikolaevich watching with a kind smile the dancing couples...

Count Ivan Stepanovich
LAVAL
1761 — 1846

Countess Alexandra Grigorievna
LAVAL
b. Kozitskaia
1772 — 1850

The front hall
of the Laval's home
on the English Quay
St. Petersburg

XIII

Prince Serge Petrovich
TRUBETSKOY
Decembrist
1790 — 1860   (ca 1820)

Princess Ekaterina Ivanovna
TRUBETSKAIA
b. Laval
1800 — 1854   (ca 1820)

The house of the Trubetskoys
now Museum of the Decembrists
Irkutsk — 1981

Katacha TRUBETSKAIA
in Siberia
(ca 1850)

Serge Petrovich TRUBETSKOY
in Siberia
(ca 1850)

The grave of Katacha TRUBETSKAIA
with the author's daughter
Irkutsk — 1981

The entrance to
the Znamenski Monastery
Irkutsk — 1981

XV

SABLY
The back of the house
1913

SABLY
The alley of chestnut trees
1913

SABLY
The front of the house
1913

SABLY
The front of the house
1981

SABLY
The alley of chestnut trees
1981

SABLY
The house in winter
1981

Olga Alexandrovna DAVYDOVA
b. HSH Princess Lieven
the author's mother
1857 — 1923

Vassili Petrovich DAVYDOFF
the author's father
1852 — 1900

Портретъ кн. Ливенъ (собств. кн. Ливенъ).

Princess Maria Alexandrovna
LIEVEN
1899 — 1941
(portrait by V.A. SEROV)

Prince Karl Andreevich
LIEVEN
1767 — 1844

Princess Daria Kristoforovna
1785 — 1856
LIEVEN   b. Benkendorf
(Drawing by Sir Thomas Lawrence)

Prince Alexander Karlovich
LIEVEN
The author's grandfather

Princess Ekaterina Nikitichna
LIEVEN   b. Pankrateva
the author's grandmother

Elisaveta Sergeevna DAVYDOVA
b. Princess Trubetskaia
the author's grandmother
1834 — 1918

Princess Elena Alexandrovna
LIEVEN
1842 — 1915

Aunt Lina and friends

YURCHIKHA

At the start of these memoirs I stated that when I was three years old my grandmother Elisaveta Sergeevna Davydova had, at the instance of her sister Zinaida Sergeevna Sverbeeva, convinced my grandfather to give my father a part of the domain of Kamenka, the estate of Yurchikha with half of the «Big Wood». It was a splendid estate which brought in enough to allow our family to live comfortably but it had no house and at first when we went to the district of Tchigirin we were forced to stay at uncle Nicholas' house in Kamenka.

I do not know for what reason the house at Yurchikha was only built much later when I was 7 or 8 years old. I remember how I used to run on the foundation stones and stare at the gardeners who were digging holes for the trees in the park. Once the house was ready we spent each summer there and later when I was a student I even went there sometimes in winter.

Many personal memories are linked to Yurchikha, memories of my childhood, my adolescence and my youth. It is there that I became conscious of my surroundings and started to criticize them. It is there that I started to feel the basic contradiction that I had inherited from my parents, the meeting of two totally different worlds, the Davydoffs' and the Lievens', with their diametrically opposite characters. I noticed very quickly, and my mother never denied it, that everything that had to do with Kamenka was not only alien to her but even almost unacceptable. In Moscow, on a territory that one

145

might term neutral, the contradictions between the Davydoffs and the Lievens were less evident, but in Yurchikha an insurmountable gulf seemed to separate Kamenka from the Bliden palace. My mother remained insensitive to the beauty of the history of Kamenka, be it that of the Decembrist-Pushkin period or that of its flowering under the effect of Tchaikovsky's genius. Its inhabitants, his «angels» and his «doves» as Piotr Ilyich Tchaikovsky called them, did not awaken any echo in her either. She even had a rather hostile attitude towards uncle Nicholas.

Nowadays this does not surprise me any more. I can understand that for a woman brought up in the respect of true monarchism the Decembrist plot was inexcusable and my great-grandfather was in her eyes nothing but a state criminal who had violated his oath. I also think that for my mother my great-grandmother Alexandra Ivanovna had always remained a serf, that is a woman who was not of her class and who furthermore had had «illegitimate» children. During the years of my adolescence and my youth I could not share unconditionally my mother's views on Kamenka. In me flowed the blood of the Davydoffs and somewhere in my subconscience awoke this personal feeling that grew gradually until it became a love for the beauty of Russian culture and explained my feelings for Kamenka. Neither could I understand my father's attitude towards Kamenka. He seemed to nurse a personal resentment towards it, almost a feeling of hate. I never noticed any interest on his part for Kamenka, whether for its inhabitants or for its personal charms. I must add that very shortly after we moved to Yurchikha my father's character changed completely and very quickly. From a weak man without any will power he became overbearing and so irritable that to us he seemed almost frightening. At first I attributed these changes to his discord with my mother but later it became evident that these fits were the premonitory signs of the distressing mental illness that flared up when I was 14 and ended in his death in a clinic abroad.

Until my father left Yurchikha life there was not very gay. Our neighbors were all Poles and my father had inherited from my grandfather and from uncle Nicholas their hatred for Poles so they never came to see us. As for my relatives in Kamenka they felt my mother's lack of goodwill towards them and my father's hostility and rarely came to Yurchikha. From time to time we were taken to see my great-grandmother, my aunts and uncle Nicholas. We only saw very seldom the younger generation of Davydoffs in Kamenka. The family of uncle Lev and aunt Sasha particularly irritated my father and as for my mother she thought their company was bad for us from a moral point of view.

When my father was forced to go abroad my mother took over the management of the estate and moved to Yurchikha to live there permanently and the atmosphere in the house became more relaxed. This manifested itself first by the fact that a few occasional visitors started to come and see us whereas before they used to make a great detour to avoid us. Nevertheless for us adolescents life continued to be monotonous. We filled it as best we could with hunting in the company of our friend F.F. Tchernai who had been our first tutor and who had taken on the job of forester, with horseback rides and with family picnics in the «Big Wood». None of these pastimes could satisfy us for long and, if one can use such an expression, we stewed in our juice and were bored. The one who suffered most was my brother Piotr who could absolutely not bear solitude and loved company. Thanks to him, and partly to me, life in our Yurchikha home changed and the isolation of the Davydoffs from the Polish landowners of the Tchigirin district came to an end.

This all started by chance. One day my brother who was already in his first year at university and who happened to be staying in Yurchikha during the month of September received an invitation to a shoot from the head game warden of the Raevskys, Mattiskin. There he met Edward Rostsichewsky, who was a student at the Technological Institute and the son of our neighbor the owner of Kossar. My brother invited him to our home in Yurchikha and my mother, who felt no animosity toward the Poles, received him cordially. From that day on we fell into the habit of going to Kossar and through the Rostsichewskys we got to know other Polish neighbors.

The younger generation of Davydoffs in Kamenka soon followed our example and a pleasant and gay life started at home. Only the older people of Kamenka did not take part in this change in our lives and uncle Nicholas remained as obdurate as ever though he never reproached us our friendship with the «liahi».

The Poles were pleasant neighbors. They had all the characteristics of their race. Perfectly brought up, with maybe sometimes a slightly too pronounced touch of the Western man of the world, loving life and company, extremely hospitable, warm, excellent comrades and good friends, they were at the same time in love with all that made up the charm of the old seignorial life of that time. Their main pastimes were hunting, horses, dogs and joyous lunches and dinners with friends where more than one bottle of «starky»[1] was drunk along with Hungarian wines and remarkable French wines that they imported. At the start of our friendship only one essential thing was lacking, the quality of the food, which had only a very limited national character. Furthermore the very low level of the culinary talents of their chefs who came from places like Hapok and Oleks was the cause of the catastrophic taste of the dishes served in Polish homes. When they started coming to Yurchikha, where we always had an excellent chef, the Poles realized that one could also eat well in the country, acquired Russian chefs from Kiev and started to serve us first-class meals.

I loved the Poles, attachment to old customs and traditions, which manifested itself sometimes in small details of everyday life. I remember that at the beats they organized, the host would stand at the edge of the forest waiting for his guests with a small glass and a bottle of «starky» in his hand and a Cossack by his side dressed in a «kuntuch»[2] with a very large leather belt holding an enormous pot of «bigos»[3]. Each guest after passing his tongue three times over his lips as also did the master of the house had to drink bottoms up the small glass of starky and eat a piece of bigos while the host said:

---

1. Starky = very strong vodka.
2. Kuntuch = a Polish caftan.
3. Bigos = A stew made of cabbage and smoked sausage.

«Thine eye be clear!». I remember how, along with a zakusky before dinner, everyone drank vodka out of the same small glass that was passed from guest to guest by order of age. Finally I remember the old tradition, dangerous for an inexperienced bachelor, according to which in noble Polish families when a daughter was born a few bottles of Hungarian wine were walled up in the cellar and only drunk on the day of her wedding. To say to a young girl «May I taste your wine» was the equivalent of proposing to her.

The Polish women and young girls had nothing to envy of the men. They had refined manners, a great deal of savoir-faire, education and taste for literature and music. They often travelled abroad, preferably to France and Italy, with a particular love for the latter, probably because one of the Queens of Italy had been Polish, Komar, a relative of the Krassinskys. The young girls were delicately charming and almost always pretty, gay and coquettish, and easily turned men's heads. Country balls in Polish homes were joyous events. To the sound of a Jewish orchestra which, because of the lack of space in the room, played outside the open windows, we danced all night, until 6 or 7 a.m., unending mazurkas danced in the old manner with «the heels» the «kneeling» and all the rest. Quadrilles with a cotillion took over from the mazurkas and in the last figure the young girls would give their dancing partners in lieu of a medal or of a decoration a small glass of Hungarian wine.

Only two small clouds cast a shadow over the pleasant memories I have of my Polish friends. The first was their passion for and pride in «high birth», which could reach such a pitch that people who bore excellent names of noble Polish families with old coats of arms would disfigure these so as to make believe that they came from titled magnates. The second was the incredible chauvinism of the women that manifested itself by the fact that even to us who had been the first to hold out the hand of reconciliation they never spoke Russian but only French. I remember how a Polish woman married to one of my good Polish friends wrote to me a short time after the revolution a letter in Russian that was grammatically perfect. When I ran into her one day I said to her that I had not realized that she knew Russian so well.

«But I studied at the university of Kiev» she answered and we both burst out laughing. We Russians did not pay any attention to this form of protest of Polish women and thus removed all meaning from it.

One of the most important pastimes of our group was what we called «the rounds of the estates». These rounds consisted of the following: one of us would suddenly realize that he had not visited his friends for a long time, so we would get together, pack a few clothes and necessities in a small trunk and go and visit our nearest neighbor where we would spend the night. The next day this neighbor would join us and after dinner we would all go together to the next neighbor who would join us in turn and we would go and visit a third one and so on. This round of calls would sometimes last a week. A whole line of coaches would arrive at the last neighbor visited and from there we would all go home. I don't know why, but only bachelors, that is to say mainly young people, would participate in these rounds. They were the occasion for noisy frolics, music, songs, sometimes card games but especially dinners and suppers at which were drunk vast quantities of wine. Sometimes when we wanted to change atmosphere the whole company would got to Kiev. In the best hotel, «the Continental», we would rent several rooms, lunch and dine together, and in the evening visit the famous «Castle of Flowers» where sometimes we would stay until dawn.

On July 11th, my mother's name-day, it was a tradition for all the young Davydoffs and our Polish neighbors to get together at our home in Yurchikha. At our table, very well supplied in spite of the heat, would be seated up to 30 people and the guests would only leave late at night after supper. I remember how the old «pan» Adam Rostsichewsky, owner of part of the estate of Timachevka, would come and congratulate my mother. He would arrive in a splendid carriage drawn by two thoroughbreds with a coachman dressed in the Polish style and seated at the back a shabby looking little Jew. This conformed to an old Polish custom according to which a great lord should always have by his side his personal factotum to gratify his slightest whims. When he visited my mother, pan Adam bore a festive air. Dressed in a dress-coat with white gloves he would offer her wonderful roses from his garden and would leave Yurchikha with a basket of selected peaches, for which Yurchikha was famous.

Our only Russian neighbors were our Davydoff relatives. Among them were the two brothers Dimitri and Yuri, the children of uncle Lev and aunt Sasha (Tchaikovsky) who lived on their estate of «Verbovka». There also stayed the children of uncle Alexis, Lev and Grigori, who used to come and spend the summer months in Kamenka. At first when uncle Lev was still living and his sons were not married, their comrades would also come to Verbovka. Modest Ilyich Tchaikovsky would arrive with his deaf and dumb pupil Conrad. Life would become very gay at Kamenka. The young people would invent all sorts of pastimes. Apart from the «rounds of neighbors», the picnics and the joyous dinners, I remember the staging, in one of the barns of Verbovka, of scenes of the opera Mazeppa in which my uncles took part while Modest Ilyich accompanied them on the piano. I remember also real horse-races on the big field of the estate that adjoined Kamenka with even a betting system and many varied objects in lieu of prizes.

Our house in Yurchikha was neither beautiful nor luxurious. It was a rather large one-story H-shaped house surrounded to the North and East by the park with the entrance on the West side and the outbuildings on the South side. Like the exterior, the interior was simple but large and comfortable. The house was better than the one in Kamenka in the sense that it was situated in the middle of the country on a hill far from the village and the administrative buildings. The view from its terraces was not beautiful but vast. From the terrace on the North side that gave on to the park one could see a large road that led from Kamenka to the small village of Alexandrovka and further on the river Tiasmin and the surrounding fields. Still further on the right, one could see the dark mass of the Gruchev forest and on the left the village of Kossar with the large house of the Rostsichewskys and the chimneys of their distillery. Beyond the Tiasmin spread the large plain through which passed the railway track.

151

The climate of the Ukraine, so good for agriculture, was not a pleasant one to live in. In summer the heat was stifling and when what was called «the dry wind» would start to blow one could not escape the clouds of dust of black earth that it raised even by closing the windows, while in winter it could become very cold with some snow and again the north-east wind would completely cut through one. The spring and summer nights so well described by Pushkin in «Poltava» were beautiful. During those nights it was wonderful to ride on horseback in the moonlight over the scented steppe when the silence was broken only by the distant bark of foxes or the cry of a bird caught by a nocturnal predator.

During the 25 years that I knew Kamenka and Yurchikha I was able to witness the development of agriculture and the increasing prosperity of the region. I can remember how at first to go to Kiev from Kamenka we would be shaken up for 14 hours in small uncomfortable train carriages whereas just before the 1914 war on that same railway line passed an express train with dining-cars and wagons-lits that led directly to the Caucasus. I remember how, after «zemstvos» [4] were created in villages, excellent schools made their appearance as well as paved roads for cars whereas until then the roads had been completely covered in black mud. I remember how the homes of landowners were linked to each other by telephone.

During those same 25 years agriculture made rapid progress, as much so for the big landowners as for the peasants. This was first due to the natural conditions of the area. The deep layer of black earth, the large forests, the favorable climate, made possible the intensive culture of various products from different sorts of wheat to sugar beet. Under these conditions the agricultural returns were interesting and advantageous and this encouraged people to use increasingly perfected methods of farming and to create industrial establishments. I particularly remember the improvement in the fight against that real scourge that were the longicorn xylophages which destroyed our plantations of sugar beet. In olden times the young shoots of the beet had hardly sprouted

___
4. Zemstvos = Local administration councils.

when a host of longicorns would descend upon them and within a few days nothing was left of the plantation. The fight against these parasites was effected in a most primitive fashion. A ditch was dug around the field of beets with the idea that the longicorn beetles would not be able to jump over it and dozens of farm hands were sent on the field itself with small pails which they had to fill with the parasites they caught. This method was a very expensive one and yielded poor results. Already long before the 1914 war small barrels containing a green colored French chemical product were carried on to the field of beets shortly after they had been planted, the chemical was sprayed on the young shoots and this made the longicorns disappear forever. Thanks to a good selection of the grains and to an improved preparation of the earth the yield of wheat was almost doubled and the improvement in machinery brought about a faster harvesting and threshing. I remember how just before the 1914 war on our estate of Yurchikha the wheat was threshed day and night by two machines powered by electricity produced by a generator. We had two of these generators, one at Yurchikha itself and the other near the village of Kamenka.

The two key agricultural industries of the Ukraine were sugar refining and distillation. Uncle Nicholas had a sugar refinery in Kamenka and my elder brother had on his estate of Pokrovsk a distillery that had been given him by my grandfather. Though I was young I ran this distillery for a while at my mother's request. In the early 1900s it only produced 10 million degrees of alcohol. When in 1912 my brother founded a company with Edward Rostsichewsky and they started to export their products, the production of the factory reached 100 million degrees.. Already at that time they owned tank-cars for molasses and alcohol as well as a private railway line and sidings in Kamenka.

With the development of agriculture the well-being of the peasants improved, especially during the years between the first revolution and 1914. During this period the economic development of Russia made a great surge forward. In Ukrainian villages the thatched roofs of peasant houses started to be replaced by metal ones. the old antique ploughs were changed to steel ones, the horse-threshers took over from the old chains and finally, imitating the landowners, the peasants started to grow beets. These improvements can be explained by the fact that apart from a few exceptions both the Russian and the Polish landowners lived on their estates and cultivated the land themselves and had no confidence in salaried intendants. I must say that agricultural methods applied in estates run by their owners like Kamenka and Smeliansk were cited in example. In spite of their lack of land there were few poor people among Ukrainian peasants. The reason was the richness of the soil and the fact that in prosperous Ukraine the peasants managed their land better and were more developed economically than in Great Russia which was poorer. Even if the Ukrainians liked «starky», collective drunkenness was unknown and they did not consciously drink the product of their harvests. It was only on fête days that one might run into a few isolated drunkards but never would a whole village get drunk. Furthermore, for their winter income the peasants did not need to go into town to find supplementary jobs. The large number of sugar refineries and distilleries in the area guaranteed that they would find them right there on the spot.

Another element also contributed to the general progress in the area. This was the sedentary type of life of the Jews. At the time of the Polish domination the Polish kings had given the Ukrainian Jews the privilege of settling in specific places that were called «small villages». The Russian government also limited the places authorized to Jews and maintained the system established by the Poles according to which the Jews were authorized to live in villages and towns in certain specific areas among which was the south west region, that is to say the provinces of Kiev, Podolsk and Volinsk. This limitation did not extend to the right of free circulation in these specific areas, so that a Jew who lived, for instance, in the village of Kamenka, could travel without restriction through the region visiting towns and living temporarily outside his village. Only his fixed residence had to be in a specified town or village. The result was that what was known as the Jewish ghetto did not exist in the Ukraine and the richness of this region gave the Jews a large field of action both for their activities and their spirit of initiative, all the more so as in this field there was no restriction except inasmuch as they were not allowed to own land. This does not mean that there was no poverty among Jews. On the contrary, I have never seen such poverty as in our «little village», but this was due to the density of the population and to the incredible number of Jewish children.

One of my friends said to me one day that the Jews form the basis of civilization and in my opinion he was perfectly right. At least this was the case in the province of Kiev. Of course the Jews who were not allowed to work in agriculture had monopolized commerce and credit. People used to criticize them for this and say that they sucked the blood of the natives but the answer to this is that, in spite of this imaginary bleeding to death, the population got richer and if it suffered it was not because of the hold of the Jews but because of the lack of land. As for credit, in the matter of usury, with which the Jews were reproached, the interests that they applied to their loans were not all that high and the law protected the population from bankruptcy by forbidding the peasants from signing I.O.U.s. Furthermore, nothing prevented the government nor any Russian private initiative from depriving the Jews of their monopoly. A few years before the 1914 war the government had created commercial cooperatives for farmers where the peasants could buy cheaply all the goods they needed, with savings banks that gave them credit at very low rates of interest. Even my uncles had the idea of opening at Kamenka under the name «the Davydoff brothers» a shop where the local landowners and peasants could buy everything that until then they had had to buy from the man who had the monopoly of this commerce, a certain Goldstein. The Jews were also accused of having monopolized the commerce of wheat but in fact it was very practical for the landowners not to have to look around for a buyer and not to have to contact the distant wheat agencies of Nikolaevsk and to know that as soon as their wheat was ground some «yankel» would come to them and suggest a price that after checking would turn out to be only 1 or 2 kopecks below the price offered in Nikolaevsk. I remember how a Russian merchant attracted by the rumors of the profits made by Jews on the wheat market arrived in Kamenka and bought the wheat at a price higher than the one proposed by the Jews. He sent a large quantity of this wheat to Nikolaevsk and as he wanted to make a large profit he waited for the prices to rise. He waited a long time and still the prices did not rise. He finally had to sell his merchandise at a loss. We never saw him again. No doubt when he returned home he put the blame on the Jews and accused them of having secret agreements to put pressure on the peasants.

And yet life for Jews in these «little villages» was not easy. Firstly, all of them did not manage to take part in commerce and credit. Many of them had to earn a living by doing other work. In our village almost all the locksmiths, the carpenters, the painters and the tailors were Jews. The earnings of these poor fellows were meagre and they led a very sad life. Furthermore, the threat of a pogrom always hung over their heads. Antisemitism was very widespread among the people be it the landowners or the peasants. If for the landowners this feeling was basically linked to a sort of scornful atavism towards the Jews and manifested itself by an insolent attitude and even occasional beatings, for the peasants it was a tradition inherited from the Polish domination when the uprising of the Cossacks against the Polish «pans» was always accompanied by pogroms against the Jews, as for instance at the time of the Uman massacres. I remember how, on the road that passed at the end of our garden, towards evening caravans would start to roll loaded with Jews going from Alexandrovka to Kamenka or vice versa. We wondered what was happening and were told that at Alexandrovka a girl had disappeared and had been found dead behind a hedge and among the people it was said that the Jews had killed her to get Christian blood. During the 25 years I spent in that region there was fortunately no pogrom, not a single one, neither in Alexandrovka nor in Kamenka but the threat was always there. What would happen if, in spite of the subvention he received from the Jews, the chief of police did not manage to stop a pogrom? On the day of the 1917 revolution, after the police chiefs and their subalterns had disappeared, the villages of Kamenka and Alexandrovka were completely looted and most of the Jews massacred. Thus ended very sadly their illusions about the liberty and equality that the revolution was supposed to bring them.

In my family, it was my father and my elder brother who were antisemites. My mother was indifferent towards them and later when she ran the house of Yurchikha she admitted that they could be useful and did business with them. My second brother had a strange kind of friendship with them and as for me I was interested in their tastes and in their customs and especially I tried to understand and to assimilate their extraordinary talents, their absolutely unique business sense and the business procedures that made their strength. To reach my objective I shook off all the partly emotive reactions that guided the antisemites. I never tried to understand the whys and wherefores of the Jewish problem nor in what way it could be solved. I accepted it as a basic fact that had to be taken into consideration and that had to be faced not with the intention of exterminating the Jews nor of enslaving them but with the purpose of appropriating their business procedures. The results of my observations totally confirmed my point of view. In all my future enterprises when I had to do business with Jews I was never «had» by any of them as we used to say in the South and often I would hear them say «Where did you get such a Jewish manner of thinking?». With no other representative of any other nation including the Russian did I make or conclude so easily and so simply many successful deals as with the Jews and no one stood by me in difficult moments as they did. Later on certainly I was forced to ponder over the Jewish question, approaching it from another angle, both ideological and political, but there again I did not follow the easy path of their enemies nor the humanitarian one of the progressives. The first was unacceptable to me and the second, in spite of all its good merits, seemed to me to be worthless and incapable of solving this difficult problem for our culture. But I will return to these matters later in my memoirs.

During the last years of my studies the circumstances of my life took me far away from Kamenka and Yurchikha and during the brief visits I made there I was more a guest than one taking an active part in what was going on. It was only during the First World War that events took a turn that forced me to return to Yurchikha on business. But by then I had already made the experience of life and my attitude towards everything that surrounded me had become totally different.

TALE OF A VOLUNTEER PRIVATE

«May God elevate you in his time»

Inscription on the medal of soldiers
who fought in the 1904-1905 Russo-
Japanese war.

Whereas in both world wars several thousand soldiers and an impressive amount of artillery and tanks took part in every battle, be they unimportant ones, in the Russo-Japanese war even a battle between two small groups of men could play a decisive role in the issue of the campaign. This remark applies to the battles that took place during the night of the 20th to the 21st of August 1904 in an attempt to get back from the Japanese the positions they had captured from us the day before, the village of Synkvantun and its neighboring mount, which stood on the right flank of the left wing of the Russian army that defended the position near Liao-Yang. The first Japanese army under the command of General Kuroki had moved two days earlier along the right bank of the river Taitse and, having worked its way round the left wing of the Russian army at the Yentai mines, was trying by every possible means either to overtake it if it should retreat towards Mukden or to cut its communications. The fate of the Russian army depended on the recapture of the village and the Mount Synkvantun. The battle that took place on the night of the 20th to the 21st of August 1904 was won by the Russians and all the attacks of the Japanese against the center and the right wing of the

159

Russian army were repulsed with heavy losses for the Japanese. It became evident that a winning action on the left wing could bring about the total defeat of Marshal Oyama's troops and victory for the Russians in an important battle. To achieve this all that was required was for the 17th army corps under the command of General Bilderling to attack on the 21st of August and take the bridge that the Japanese had thrown over the river Taitse a few kilometers from Mount Synkvantun, a bridge that was plainly visible from that mount and from the nearby hill 131. General Kuropatkin, who commanded the Russian army, had this very idea of attacking on the left wing the morning after Mount Synkvantun had been recaptured only a few days before it was decided to abandon Liao-Yang, but General Bilderling opposed this plan and advised against such an attack on the pretext that his troops, which had suffered heavy losses the day before were exhausted. The losses for that time and for the number of men that made up this army were indeed large but in all probability it was General Bilderling himself who was tired as no trace of fatigue could be seen among his troops. That is how the indecisiveness and the apathy of the Russian high command let slip the occasion if not to win the whole campaign at least to regain the initiative, a rare enough occasion in the Russo-Japanese war. As for me, who took part in the battle of Synkvantun as a special volunteer, I could perhaps not realize in the heat of the action the whole strategic meaning of this battle which I only found out later, but at least I did live through all these events in person and I witnessed many things that are not mentioned in the official reports.

On August 19, 16 battalions, 93 pieces of artillery and 4 squadrons, under the command of General Dobrochinsky, held the Synkvantun position, and 7 battalions, 8 guns and 200 soldiers under the command of General Ekk stood in reserve in the villages of Tudago and Tsovtchinzy. Mount Synkvantun itself was occupied by the infantry regiment of Nijinsky. The Tchembarsk battalion from General Ekk's division, to which I belonged, had been transferred from the right wing of the army and had only arrived late in the evening after a long and tiring march and was bivouacked near the

160

village of Tudago. It had been a particularly hard march because it had been a very hot day and the men, who had very soon emptied their flasks because of the heat, had not been able to refill them along the way as a guard stood in front of each well in every Chinese village to prevent them from doing so as the water had been poisoned by Chinese bandits. The reason for this was that the Russian high command had refused to pay the chief of the bandits the two million roubles he had demanded for his cooperation, and this sum had been paid to him by the Japanese. Tired and thirsty, the soldiers trudged along the road continuously asking their officers if the place where they were going to set up camp was still far, to which question they invariably received the same answer: «Not far, only two versts.»

The road ran eastward along a valley bordered on the left by low hills and on the right by mountains which separated the valley from the river Taitse. We had had time to get used to the monotonous landscape as we marched along the road from the station of Yentai where we had disembarked from the train, to the village of Chahe-North where our battalion of the Siberian Fifth army had stopped on August 10 by order of Kuropatkin. The same eternal fields of tall millet covered the center of the valley, the same Chinese hamlets with their small houses with roofs slanting on both sides in the Chinese style dotted the road, the same oblique-faced Manchus spoke to each other in a guttural tongue and the same «edible» chows leapt out of courtyards barking as we passed. We all prayed for evening to arrive and the coolness that would come with it, but when it did finally come it did so with a terrible Manchurian storm and an incredible torrential downpour that in a second drenched us to the skin and turned the road into a clayey and muddy torrent so that at each step our boots picked up a lump of mud weighing one pood [1]. It became so dark that one could not see one's immediate neighbor. When the storm passed it became obvious that we had lost our way. Before trying to find it we decided to take a rest. The heat of the day had turned into a bitterly cold

1. 1 pood = 36 lbs.

161

night and as we had not had time to dry ourselves we were shaken by fits of trembling as if we were having an attack of malaria.

It was then that an event occured that was totally incomprehensible and always remained a mystery for me. I was sitting on a rise by the roadside talking to the commanding officer of the battalion when suddenly out of the dark appeared an officer riding a grey horse. He asked my commanding officer if we belonged to the Tchembarsk regiment and, on being answered in the affirmative he said he had been sent by our headquarters to guide us to the place where we were to set up camp. The order to start was given and, leaving the road we were about to take, we turned right and followed the officer who without saying a word rode ahead of us. When we got close to the mountains that separated the valley from the river Taitse and the road started climbing towards the pass, the doubt I had felt as soon as I had set eyes on the unknown officer became a certainty and I went up to the officer who commanded my company and told him about it, pointing out that neither the officers nor the ordnances of our regiment had grey horses. The officer listened to my report then reported it to the commanding officer of the battalion, who at once ordered the battalion to halt. When we tried to find the officer who was supposed to have been sent by our headquarters no trace of him could be found. At that moment the moon rose and we were able to find out exactly where we were. It became obvious that we should on no account cross the mountain range that separated the valley from the river Taitse where the Japanese were waiting for us, but that we should turn right and follow the road that ran along the foot of the mountain and led to the village of Tudago.

In this village, objective of our long march, we hoped that we would be able to rest and dry ourselves. The tents were raised and in no time, in spite of the roar of the guns and the crackling of rifle fire, we fell into a deep sleep. We were not allowed to rest for long. The sound of firing ceased all of a sudden and was replaced by the whistling of shells over our heads. An officer, whom this time we knew to be the aide-de-camp of the commanding officer of our division, arrived on horseback with orders that we should strike camp forthwith. A short while later we encountered scattered elements of the Nijinsky regiment that only a short time before had occupied Mount Synkvantun. They were now fleeing and we had great difficulty in stopping them. It turned out that on August 19 out of the whole Japanese army under General Kuroki only the 12th division and a brigade of the 2nd division under General Okasaki that formed the left wing of the combat formation remained on the right bank of the river Taitse. They had been ordered to attack hill 131, the village of Synkvantun and the neighboring mount, and the battle had raged all day. By afternoon the brigade of General Okasaki had been unable to capture our positions in spite of reinforcements it had received in the form of the Matsunagi brigade, and it was only in the evening, at the very moment when we were trying to find our way in the dark, that General Okasaki succeeded in bringing his troops close enough for a bayonet attack. The appearance of the moon, which had enabled us to find our way, was the signal for the Japanese attack. The Nijinsky troops, exhausted by the battle that had lasted all day, were unable to withstand the onslaught and fled from Mount Synkvantun, sweeping away in their flight the ten companies of the «Novoingermanland» regiment that occupied the village of Synkvantun. The entire Synkvantun position (hill 131, the mount and the village of Synkvantun) fell into the hands of the enemy. It was then that the commanding officer of the 17th army corps, General Bilderling, had ordered our regiment to strike camp, stop the runaway troops and recapture the lost position.

After striking camp, our regiment marched on Synkvantun. When dawn broke, it had reached the village of Erdago that lay at the foot of hill 131 where a halt was called so that the men could be fed. The enemy was neither to be seen nor heard. No one was visible on hill 131, which towered above us, and only one piece of artillery could be heard firing at irregular intervals in the direction of the Taitse river. After the soldiers had emptied their mess-tins and the itinerant canteens had been moved back to the rear, orders were given to strike camp and occupy the north slope of hill 131. It is only then that

Japanese shells started to fall on that very slope. I can see as if it were to day the tall and thin silhouette of General Ekk walking slowly down the hillside with two adjutants who had accompanied him to the top of the hill to observe the situation. In spite of the shells that exploded all round him, he never quickened his step in the slightest and he seemed to be so deep in thought about the impending battle that he did not even notice the shells.

After reaching the summit of the hill we lay down in a line along the crest itself. The Japanese shells that were exploding at an ever increasing rate in front and behind our lines finally reached us. We received the baptism of fire. We had our first wounded and our first dead. It was only one hour later that the signal to attack was given. We climbed over the top of the hill and discovered in front of us a lone peak that rose isolated from the mountain range that bordered the valley of the Taitse river. In front of this peak a road led to the pass and further to the right one could see the Japanese bridge over the Taitse. This was Mount Synkvantun, which we were to attack and recapture. In front of us the Vyborg regiment, which had preceded us and had occupied hill 131 and the village of Synkvantun, was already advancing in line.

Before describing the battle itself I must explain what the regiments that took part in it were like and particularly the Tchembarsk regiment to which I belonged.

General Ekk's division included the regiments of Vyborg and of Tchembarsk. They belonged to two different army corps and they were completely different as much by the quality of their elements as by their military preparation. The Vyborg regiment had as its honorary chief the German Emperor Wilhelm II and formed part of the troops that were stationed in the military district of St. Petersburg and in peace time had their quarters in that city. The Tchembarsk regiment belonged to the 73rd infantry division of the Siberian 5th army corps that had been formed during the war with reservists of battalions from the western provinces of European Russia. Thus the Vyborg regiment was made up permanently of subalterns and officers and of recruits who had just reached the age of mobilization. There was a predominance of very low grade cadres who had had a few years of military instruction and were welded together by a true discipline. The officers formed a united family who knew the traditions of the regiment and its military past. Also, certain factors like the fact of being stationed in the capital, the proximity of the high command and above all the honorary command of the German Emperor, played an important role in its military preparation. The Tchembarsk regiment, on the other hand, in the first unit of which I had been sent as a volunteer private, had all the faults of a recently formed regiment. It had no combat experience and there could be no tradition as the officers were men who had only just met and had nothing in common. There were also among them men who had been failures in their job. Things were particularly bad in the ranks of the subalterns who, apart from a very small number of reservists, consisted of very young peasants who had long forgotten what military discipline was. Nevertheless as far as I was concerned I was very fortunate both in regard to my immediate military commanders and to the men who formed the first detachment of my company. As if they had been handpicked, these men were all tall, young, healthy, wonderfully disciplined and united by the solidarity of the Russian soul. The officers were all reservists on the active list . The oldest of my immediate superiors was the commanding officer of the battalion whose name escapes me, a lieutenant-colonel who had taken part in the Russo-Turkish war of 1877, and the company commander was an officer who was not all that young, Captain P.I. Bogo-liubov, one of those officers whom soldiers respect, love and call «father». The chief of my half company was a reservist, ensign Betchko-Druzin, who, in civilian life, had been chief of administration and whose actions in military matters were those of a civilian but whose generous soul had won the heart of his subalterns. The doctor, a German from the Baltic provinces who had finished the university of Dorpat and was a man of great culture, was pleasantly outstanding among the officers of my battalion. As I spoke German very well and had many relatives in Courland, we quickly became friends.

I must also mention our regimental sergeant-major, Ivan Kuzmitch, a strict but good-natured man with whom I had managed to get friendly already in Penza before being sent to the front, through drink and money.

From what I have just said, it is obvious that it was difficult for the Tchembarsk regiment to compete with the Vyborg one and everyone spoke of the fact that, however valiant our regiment would be in combat, the merit of the outcome of the battle that was imminent would not be attributed to us and the congratulations and decorations would not be for us. It was difficult to compete with the regiment that had as its honorary chief the German Emperor and had been sent to attack before us.

After describing the participants in the coming battle, I must now describe the battle itself. After going over the crest of hill 131 we had to scramble down the south slope under the fire of the Japanese artillery. We could not say where it was firing from but we could see that Mount Synkvantun was completely obscured by the smoke of our shells. It was amazing to see with what precision these were being fired, making like a crown around the summit of the mount. After reaching the bottom of the slope of hill 131 and crossing the road that led to the pass, we plunged into the high stalks of millet and, turning left to circumvent the mount, we started to advance by leaps and bounds, flattening ourselves in the folds of the terrain. The fire of the Japanese artillery became heavier and heavier and its aim adjusted itself to our displacements. Fewer and fewer soldiers rose after each forward leap. Many remained lying on the ground, some without saying a word, others moaning and writhing in pain. It was a natural thing and each of us knew that the same thing could happen to himself any minute. What surprised me was that, as we advanced, we ran into more and more soldiers of the Vyborg regiment who lay deep in the folds of the terrain quite uninjured but refusing to expose themselves to any further danger. As our section had with reason the entire confidence of our company commander, neither he nor our ensign ever came to watch us during the attack. We had to decide on our own what to do with the men from the Vyborg regiment. Our first reaction was to leave them alone and not pay attention to them but then a feeling of injustice took hold of us and we started to prod them on with our bayonets and in that way forced them to join us.

Hill 131 that seemed so close to Mount Synkvantun was in fact quite a distance from it. We had been advancing already for several hours and had not yet reached the foot of the mount. Darkness started to fall and the flares that burst over our heads began to shine with a blue light and the Japanese machine-guns and rifles kept on firing at us. We reached the end of the field of millet and the terrain offered no more protection. At last the firing of the guns ceased but that of the machine-guns and of the rifles increased. Having rounded in the darkness the left side of the mount, we started to climb up it, but we had not progressed more than fifty feet when from behind us, from the village, which was barely visible, someone started firing on us. We threw ourselves down at the foot of the mount but soldiers from I know not what company ran up to us shouting and firing their automatic rifles and jabbing the men they encountered with their bayonets. Panic set in and only a few of the men were not affected by it and continued to advance. In the darkness it was difficult to distinguish what was happening and who was firing on whom. Fortunately order was re-established fairly quickly thanks to the coolness of the leader of our regimental band, a little Jew from Zlatopolia in the province of Kiev, and of his musicians. One of the commanding officers of our battalion ordered him to play the national anthem and, as soon as the soldiers heard these familiar notes, they pulled themselves together.

The attack had been lasting a long time and we were very tired. It was especially the thirst that bothered us and the small amount of water that the men had had in reserve in their flasks had long been drunk. Instinctively I bent down over one of the dead bodies that lay at my feet and started to feel around for his flask. As I bent down more I realized in the dark that the soldier was Japanese and I discovered that his

167

flask was full of rum which I drank avidly. Having thus regained some strength I resumed my climb towards the summit and after a few steps fell upon soldiers of my section who were standing and arguing around a body that was stretched out at their feet. I asked them what had happened and they answered that the body was that of our ensign Betchko-Druzin who had been wounded and was unconscious and that they did not know what to do with him as no stretcher-bearer was in sight. At that moment our company commander P.I. Bogo-liubov, who had noticed that we had stopped, came up to us. The oldest N.C.O. told him what had happened. P.I. Bogo-liubov hardly had time to start giving his instructions when I said to him: «Don't worry, Your Excellency, I will carry him away from the combat zone», and no sooner said than done, I lifted the body, slung him over my shoulder and started to clamber down the mount towards the village of Erdago where I knew our infirmary was. The ensign was not tall but he was stocky and rather plump and it was not easy to carry him, especially as an unconscious person weighs more than a conscious one, for he does not hang on to the person who is carrying him. The situation was further complicated by the fact that I could not abandon my rifle and that bullets were whistling around me. My strength started to ebb but the knowledge that at my very first battle I would have merited the St. George cross or better still a decoration of the Order of War as one then called it officially, gave me energy. Fortunately, after I had carried the ensign almost one verst, I ran into some stretcher-bearers to whom I handed over my burden with a sigh of relief. After resting a short time on a rock, I walked slowly back up the mount but already from its summit came the sound of cheering that told me that we had captured the mount and that the battle was over. When I rejoined my company I learned that we had received orders to return to our starting point, that is to say hill 131, and occupy it. It was already two in the morning and, tired as we were, we climbed up the hill and reached the crest where a pleasant surprise was in store for us. While we were fighting our cooks had prepared something for us to eat and soldiers sent by our officers brought us hot cabbage soup and a ration of meat.

The night was cold and clear. After this tiring day we yearned for sleep but anxiety gripped our hearts. Far away to our right we could see Liao-Yang in flames, and even farther to the right burned the frontier signal posts at the Yentai junction. We did not know the meaning of these fires but we had a feeling that they boded us no good.

The morning of August 21 arrived, quiet and calm. In front of our cantonment the doctor of our battalion was dressing the wounds of the injured who had dragged themselves from the field of battle the evening before. As I had nothing to do I helped him and we exchanged our impressions of the events of the previous evening. Suddenly the order was given to strike camp. At first we thought we were going to attack but we very soon found out that the Russian army was going to abandon the position of Liao-Yang and that we were going to retreat. It was with a heavy heart that we marched back along the valley where two days earlier we had marched so full of hope and of expectation of the unknown.

When at last we halted to rest, we learned that the whole merit of the capture of Mount Synkvantun had been attributed to the Vyborg regiment and rewards were heaped on it in spite of the fact that it was our section that had reached the summit first. I learnt later that it was not for nothing that, at the start of the attack, when we were scrambling down the south slope of hill 131, the German representative and P.A. Polovtsov, a captain from headquarters, had stood looking at the Vyborg troops. One had to please the honorary chief of the battalion, Emperor Wilhelm II. I cannot remember how many war medals were given to the Tchembarsk regiment. I only know that one of them was for me «for having saved a wounded officer during the battle under the fire of the enemy», and another for the band leader for having played the national anthem under similar circumstances.

A few days later, during a halt in a small railway station where the hospital train of Empress Alexandra Feodorovna was stopped, I was sent by the officers to try and get some tea and sugar from that train. The officers were convinced that my appearance would be enough to ensure the success of this enterprise. It really was impossible to doubt that I had just taken part in a battle. My vest was torn, on my left sleeve was a large bloodstain from the dead Japanese who had given me his rum and my epaulettes and cap were soaked. Wounded men were being taken aboard the train and, as I did not want to disturb the personnel of the train with my business, I stood on the platform where two generals were strolling and chatting. When they had passed in front of me for the second time and I had stood once more at attention and saluted, one of them came up to me, shook my hand, and asked me in what battle I had taken part. After I had told him it was Mount Synkvantun, he said: «Never forget this—it is a great honor for you!».

THE IMPOSSIBLE KOLKHOZE

Life sometimes places a person in a position where he is forced in spite of himself to take part in events for which he has been in no way prepared. This can happen particularly at the time of a revolution when it is difficult to predict how and in what direction any situation will turn under the psychological influence of the masses that act, as one knows, against all laws of logic. Occasionally this sort of situation will become dangerous for the person who is obliged to take part in it and it often happens that for a person to get himself out of just such a situation he will have to make rapid decisions which may later on, when all is quiet again, seem contrary to his own convictions. This occurred a long time ago when I had to take part against my own wishes in events that have become one of the evils of the bolshevik revolution but the memory of which has left me paradoxically a feeling of moral satisfaction.

In the spring of 1915 I was living in St. Petersburg and while working at the Chancery of Credit I also worked for the Red Cross. I was completely discharged from all military obligations at the time of the general mobilization of 1914 and I was therefore free to do what I liked. At that time my mother, who was managing our estates in the South of Russia and who, for that reason, lived permanently in the province of Kiev, arrived in St. Petersburg. She informed me of the bad state of our affairs due to the difficulties caused by the war and to other failures and told me that this situation was a very alarming one. For her, a woman no longer young and not in the best of health, it was difficult, under conditions she was not used to, to bear alone the responsibility of our possessions. Of my two older brothers one was at the front and the other one did not possess, in my mother's opinion, a sufficient business competence. Because of this she asked me to take over the administration of our properties. Although I was eager to help my mother I knew her domineering character so I did not accept right away her suggestion but asked her what she would do if I accepted. She answered that she would go on living as before on our property of Yurchikha, that is to say in the very place where I would have to accomplish a job that was new to me and difficult. This meant that I would have no freedom of action and that I would have to act continuously under the critical surveillance of my mother, which would inevitably lead to a worsening of our relations and consequently an aggravation of the state of our affairs. With such an outlook, to abandon my well-established position in St. Petersburg not only was not worth my while but was even risky. My post at the Ministry of Finance where I often had to assume responsible jobs, my friendly relations with important businessmen and with the banking circles, and finally the habit I had of defending my own interests myself, had given me not only experience and knowledge but had also accustomed me to independence. My mother knew this because many times in difficult moments she had turned to me and to my acquaintances in the banking world and her requests had always been satisfied. There was another obstacle that prevented me from collaborating with my mother. This was the very special manner that the provincial Russian landowners had of approaching business matters and the opinion people who lived and worked in the capital had about this. Whereas the latter were always used to facing squarely and examining for themselves all the details of an affair, even the most insignificant ones, finally only taking into account the essential elements, provincial landowners were suspicious of everything, relied on petty busybodies whom they took for great businessmen, listened to their advice and considered them to be experts on every matter.

I therefore concluded that the responsibility involved was too great and without having recourse to any diplomatic excuse I told my mother very squarely all these considerations I have just outlined and said I could not accept her proposition. However, I did not want to refuse my help entirely, so I compromised and offered to take care of the estate that caused her the most trouble but on condition that, should she agree to this, she would first of all never interfere in any way in my affairs and secondly I would take for myself all the profits and all the losses. I got the impression that my mother was delighted with my offer and she answered right away that she would be very happy if I took over the management of our Crimean estate Sably where business was very bad and in which she had had to invest every year large sums of money. We quickly reached a complete agreement and it was decided that early September after having cleared my affairs in St. Petersburg I would move to Sably.

When I acceded to my mother's wishes I realized perfectly well the pros and cons of my future occupation. Among the pros was the fact that Sably was a wonderful estate situated on the Crimean peninsula 14 versts from Simferopol at the foot of the Yaïla mountain range on both banks of the river Alma and covered 2.600 dessiatines of land. Although the major part of the estate consisted of oak forest that was only good to be used as fuel for heating, it was very interesting from the point of view of agricultural exploitation. It included 90 dessiatines of orchards, 40 dessiatines of vegetable gardens which were very fertile because of the frequent overflow of the river, tobacco plantations, a herd of pedigreed cows and, although not extensive, fields of cereal. Another favorable element was that Sably was close to the railway station of Simferopol where express trains stopped, enabling one to be in St. Petersburg in 36 hours, Moscow in 24 and Kharkov in 12. Finally it included a fine house with a beautiful park and the paved roads that linked Simferopol to the south coast

173

would enable me to go to Yalta by car as well as to the other towns on the coast. Needless to say the wonderful temperate climate allowed one to live pleasantly in the country the year round.

There were several more or less important unfavorable elements. In the first place there was the fact that the property had been left us by my father at a time when my grandmother was still living, which had forced by mother to pay rent to her in the form of a life annuity. My grandparents had lived in Sably for almost 60 years and after my grandfather's death in 1912 my grandmother, who had reached her eightieth year, continued to live there and it was only in winter that she would move to Simferopol. Therefore I would have to spend six months of the year at Sably as her guest without being really independent. This situation in itself did not really disturb me all that much and was even in a way a good thing as it would leave me free at the time of the big domestic labors. What troubled me was that until now none of my grandmother's offspring had been able to live with her because of her very bad character, aggravated by the fact that she was a tottering old lady, blind and in ill-health, forced to live alone in the company of two nurses who were strangers to her. My mother, when she agreed to have me manage Sably, reminded me of this state of affairs that had caused her a lot of trouble in her business relations with my grandmother.

The second unfavorable element was the very bad condition of the estate and the need for my mother to have to disburse every year large sums of money, a fact that was totally incomprehensible to me. These two black marks, though disagreeable, did not appear too serious to me, but the third one seemed much more complicated. The peasants of the village of Sably, which was close to the estate, had a very bad reputation with the landowners of the Crimean peninsula. They were called nothing less than robbers and thieves and political agitators. The relations between them and my mother's manager were very strained and there were constant quarrels. In 1905, at the time of the peasant rising, the peasants of the village of Sably had attacked the manager's house and had ransacked it. The manager and his wife had barely had time to flee.

174

I remember that after the looting the peasants did not touch either the estate or the surrounding buildings or any possessions on the estate other than the manager's house. That same day the governor had arrived at the estate accompanied by the judicial and the military authorities. The procurator and the examining magistrate 'had noted down the facts and the administrative authorities had done their job and inflicted a corporal punishment on the instigator of the attack, a certain Piotr Gutienko. A few months later the participants in the attack were judged by the Odessa law courts before state representatives for political crimes. As I was then living temporarily in Simferopol and had nothing to do with the running of the estate, I went more out of curiosity than anything else to see the place that had been attacked. Fortunately I arrived there after the punishments but, after talking with the governor and with the procurator, I gathered that both these men considered that this incident was a normal thing that was part of the «peasant agitation». The law courts reached the same conclusion. Personally my impression was quite different and later on I turned out to be right.

At the time this incident took place and even later when I lived in St. Petersburg and worked at the Ministry of Finance my thoughts were far from the peasants and from the agrarian problem but in spite of this, when I happened to think about it, I always had the impression that the interested parties did not face the problem in the right way. Among these parties I included the men in power just as much as the landowners and the populist radical intelligentsia. As I worked at the Chancery of Credit, whose main concern was to maintain the international rate of exchange of the rouble, I was in favour of the government's agrarian policy on the peasant problem. I knew that to divide all of a sudden the large estates into small agricultural holdings would be very risky for the rouble because it would threaten the export of wheat, which was the main basis of the Russian trade balance. It seemed to me that the government had to find another way of solving this problem of primary political importance. I think that just such a solution was found in the «khutors»[1] of Stolypin. In spite of all my political objectivity, it seemed to me that the way the radical populist intelligentsia and especially the revolutionary parties approached the problem was ill-founded and irresponsible. As I had learned in my government post to face state problems in a realistic fashion I accepted totally the fact of the decay of the autocratic regime in power and because of that I accepted and understood entirely the logical fight of society against this regime, but I could absolutely not understand how it was possible to try and realize this objective of a political revolution by means of a social revolution. Because of my realistic approach to the problem, the belief in a «peasant truth» and the existence of a «socialist peasant» seemed to me to be a chimera, but what surprised me most in the method of approach to the peasant problem by the populist revolutionary parties was their ignorance of the budgetary economic problems of Russia. This surprised me all the more as I knew their great and sincere patriotism. Without mentioning the fact that the parties were completely isolated from the people and lived with utopian notions about them, they had no idea of the Russian budget nor of the consequences of the division of the land according to the slogan «land and liberty». For these idealistic patriots any means were good to overthrow the abhorred autocrat.

Regarding the third unfavorable element that was directly linked to the agrarian problem, what surprised me most was the ignorance of the problem among the groups of landowners, especially the nobles who ruled over ancestral lands. Their manner of approaching it smelled of damp decay and moldiness. In spite of the obviously poor returns of their method of running their estates, which brought in at the very best an income of 3%, barely compensated by the increase in value of their land, they hung on to them either for sentimental reasons or for love of their old homes or because they understood that by leaving the land they would definitely lose their predominant position in the government, a position which in fact they had already mostly lost. Underestimating the threat

---

1. Khutor = a small metairie.

of the rising revolution, they hung on to the land with feeble hands. But what had already surprised me personally in my childhood were the relations between the landowners and the peasants and the psychological aspect of these relations. It is common knowledge that if children or young adolescents are not able to judge and to analyse their impressions they do feel them in a much stronger manner than adults and these impressions leave a deep mark on them and on their conscience for the rest of their lives and often contribute to the formation of their future convictions. When I was a child and later a young man I used to spend the summer months in the country and without realizing it I would observe the relations between the landowners and the peasants, particularly between my father and our neighbors, the peasants of the village of Yurchikha in the district of Tchigirin. In those times one currently applied the old custom of solving any misunderstanding with the «moujiks» by slapping them and when this occurred in front of me I would be so revolted that for a long time I could not dispel a feeling of shame and uneasiness for the person who had allowed himself to beat in this manner a practically defenceless human being. But apart from this acute sentiment induced by the sight of the humiliation of the human dignity of the weak, what impressed me enormously was the profound hypocrisy of the relations between landowners and peasants, as much on one side as on the other. I remember that when one or more peasants came to see my father about some problem or other he would «make his appearance» in the «refreshment room» or in the courtyard where the «petitioners» awaited him. My father's expression, like that of other landowners, would change completely under these circumstances. Automatically his face, which had been smiling a few seconds earlier, would suddenly take on an expression of severity and aloofness such as befits a superior being who addresses himself to his inferiors. Apart from the fact that the landowners would always address the peasants by saying «tu» to them, they had always in addition a certain arrogance and a sententious tone of voice when they spoke to them. I must add that all landowners did not adopt this serious tone of voice in their talks with the peasants. Some on the contrary like Maniloff would use in their speeches a honeyed sentimental style that was even falser. The peasants answered the landowners no less falsely. They would twist their hats in their fingers and in my childhood would kiss the master's «little hand» or «little shoulder». Their faces would take on a miserable or begging expression full of voluntary humiliation. If in my time the saying «You are our Father and we are Your children» was no longer used, nevertheless the peasants continued to answer the sententious remarks of the landowners by «Well, what do You expect. You are educated, You know better». It is evident that each side tried to cheat the other but whereas the peasants guessed perfectly well the thoughts of the landowners, the latter were incapable of piercing the stone wall of the dissembling character of the peasants to guess at their psychology. This sort of relationship was evident in everything. When a landowner acceded to a peasant's request, this took on a character of charity, whereas if for some reason or another a peasant did something that displeased him, the thunder and the lightning of his wrath would fall on him. All this was disgusting and provoked in me a feeling of intense pain that remained forever.

As I have already said, when I lived in Petrograd I had other interests and the question of the relationship between landowners and peasants only had an academic interest for me. From the moment when the question of my managing Sably was settled, I started trying to put my ideas on this problem into concrete form. First of all I came to the conclusion that the hypocrisy in the relations between landowners and peasants was a relic of the right to slavery. It was not without reason that when the landowners spoke of the neighboring peasants they called them «our people». Fifty years after the liberation of the peasants the landowners kept on considering them as persons who were dependent on them and towards whom they had certain tutelar moral obligations and also certain rights. As for the peasants they thought with reason that they were in fact defenceless before the landowners as power would always be on the latter's side and they persisted in adopting towards them a servile psychology that expressed itself by trickery, the usual weapon of the weak against the strong. Furthermore I started to think that the peasants no longer held any respect for the landowners. In truth what respect could they have for masters who lived most of the time in town and handed over the management of their estates to salaried managers? In addition the peasants could see that the landowners did not take care of the farming as they should have done. They were aware of the fact that the estates were in debt, a state of affairs that occurred mainly when they were not supervised, and of the fact that the landowners led lives well beyond their means. The peasants, at least those who lived in our part of Russia, possessed a great sense of economical psychology and the landowners who had none could not enjoy their respect.

It was with these thoughts in mind that I left Petrograd intent on checking my conclusions on the spot. What bothered me was the reputation of the Sably peasants and the fear that, if that reputation should turn out to be exact, then I would face obstacles in establishing correct relations with them. I wanted to rid myself of the biased feelings that others had and that encumbered me. I do not know for what reason it seemed to me that this opinion was also the result of inveterate provincial points of view and that there was no real basis to it. Without reaching a definite conclusion beforehand I had established for myself a rule that whatever happened I would try on the one hand to be respected by the peasants by giving them the example of a simple and hard working life and by a good management of the estate, and on the other hand avoid all hypocrisy in our relations by establishing between us complete equality on a social plane. I did not think then that the application of these conditions would lead me to such unexpectedly good results and provide me with a deep moral satisfaction during that most delicate of periods for a master—a revolution.

When I arrived at Sably in early September I wanted to get down to my new occupations right away and before all else overcome the unfavorable elements I have spoken of. I also had to accomplish my other tasks as delegate of the Red Cross, which I had agreed to be so as not to break off all contact with this organization in time of war, but fate prevented me from realizing these intentions and a situation arose that greatly complicated my work. First of all, only a few days after my arrival, my chief at the Red Cross suddenly died and I was obliged to handle his work, which lasted several months until I was transferred in my role of deputy to the prefecture of Sebastopol. Then, a very short time later, I received a cable from my mother requesting me to join her at once because of the alarming worsening of our affairs. Therefore I had to go regularly during eight months to the district of Tchigirin and to Kiev. During that time I passed no less than 25 times through the railway station of Sinelnikov. Because of this I was only able to look after Sably intermittently.

The first unfavorable element in my new situation—my relations with my grandmother—I managed to smooth out easily and rapidly. Instead of the authoritarian and cantankerous old lady I was expecting, I found an ailing and blind old woman who already had one foot in her grave and who saw everything through the eyes of her nurses. Tenderness and attentiveness did their work and in a very short time my grandmother was raving about me. The question of the running of the estate was a much more difficult one to solve. On the one hand I had to cover my expenses and on the other hand I had to solve the problem I had so much at heart, that of my relationship with my peasant neighbors. From the moment of my first contact with the management of Sably I was convinced that it was run on the principle of «bluff», that is to say for show. The whole business was entirely concentrated on the spectacular angle—the fruit-trees—whereas all the rest like the culture of wheat, of tobacco, of vegetables, and all the active and inactive potential, were completely left to waste. The harvest of wheat, barley and oats did not exceed 25 to 30 poods per dessiatine[2] and the dray-horses were in such poor condition that after the Society for Prevention of Cruelty to Animals had lodged a complaint the police authorities had imposed a fine on the estate. When I found out about this situation I asked the manager the reason

---

2. 1 pood = 16.380 kgs. 1 dessiatine = 1.1 hectare.

for these disorders and I became convinced that the whole fault was his.

The manager was a German Balt who had finished agricultural school in Germany and who had worked for my family for over twenty years. At one time he had worked in one of our Kiev estates, watched over closely by my mother, and he had accomplished his work rather well but when he found himself far from «the master's eye» he had felt independent and decided to satisfy his ambition and try to create for himself a position in the community and among the landowners. Furthermore, being lazy, he did not spend much time thinking about the running of the estate. The fact is that he was a stubborn and stupid German who despised in secret all that was Russian and particularly the Russian peasants who hated him as much as he despised them. This was the same manager whom the peasants of Sably had tried to get rid of and whose house they had ransacked. When I asked him the reasons for the disorders in the management of the estate he answered in a superior tone of voice that he ran it «in the Crimean manner». It surprised me that my mother had not guessed that the uprising of the peasants of Sably in 1905 had only been a settling of accounts with the hated manager and that this explained why the peasants had spared the farmland and the house. I could not understand either why my mother, in spite of the constant deficit of the estate, had continued to have confidence in Mr. Zichman—that was his name—for the management of the estate. Now my impressions on the 1905 incidents were fully confirmed and it was with pleasure that I would have got rid of Mr. Zichman immediately if the affair of the Kiev province had not monopolized my time so completely. It was only eight months later when I had finished the Kiev affair successfully that I succeeded in putting my plan into execution. Nevertheless during the short intervals of time that I spent in Sably, in spite of Mr. Zichman's opposition, I managed to proceed to certain urgent reforms in the management that gave good results later.

There remained the third and perhaps the most serious of the unfavorable elements, the question of my relations with the peasants of Sably. It seemed to me that in this matter I

181

should not act with precipitation and I first started by checking as if there was nothing to it, with the most subaltern employees of the estate, whether the reputation of «brigands» really applied to the peasants of Sably. I checked in the same way with the local authorities. It turned out that no criminal tendency had been noticed in the peasants. They were no more «brigands» than those of the villages and boroughs nearby on the Crimean peninsula, that is to say that in truth they were not brigands at all. Nothing particular marked the village of Sably on the political plane and the only «nefarious» element, Piotr Gutienko, that same one who had been subjected to a corporal punishment in 1905, distinguished himself only because at the time of the general mobilization he made believe he was dumb and acted his role very well for one year. When I arrived in Sably he had recovered his voice and was quite successfully engaged in the illegal sale of wine. Thus was dispelled the myth that had originated without reason in the imagination of the neighboring landowners.

As they hated Zichman and only found in him arrogance and brutality, the peasants of Sably during my short stays there started to consult me directly about their problems without going through the manager. This enabled me to try out the way in which I had decided to speak to them. To start with I began saying «You» to them. Secondly I did not «make an appearance» to meet them but called them to a special room that I named «the business office» where I was in the habit of receiving the manager and in general anybody who wished to see me. Thus there could be no «fumbling of hats» because the peasants when they entered the house had to leave their hats at the entrance. The first few times I invited them to sit in my office they were very intimidated and started talking in the same hypocritical tone of voice I mentioned earlier. I had to explain to them that if they wished to do business with me they should speak simply and if the business suited me there was no reason why we should not come to an agreement. I made them understand that the days of serfdom were over, that I considered them to be free people, masters in their own rights, and that, for that very reason, there was no question of my doing things for them «out of charity» and that our relations should be based on the strictest equality. Little by little my policy started to give results and the hypocrisy I abhorred so disappeared completely from our relationship. Eight months later the dismissal of Zichman and his replacement by a young man who had acted as accountant in the estate of a neighbor in the province of Kiev and who furthermore belonged to the socialist revolutionary party made a strong impression on them. They saw in this act not a submission to them but the fair understanding on my part of the harm that a person so incapable and lazy as Zichman could cause as manager.

Having got rid of Zichman I attacked with zest, in collaboration with my new young manager, the problem of improving the state of affairs in Sably where I now spent most of my time, only going twice a week to Sebastopol for my Red Cross affairs. We worked like mad in a new relaxed atmosphere. The results of this beneficial situation were rapidly felt and at the same time my relations with the peasants improved. Slowly but surely, without any unnecessary words on one side or the other, these relations took on a character of esteem and mutual respect. I learned that the peasants had named me «Davydchuk» and had approved of the measures I had taken for the administration of the estate. The «nefarious element» Piotr Gutienko also started to come and see me and, having been received in the same manner as the other peasants, he started to propose to me «schemes» that were so shady that it was absolutely out of the question for me to accept them. This fact provoked no animosity on his part for, being far from stupid, he understood very well the reason for my refusal.

Thus passed another six months and the end of February 1917 arrived. In town there were rumors that «something» had happened in Petrograd. What this «something» was no one knew but everyone guessed that it was something of the utmost seriousness. In the first place there was no longer any news from the capital nor from Moscow. The newspapers and the mail did not arrive and the local press could not even report the rumors as the local authorities controlled it very strictly. At last, I can't remember on what day, the local progessive press reported in a special edition the news that

183

the tsar had abdicated. I remember that this edition was brought to me from town by one of the employees of the estate who used to go and fetch the mail. Although I was prepared for the news I had just received I was nevertheless terribly distressed by its enormity. Independently from the very understandable reaction on the historical plane I could not fail to appreciate all the changes it would bring to my life and all the new problems I would have to solve. For an hour or two I remained motionless at my desk meditating on what had happened. My first thoughts were for my mother who lived alone with my elder brother's daughter and her governess in her estate 300 versts from Kiev next to the peasants of the village of Yurchikha who were antagonistic to her. As I realized I could do nothing for them, I returned to my personal problems. Should I leave the house and go either to Simferopol or to Sebastopol, or should I stay in Sably? To answer this question I lacked one certainty which was whether the peasants would, as in revolutions of the past, immediately kill the landowners, destroy their homes and loot the agricultural buildings, or would wait and see the turn of events realizing that their old desires could not now fail to be accomplished by legal means. After thinking it over I decided to remain in Sably and to continue my farming activities. It seemed to me that to flee at this moment would be to show cowardice and would be the complete negation of all I had striven to attain in my relations with the peasants. Furthermore as I understood that something had happened in Russia that would uproot deeply its whole structure and that this had happened at a difficult moment for the country, that is to say in time of war, I was of the opinion that even the most insignificant person in his sphere of activity should do his duty, take part in the revolution, prevent its excesses as best he could and try, even in a minimal role, to preserve the economic strength of the nation. Because of this and of my two responsibilities, that of my work in Sebastopol and that of my personal work in Sably, in spite of the distracted telegrams from my Red Cross collaborators, I decided to stay.

My supposition that for the moment in the Crimea the peasants would not touch the estates turned out to be correct.

Only a few landowners went to live in town, the others continued to live on their estates and only encountered minor difficulties with their peasant neighbours. The same thing happened in Sably. The day after I received the news of the revolution I went into town for news and returned home without any problem. The following day I had just woken up early in the morning and was still in bed when I was told of the arrival of a police guard who lived on my land and was kept by my grandmother and with whom I had no contact. He was shown into my room and told me that Piotr Gutienko had just been to his home and had taken his rifle which he had let him do without resisting, and that the estate was surrounded by peasants who had decided not to let me go out of the estate and wanted to finish me off on the road. I told him he had acted in an intelligent manner by not resisting the theft of his rifle and I advised him, so as to eliminate all danger to himself, to remove his police uniform and to present himself to the army recruiting office and state that he wished to enlist. As for myself I told him not to worry as I was absolutely not afraid and thought that nothing threatened me. As proof I cited the fact that Piotr Gutienko had not stopped at my house on his way home. That same day I went into town once more and returned late that evening with no difficulty.

Thus started my life in the country during the revolution. It lasted until January 10 1918 when I was obliged in dramatic circumstances to leave Sably. During that time, under new conditions, I succeeded in smoothing out the work of the Red Cross in Sebastopol and in taking part in the political activities of the Cadet party as a member of the government committee to which I had been elected. A journal of the party was even edited and I wrote articles for it, and a university for the people was created to which I gave money and where I gave lectures on financial law. This new activity pleased me immensely and brought me closer to many public groups.

In the country, I continued to look after the estate and to make improvements as if nothing had happened. Apart from that, as I have already said, I thought it was my duty to uphold even on a small scale the economy of the state and I did not want to lose in the eyes of the peasants my reputation of being a good manager and in so doing lose their respect. Our relations continued to be friendly and the members of the village council often came to discuss with me current events and the «installation» of the revolution. During these talks I would endeavor to restrain them from making any show of impatience and I would exhort them to have confidence in the interim government and to wait for the decision of the Constituant Assembly which could not fail to satisfy their desires. I spoke to them of the absolute need to uphold by every possible means order at the rear so as to continue the war against the Germans who, if the front were to collapse, would immediately reach the Crimea and would apply there their type of rules that would have nothing in common with the newly acquired liberties. The peasants would listen to me and seemed to agree with me. Sometimes however, probably under the influence of more agitated elements, they would provoke me with questions relating to the relations between them and the estate. Most of these questions were devoid of all meaning and were easy to answer. There were also comical ones. For instance one day the peasants asked me to whom the village church belonged that had been built by my grandmother, to the owner or to the peasants? To my great surprise they were satisfied with my answer that of course it belonged to God!

I was somewhat worried by the arrival in the village of deserters from the army. They were noisy, drank a lot, sang and shouted in the evening but their armed attacks were limited to the fish of the Alma which they killed with hand grenades they had brought back from the front. Spring came, then summer. The work in the garden and in the fields continued quietly and without complications. At last the moment arrived for the elections to the zemstvo[3] that had been set up by order of the government. The concept of the zemstvo that had already been planned under the old regime and which at that time was said to have to be «composed of all the classes», had always appealed to me and I dreamed of taking part in it. It seemed to me that a collaboration between the forces of the intelligentsia and of the peasants in the not

---

3. Zemstvo = a local administration.

too big area of a rural district would be a good thing not only for the farming but also for agricultural development. I thought that the peasants who made up the majority of voters would find among the landowners some decent and honest people. At the time of a revolution the zemstvo of a rural district could take over from the «soviet»[4], which applied an irresponsible and harmful demagogy, and could incite the peasants to accomplish serious and productive work. A small isolated rural district seemed to me to be the lowest scale of state activity capable of teaching the peasants how to seek personal satisfaction in work that was done for the benefit of everyone. I thought that under the new structures my dream could not become reality as the peasants would probably not vote for a landowner and this saddened me. What was not my surprise and pride, therefore when that same evening, after the local inhabitants had convened to designate the candidates for election in the village of Sably, which had its own voting office, a deputation of peasants came to see me and showed me the list of the five candidates, the third of which bore my name. I did not hide my surprise from the peasants and I asked them why they had chosen me. They answered that in the new zemstvo there had to be educated men who were also good masters and who had proved by their attitude their good intentions towards them and that for them the person who fulfilled these requirements was myself. In addition they had confidence in me because they knew that «I was not going to steal their money» and that with my help the zemstvo would build the roads they needed as well as the schools and the hospitals. Although I knew that the decision of the peasants could not be fulfilled as far as I was concerned because the government council in Simferopol would veto my candidacy, nevertheless I felt a tremendous moral satisfaction. My conviction that it was possible to establish confidence between the peasants and the landowners through a work done in collaboration had had its first concrete confirmation. As was to be expected the next day a member of the government

---

4. Soviet = committee of a rural district.

council arrived in Sably and forced the peasants to remove my candidacy.

My next official meeting with the «council» took place in September when one of its members brought me an invitation to the meeting that had been convened to report on a circular from the Minister of Agriculture, Tchernoff, that related to the guarantee of the autumn cultivations. The peasant who brought me the notice was also going to the meeting as a delegate of the rural council and I invited him to go with me in my car. When we arrived at the meeting we saw that the praesidium that was already in session was composed of peasants and of the rural intelligentsia. The hall was filled with representatives of the rural councils. The first row of seats was reserved for the landowners of which there were only three not counting me. At the opening of the meeting the president communicated the contents of the minister's circular which stated that if one of the landowners, because he expected an imminent agrarian reform, had not started his autumn sowing, then the land that he had not sowed should be given free of charge to the peasants so that they could start the sowing. Immediately after the president had finished reading, one of the agitators present asked for leave to speak and made an impassioned speech in which he stated that at last the landowners' land was going to be given free of charge and in full ownership to the peasants. After he had finished I in turn asked permission to speak and remarked that the orator who had preceded me had obviously not understood a word of the circular and asked the president to please read it over again. To my great surprise my intervention did not provoke any protest and the president complied with my request. Then started the questioning of the landowners. How much land did each of them have for the autumn sowing and did they intend to sow it? When it came to my turn I stated that as far as I was concerned this question arrived too late as I had already finished sowing my fields two weeks before and, to apply the measures decided upon by the government, I requested the right to use the land of the peasants of Sably which covered 800 dessiatines, only 69 of which had been sowed by them. My statement had a shattering effect for the space of a second on the praesidium and silence reigned in the hall. The president then asked the Sably delegate if this was true and he confirmed it very sincerely. The fact was that my peasant neighbors worked as waggoners and in truth had no time to sow their land. Naturally my request was not granted which pleased me greatly as to sow the peasants' land, I would have had to have grain which I did not own and it was impossible to obtain any because of the measures taken by the interim government on the wheat monopoly.

The atmosphere in the Crimea was becoming more and more alarming for, after the bolshevik revolution that had taken place in Sebastopol, soviet power had installed itself there. However the Crimean peninsula had not yet recognized this power and it was a self-elected Tartar committee that governed the Crimea with the help of the Crimean battalion of Tartars garrisoned in Simferopol. Although life had become difficult because of the nervous tension that prevailed and because one could not help but wonder what would happen later, I continued to live in Sably where the house was full of acquaintances and friends, refugees from Petrograd. In those agitated times my grandmother lived in her apartment in town with her nurses.

By mid-December it became evident that the peasants of the village of Sably, except those who owned a lot of goods, had become bolsheviks. Piotr Gutienko was chosen as president of the rural council. He did not hide his political beliefs and all the members of the council followed him. Bolshevism had even penetrated the employees of the estate and the household servants. The situation had become dangerous for me and my guests but until then I had no reason to complain of any excesses on the part of the peasants. The new tendencies only manifested themselves by the fact that the peasants tried to oppose the export from the estate of negotiable products but even this ceased after I had had a peaceful talk with them.

January 1, 1918 arrived. The day before we, the occupants of the house, had wanted to hide from each other how worried we were and we had seen in the New Year with mutual wishes which we knew very well could not come true. The following day at twelve noon Piotr Gutienko sent me a note inviting me to be present at the village meeting. After some hesitation I decided to risk it and left for the meeting. Not wanting to be alone in a situation that might become dangerous I took along with me my driver, a man who was faithful and devoted to me. We were both armed with revolvers and I asked him to remain at the door of the rural council house where, in case of absolute necessity, he could cover my retreat. I intended to sell my life dearly. When we arrived at the meeting the courtyard was full of people and no particular atmosphere of agitation was noticeable. Piotr Gutienko came up to me and invited me to enter the council house. There he announced to me that the Sably rural council had decided to «socialize» the Sably estate and the neighboring «khutor» of Count Mordvinoff and he suggested that I go with him to the meeting so as to fix the details of the procedure. I answered by asking him why the peasants had refused the idea of sharing between themselves the estate and wished to keep it for a general use on a socialist basis? To that Piotr Gutienko retorted that the peasants realized perfectly well that a farming estate such as mine would lose a great deal of its value if it were divided. We then went together to the meeting and stopped at the entrance to the council hall. Having taken a quick look around at the group of peasants assembled in the courtyard I noticed on the right a small soldier, well dressed, who held in his hands rolls of propaganda notices on which one could decipher bits of sentences obviously bolshevik. Now I knew from where would come, if not danger to my life, at least a verbal attack. I was ready for the latter, for I had decided beforehand to have done with this difficult affair in a peaceful manner and I could not accept the intrusion of an alien element in the person of an agitator sent from the city. Stepping out on the porch Piotr Gutienko announced to the people who were assembled in the courtyard that he had informed me of their decision and, turning in my direction, he asked me if I was in agreement with it. I answered that in view of the situation that prevailed in Russia one could not speak of any right and that it was only force that was on the side of the peasants

190

and that for that reason my agreement was absolutely not necessary. I also pointed out that, if one spoke of rights, I personally had none as far as the decision to socialize the estate was concerned as I was only my mother's agent and she rented it from my grandmother, the yearly agreement having been signed the day before. Because of all this I stated that «taking advantage of the freedom conquered by everybody I would in a few days time leave the estate taking with me only my personal effects that had no bearing on agriculture». Obviously displeased with the turn of events, the agitator tried several times to interrupt the peaceful talks with provocative remarks but each time he was stopped by Gutienko. When I had finished speaking Piotr Gutienko answered that my grandmother had enjoyed enough advantages from the estate and that in my mother's absence I had to give my agreement to the socialization of the estate, this being absolutely necessary for the maintenance of the friendly character of our relations. «Furthermore», he said, «we absolutely do not want to get rid of You. Although we understand that You are free to do as You choose we ask You to stay with us because we need You to organize a socialist administration and the future running of the estate». Such a statement coming from Piotr Gutienko was too much for the agitator and, foaming at the mouth, he started to shout that what was happening was a mockery of the revolution and that no preliminary agreement with the landowner, blood-sucker and exploiter that he was, was acceptable. There it was not only Piotr Gutienko who stopped him, it was also the crowd of people from whom came cries that «Davydchuk had never drunk the blood of anybody and that they needed him as a useful and honest master whom they knew well». When peace was restored I asked Piotr Gutienko what would be, in the event that I accepted their decision, my position in the administration of a socialist agricultural development and what would I have to live on? Piotr Gutienko answered «You will be a member of the managing committee of the estate and its president. You will run this organization, you will sleep in your home and you will enjoy as before the proceeds of the farming. As far as your salary is concerned it is up to you to fix the amount». I did not answer immediately Piotr Gutienko's statement.

Needless to say the peasants' wish that I, landowner and master, should collaborate with them in the enthusiastic atmosphere of the revolution could only surprise me immensely. It was the proof that all my surmises on the relations between peasants and landowners were right. I had won a great victory that had given me a great moral satisfaction but from there to participation in the establishment of a communal agricultural organization was a big step that I was not ready to take. Never having been a socialist and certainly not a communist I could not bring myself to take part in a bolshevik enterprise. It was obvious to me that the socialization of our estate was the work of the bolsheviks who were in Simferopol and who wished to turn the estate into a future «sovkhoze»[5]. The present plan was a delusion the reason of which was to prevent the looting of the estate by the peasants and the sharing out of the land between themselves. The presence of the agitator at the meeting confirmed this. There was only one thing that the bolsheviks had not thought of—that was my role in the affair. By a strange concourse of circumstances my private interests coincided with those of the bolsheviks, the only difference being that like everyone at the time, I did not believe that soviet power would last and I thought that the socialization of Sably with my participation was the only way to maintain its value for my family.

All these ideas passed through my head like lightning and I agreed to the demand of the peasants. After that, I considered it to be my duty to explain to them that obviously they did not realize to what, in fact, the socialization of an organization, or as I called it, a communal rural organization, corresponded. I pointed out to them that there was no room for individual property and that consequently from now on all their land was the same as ours and Count Mordvinoff's and would become communal property. The same fate would be reserved to their livestock and equipment. All the members of the community would have to work alternately for nothing a certain number

---

5. Sovkhoze = Model farm run by the state.

of days that would be fixed during the year. «Furthermore», I added, «I will write a project of rules for the community that I will submit to the council for its approval».

As a new member of the «council» I was immediately invited to the meeting. In the meantime my wages had been fixed at 18,000 roubles a year and they suggested I invite my mother to come and stay with me in Sably. When he said goodbye to me Piotr Gutienko said «I knew you would agree to stay with us. It is not for nothing that your ancestors were exiled to Siberia because of their convictions». The mention of my Decembrist ancestors by Piotr Gutienko shocked me. For me it was a profanation.

That same day I tackled the drawing up of the rules of «the Rural Agrarian Commune of Sably» and I had almost finished it when the rural council informed me that the realization of the project had been postponed until the end of the month.

On January 10 the Crimean peninsula was occupied by the sailors and the workmen of Sebastopol who had shot on the spot without distinction all the landowners who had not been able to leave their home. I and my relatives and friends succeeded in leaving Sably at the last minute when the «armed people» were already in the park.

Soviet power installed itself in the Crimea and declared a short time later that Sably had become a «sovkhoze» and that its management had been handed over to my attendant. According to the news that has reached me, Sably is still to this day under government management and the peasants have nothing to say about it[6].

6. When the author's daughter visited Sably in 1981 she found that the estate was indeed run as a government farm with production concentrated on apples (see the chapter «My Red Apples from the Crimea») and that the house, unchanged since its description by the author, had been turned into offices and a kindergarten.

THE MEETING

The bay of Sebastopol was all bathed in sun one fresh morning of November 26, 1918 when a fleet of at least 100 ships steamed slowly into the bay. It was the victorious fleet of the Allies who had only just signed the armistice with the Germans. It was the first time after four years of war, during which Russia had lost so much blood by the side of the Allies, that their ships were entering a Russian port, yet they fired no salvo. Russia was not there and her flag flew neither on the fortress nor on what was left of yesterday's Russian fleet. The yellow Ukrainian flag flew on the Russian ships and the shore batteries had long since been destroyed by the Germans who had occupied the fortress. This was not a visit to Russia but a demonstration of wartime force in front of the Germans and their allies the Ukrainians. The admiral who commanded the fleet that had just arrived did not come ashore, as was the international custom, to visit the commander of the Russian fleet and the latter did not go on board his ship. Instead, on the small jetty next to the «Grafskaya»[1], awaiting the moment when the flagship, the dreadnought the «Superb», would lower her anchor, stood two small groups, one composed of two army officers, the commanding officer of a small unit of the voluntary army that was stationed in the Crimea and his chief of staff, the other of ten members of the regional government of Crimea and the author of these lines, who held the function of chief of protocol.

The regional government of Crimea had been formed on November 16, 1918 that is to say ten days before the morning

---

1. Landing-place built by count (Graf) Mordvinoff.

195

described above, after the armistice signed by the Allies with the Germans and the resignation of General Sulkevich, a Tartar nationalist whom the Germans had supported. Already at the time of the Germans and before coming into power the regional government's objective had been to prevent the separation of Crimea from Russia and to introduce a democratic form of government in the Crimea. Later on, when the Germans were preparing to leave, another problem arose, that of filling the gap and establishing some form of controlling power in the region. Its position was a difficult one. When the Germans left, no armed forces, not even police, remained in the Crimea to maintain order and some form of resistance was to be expected from the local bolsheviks. When the new government asked for military aid, General Denikin answered that he was unable to give any whatsoever and that all he could do was to send an insignificant detachment for «a psychological effect». The only hope left were the Allies and it was with this in mind that the government was welcoming the Allied fleet.

There was little hope that this plan would succeed. Nevertheless the government relied on the fact that the democratic forces of the region were represented by a State Assembly that had been elected after the February revolution and that members of all the important political parties were represented in the present group. But who, beyond the borders of Crimea, was aware of its existence? In addition to active local representatives the group included personalities such as S.S. Krym who was President, member of the Cadet party, ex-member of the State Council elected by the Taurid Assembly, M.M. Vinaver, minister of Transport, member of the Cadet party and ex-member of the first government Duma, and V.D. Nabokov, Minister of Justice, also a member of the Cadet party and ex-member of the first government Duma. But if these names had a great deal of meaning for local people and even in Russia, what impression could they make on the British Admiral who only had a very confused idea of what was going on? The author of these lines, only a few days before the arrival of the fleet, at the request of S.S. Krym, had been to Sebastopol to find out from the Germans or from the Ukrainian commanding officer what were the intentions of the Allies. He had been unable to get any information from one side or the other and his mission might have been a complete failure if he had not seen by chance, one morning, a British submarine enter the roadstead. The officers who came ashore went straight to the Kist hotel, where the German Admiral was staying, with the objective, as we discovered later, of coming to an agreement with him regarding the terms of surrender. We were able to intercept the officers at the entrance to the hotel and the chief of protocol informed them at once of the existence of the Crimean government, whereupon came the question «Bolshevik?». We succeeded in explaining to them in a few words what sort of government ruled the Crimea and requested them to pass on this information to their headquarters in Constantinople. To this they replied that the Allied fleet under the command of Admiral Gough-Calthorpe was due to arrive in Sebastopol on November 26 and that everything could be settled at that time. The object of the mission having been accomplished, all that was left to do was to send a cable to the government and wait for further instructions. These arrived without delay. S.S. Krym asked that everything be prepared for a dignified meeting.

For the chief of protocol this mission was not an easy one. He understood the difficulties that lay in organizing a meeting between Russian representatives who found themselves in power for the first time, and representatives of the Allied forces who, to complicate matters, were naval men and British. On the one side there was the refusal of all parade and etiquette, on the other the strict and traditional attitude regarding these matters. What appeared to be, for the Russian political leaders, ridiculous and unnecessary red tape was in a way sacred to the British. Any transgression of that etiquette, even in the smallest detail, might not only lower in the eyes of the foreigners the prestige of the Crimean government but also jeopardize the success of its enterprise. All this was complicated by the fact that the Crimean government was alien to Sebastopol, recognized by no one and even an enemy in the eyes of the commanding officers of the Ukrainian navy. It was not even on good terms with the volunteer army who, although it recognized it, thought it served no purpose.

The easiest part was to prepare lodgings for the representatives of the government and to greet them at the station. It was much more difficult to arrange their transport from the quay to the flagship. It was unheard of that the Crimean government should be taken to the ship aboard a row-boat with one oarsman and no flag at the stern. Under such conditions it would have to draw alongside the flagship on the port side and not receive an official welcome as if it were a private group. The question of the flag was the most delicate one. To hoist a yellow flag would entail not being welcomed, for the British did not recognize independent Ukraine. Nor could one raise the withe, blue and red flag for the British knew it as the flag of the Russian commercial fleet and would again force that boat to draw up along the port side. This left only one flag that the chief of protocol knew the British sailors respected, the flag of St. Andrew. But there, two questions arose. First, had any such flags been kept after the Russian revolution? Secondly, would the members of the government agree to go under such a flag? It was useless and in any case too late to ask for instructions from S.S. Krym as he had named the author of these lines «chief of protocol» for the very reason that he himself knew very little about these matters and supposed that the latter, in view of his pre-revolutionary activities, would know all about them.

In the first place a naval motor launch had to be found at all costs. With this in mind the chief of protocol went to see the commanding officer of the Ukrainian fleet, Admiral Tchernilovsky-Sokol, whom he knew well and very matter-of-factly asked him to give the Crimean government a launch with a crew to go and visit the British admiral. The admiral, after listening to him, said that it was quite impossible for him to do so but that, recognizing the delicate position of the chief of protocol, he would present a launch to him personally and would give the necessary instructions to the commanding officer of the launch. The following morning the chief of protocol, well before the arrival of the Allied fleet, went to the quay side where the launches were anchored and having chosen one of them asked the commanding officer if he had a flag of St. Andrew. He was answered in the affirmative and, after giving him a tip, asked the officer to raise this flag as soon as the launch had left the quay side with him and the members of the government aboard. After getting the officer's agreement and seeing that the Allied fleet was entering the port, the chief of protocol went to fetch the government members, brought them to the quayside and installed them aboard the launch. When the launch was some distance away from the quay he made a sign to the commanding officer and the flag of St. Andrew was raised at the stern.

The effect produced by this action on the members of the government was not the same for all. The socialists looked indifferent and turned their heads without saying a word. S.S. Krym, M.M. Vinaver and N.N. Bogdanoff put on a commiserating smile. V.D. Nabokov alone, who had remained seated up to that moment with a worried look on his face, seemed happy, got up and silently shook the hand of the chief of protocol. The launch approached the starboard side of the ship. On board by the gangway stood, all ready for the official meeting, two ensigns with telescopes in their hand. When S.S. Krym, who was the first to climb the gangway, was about to board the ship, the chief of protocol barely had time to shout to him «Solomon Samoilovich, your hat!». The ensigns stood at attention and the government members were led to the Admiral's cabin.

The officer on duty at the entrance to the cabin asked S.S. Krym whom he should announce, then let in the government members. At the end of the cabin stood by a desk a man of medium size, rather thickset, dressed in an admiral's uniform. This was Admiral Gough-Calthorpe. After listening to the words of greeting of S.S. Krym he held out his hand and asked him to introduce the other members of the government, after which S.S. Krym invited him to lunch on land. With a pleasant smile the Admiral answered that it was unfortunately not possible for him to accept this invitation as the only person in power recognized by his government in southern Russia was General Denikin. After a minute of awkward silence M.M. Vinaver exchanged a look with S.S. Krym, then read the speech he had himself written in French that had been prepared for the lunch. The Admiral listened to the speech and without answering it was already on the point of saying goodbye when something happened that had not been foreseen by the chief of protocol. A feeling of humiliation and shame had been felt by everyone but especially by V.D. Nabokov. His face expressed his suffering. At the end of M.M. Vinaver's speech he detached himself from the group of government members and stood staring out of the porthole. Suddenly he turned round and quickly went up to the Admiral. In perfect English he started telling him how during the war he and a group of members of the Duma had visited England and had been received aboard the ships of the Royal Fleet. He named the ships he had been fortunate enough to visit and the names of the commanding officers who had greeted him. The Admiral's face lit up and with obvious pleasure he started to evoke details of this meeting. The conversation might have lasted a long time if all of a sudden the door of the cabin had not opened and the orderly announced «Lunch, sir».

The interview had come to an end and the flag-officer accompanied the government members back to the gangway near which were the same ensigns who once more stood at attention.

THE GREAT-GRANDSON OF THE DECEMBRISTS*

«She opened the way for others
She drew the others to sacrifice»

Thus wrote Nekrassov in his poem «the Russian Women» about Ekaterina Ivanovna Trubetskaia, the first wife of a Decembrist to join her husband in exile in Siberia.

I never knew in person my two Decembrist great-grandfathers Vassili Lvovich Davydoff and Serge Petrovich Trubetskoy. I was born after their death but I spent my childhood and my youth in Kamenka, the Davydoff estate which in the 1820s was the seat of the Southern Secret Society of which my great-grandfather was president. In Kamenka there still lived his widow, my great-grandmother and her children who were born in exile in Siberia where she had gone of her own free will to join her husband. Her son Piotr, my grandfather, and his wife Elisaveta, daughter of the Decembrist Trubetskoy, had also lived a short time in Kamenka before settling in their Crimean estate of Sably.

A great deal has been written about Kamenka and the Decembrists, but nowhere does one find what these living witnesses told me, because for them the conspirators were either close relatives or friends. All their thoughts and their feelings were known to them. They could say what had made

---

* This chapter includes 5 lectures made by A.V.D. on the Voice of America in 1952.

their hearts beat and what had been their secret aspirations. Their stories were so alive and so clear that when I evoke nowadays that distant past it seems to me as if I had been in Kamenka myself when the members of the secret society, Volkonsky, Muraviev-Apostol, Yakushkin, Poggio, Yushnevsky and others met there and Pestel read «the Russian Truth», which he had written and which corresponded to the project of a new constitution. My great-grandmother had known them all and remembered them.

I remember her and her children, my uncles and aunts, and I can still feel the warmth they left me for the rest of my life. I have never encountered in anyone the high and pure moral sense, the kindness and the love that they had. The Davydoff and the Trubetskoy families always preserved the cult of the Decembrists' memory which convinced me very early in life that their moral qualities kept them apart from the other people of their time. My great-grandmother's tales made me understand that what inspired the Decembrists was a deep love of others, of the human being in general and their desire for the well-being of each individual. They could not conceive of such a well-being without the total freedom of the individual's personality. They became convinced of this when they discovered what was happening at that time in the rest of Europe at the very borders of their country. That was the time when, after an age-long subjection of the people, the sun of freedom was rising. The Decembrists belonged to the most cultured circles of society and were able to read everything that was being written at that time in the West on freedom and on the new governmental structures that could give this freedom. Being fervent patriots and loving their country and their people, they desired for both of them the blessings that the Western nations were already enjoying. The 1812 war and Napoleon's eviction from their country, accomplished by their people, strengthened these convictions. Having taken part in this war and shared with the soldiers all their trials they could appreciate the high spiritual qualities of the Russian people and realize what they deserved. The foreign campaigns that were made after this war and that the future Decembrists took part in enabled them to discover with their own eyes the material benefits that the people enjoyed and the way they lived in countries where the liberty of the individual had been achieved. This awoke in them the sentiment of their duties towards the Russian citizen. These duties consisted in the obligation for them to enable their country and their people, who had shown such courage, to enjoy these same benefits. They expected that at the end of the war, as a reward for what they had done, the people would be given by the Tsar their freedom from serfdom and the right to become citizens. Something quite different occurred. The Tsar, who feared for his absolute power, only tightened the screws. He put the country in the hands of his contemporary Arakcheev who became a real dictator. My great-grandmother's voice trembled when she recalled how this cruel and soulless man had ruled her country. He had only one objective—to keep at all costs and by every available means immutable the autocratic regime. The right to serfdom was not enough for him. He added the nightmare of military deportations. A peasant serf who belonged to a landowner enjoyed a certain freedom in his everyday life, but those who did their military service were completely deprived of it. The peasants were not the only ones to suffer the yoke of tyranny. Every class of society was subjected to it. The whole population had to act and think in accordance with the government's will. The government had an eye on everything and intervened in every act of public life. Such a situation could only awaken the indignation of freethinkers such as the future Decembrists. Having convinced themselves that it was impossible to achieve a better fate for the people by normal means they started on the road to rebellion. Thus was born the Secret Society.

My grandmother Elisaveta Sergeevna Davydova was the daughter of the Decembrist Serge Petrovitch Trubetskoy and his wife Ekaterina Ivanovna, Katacha. I knew her well because she only died in 1918. She was born in Siberia and at the end of her studies at the University of Irkutsk she married my grandfather Piotr Davydoff, the son of the Decembrist. Her first education was given to her by her father. He spoke to her of his reasons for taking part in the conspiracy, of his role in the activities and the formation of the Secret Society and particularly of the aspirations of the Decembrists. My grandmother remembered very well her father's precepts and cherished his memory. She told me a great many things that she had learned from him.

My great-grandfather had told her how on his return from Paris in 1818, where he had lived among a free people, he had been shocked by the lack of freedom in his own country, where only serfdom and a flagrant contempt of the individual existed. His ideas were shared by his friends the officers of the Semenovsky regiment. Their talks led to the idea of forming a secret society, the objective of which would be to eliminate all these injustices. After several changes this idea resulted finally in the creation of two Secret Societies, the Northern in St. Petersburg and the Southern in Tulchin.

The members of the Secret Society had a conception of the world that was based on two sentiments—love of one's neighbor and love of liberty. Both constitutional projects drawn up by members of this Society—Nikita Muraviev's project and Pestel's «the Russian Truth»—clearly express these sentiments. «Individual freedom», wrote Pestel, «is the first and foremost right of each citizen and the sacred duty of the government». When my great-grandfather spoke to his daughter about this conviction of Pestel's he explained to her in what, in the mind of the Decembrists, this liberty of the individual consisted and what should be the essential rights of each citizen.

In those times individual freedom meant essentially the liberation of the serfs from their state of slavery. In addition each free citizen should enjoy without any restriction whatsoever the right to express orally and in writing his opinions and his thoughts, that is to say have the right to think and to speak. In one of the constitutional projects it was said that «each writer is responsible for his opinions and for the rules that he expounds and may be judged according to the rules of the moral code». Furthermore it was said that a free individual could in no way be condemned because of his beliefs or his religion, that is to say he had to have complete liberty of conscience. In these projects it was stated that «freedom of religion was to be complete, both in conscience and in sentiment as long as one did not infringe the laws of nature and of morals». Each citizen could choose his subject of study freely, come and go as he wished in the country and leave the country whenever he chose to do so. On the basis of these rules «the equality of all before the law» was to be established. At the same time all titles and other privileges were to be abolished. Finally the right of ownership was declared sacred and inviolable.

However, the simple fact of having achieved these rights was not sufficient. They had to be protected against the risk of being abrogated and something had to be done so that no one could eliminate them either by force or by lies. Only the democratic structure of the government or, as one said at the time, the right of the people, could act as a shield against such attacks. Pestel said: «Sovereign right belongs to the people. The Russian people are free and independent. The source of all power are the people to whom belongs the exclusive right to decide for themselves. The people wield their power through representatives freely chosen by them». To avoid the possibility of arbitrary actions by the government the person of each citizen was declared inviolable. To safeguard the immunity of the individual special rules were established and anyone who violated them could be brought to judgment. Thus according to the constitutional projects no one could lose his freedom other than for a legal reason based on the laws in force. Nobody could enter a citizen's home without his authorization and he could be arrested only on a written order from the authorities explaining the reasons for his arrest. Finally no one could be judged other than by a sworn tribunal and only in a place defined by law. There could be no extraordinary tribunal nor any extraordinary commission.

It was with these rules that the Decembrists wanted to guarantee the happiness and the well-being of their people and of their country.

My great-grandmother Alexandra Ivanovna Davydova, the widow of the Decembrist, was born in 1801 and died in 1893 at the age of 92. She spent her youth in Kamenka. She remembered perfectly well all that had happened there before the Decembrist uprising as well as all that was said and done in Russian society. She liked to share her memories with her grandchildren and her great-grandchildren. I remember her quite clearly, a little old lady with a wrinkled face, seated in a deep armchair next to the round table where once upon a time my grandfather used to study. She kept until the end of her life a lucid mind and an incredible memory and she would tell us children and young people the problems that were in the minds of people at the start of the century and would focus our attention on the members of the Secret Society. According to her the main problem was the liberation of the serfs. Her husband and his friends in the Secret Society were fanatics of freedom. It was only natural that for them serfdom was totally inadmissible and if their plans were to succeed its suppression was to be one of the first measures taken. Well before 1825 they did everything in their power to draw the attention of Russian society to this problem and inspire sympathy for their ideas. These attempts were not without success. The liberation of the peasants finally became a problem so pressing that only a few people still contested its urgency. This liberation had just taken place in Europe as well as in neighboring Poland and in the Baltic provinces which then belonged to Russia. The Decembrists and the partisans of the liberation of the serfs put forward first of all its moral character. They showed how impossible it was that the right of ownership should exist over people as if they were cattle. They thought it revolting that landowners should have the right to dispose of their peasants as if they were objects, to sell them both in lots and individually, to destroy their families, to rob them and to torture them. From an economic point of view they thought serfdom was not profitable and that the production yielded by a serf's work was lower than that of a free and salaried workman.

In spite of the disapproval of the men in power and of their friends, the movement in favor of the liberation of the serfs gained momentum. It was particularly strong after the 1812 war in which the peasants, not only those who fought in the army or with the partisans but also those who simply defended their isbas, had showed an incredible patriotism. In fact the peasants had been the real victors, the ones who had expelled Napoleon and his troops from Russia. They did not listen to the alluring promises of freedom made by Napoleon and died for their country in spite of the fact that they were serfs and in spite of being oppressed by the government and by the landowners. They did not die for the Tsar but for their country. The government of that time did not understand this and after the war, fearing for its authority, only took more restrictive measures. Even simple conversations about the liberation of the serfs were considered to be crimes. One can understand why for the members of the Secret Society the liberation of the serfs became the main objective of their aspirations. Regarding this vital question there was no disagreement whatever either between the Northern and Southern societies or between the members of each society. The opinions of the Decembrists only diverged when it came to the question of allotting land to the peasants, a question that was closely linked to their liberation. The reason for this is that the liberation of the peasants could be settled very quickly without affecting the economy of the country whereas the sharing out of the land would demand a great deal of time and would considerably affect the economy. Some thought that for moral reasons it was not possible to delay the realization of a question as vital as that of the liberation of the peasants. Taking as examples England, Poland and the Baltic provinces, they suggested that the peasants only be given immediately full ownership of their home and of their individual kitchen gardens, cattle and tools. Others, and they were many, felt that such a decision would be unfair because, as the peasants paid most of the taxes, they had to have personal means to do so. They insisted that the peasants at the time of their liberation be given complete ownership of part of the landowner's estate. There were also those who like Pestel said that the land should belong to the state and that it should be given to the peasants only on a communal basis. As for the peasants themselves they insisted that the land be given to them in full ownership. One can cite as an example the case of Yakushkin, a Decembrist who wished to abolish immediately the state of serfdom of his peasants and offered them their freedom without land. Finally the idea of a liberation of the peasants with land in full ownership was accepted by the majority of Decembrists and was included in the constitutional project of Nikita Muraviev. The state of mind of the serfs in those times was brilliantly expressed in a song written by Ryleev and sung by the soldiers:

«Ah! I feel sick at heart.
In my country we are all slaves.
In that wretched condition
Must we struggle on forever?
How long will it last
That the Russian people
Be the garbage of their lords?
And how long will they haggle
Over their subjects like cattle?

Before my great-grandfather the Decembrist Davydoff was exiled to Siberia, his wife, my great-grandmother Alexandra Ivanovna, lived with her husband in Kamenka. She followed her husband in exile when she was 26, that is to say at an age when she was capable of having an opinion not only in accordance with her husband's sayings but also her own personal one on the system that was in force in her country during her youth. She returned to Russia under the reign of Alexander II just before the reforms that greatly improved the living conditions of the Russian people. Her husband died in Siberia in Krasnoyarsk before the amnesty. She lived until the age of 92 and, as I have already said, I had the joy of knowing her and of hearing her tell what she had seen and lived through during her long life.

According to what she told us the conspiracy of the Decembrists, who were organised in two societies, the Northern and the Southern, was the forerunner of a complete political and social reform of our country. The conspiracy ended in failure but the ideas of the Decembrists did not die.

My great-grandmother told us that the system that was in force in Russia in her youth had all the characteristics of a dictatorship or of a police state. The people enjoyed no freedom, neither political nor personal. The government had taken upon itself to decide every aspect of a person's private life, to rule his mode of life, to direct his opinions and to control the expression of these opinions be it oral or written

In other words every personal idea of each human being had to be incorporated in the ideas of the government. The personality of a human being meant nothing to the government. It was only an object that the state used for its own purpose. The Decembrists wanted to replace this police structure by a structure based on right, where the notion of sovereignty would be limited by a law in favor of the precious liberty of the individual and of his rights. After acquiring his freedom a person would benefit from rights that would be protected by the law. The Decembrists, who aspired at setting up just such a system in their country, worked at establishing measures that could guarantee it. For this they devised constitutional projects that defined forms of popular right and measures that protected the rights of the citizen and the immunity of the individual, and finally all that expressed clearly the notion of fair government.

In those times the law courts, whether civil or criminal, completely reflected the police structure that existed in Russia. Justice was based on the principle of a judiciary instruction where the accused was subjected to a questioning the sole object of which was the interest of the state. He could be subjected to a long detention, to all sorts of questionings and tortures to make him admit his guilt. The law courts were protected by secrecy and the accused was not allowed to be present. They made their decision known by reports made to the chancery. They were not independent and were entirely in the hands of the reigning power and its administration, and acted entirely for the latter's benefit. This sort of situation made the law courts a political weapon and was also a source of corruption and of favoritism. Such was the justice in Russia until the penal reform of 1863. It is not without reason that a poet wrote: «In the law courts Russia is black with black lies».

The Decembrists understood that in a police state such as the autocratic regime of the Tsar or the dictatorship of a party, the most perfect law court would be nothing but a dead letter, a mirage and a lie. They linked closely the reform of the laws and the general reforms of the government that they had conceived. The new law courts would reflect the new order. Independently from the subject of the inquest, at the time of

209

the debate the accused should try and convince the accuser and vice versa. The accused should have the right to defend himself and the most important element of this defence should be the statements of witnesses. The professional secrecy of the law courts should be completely abolished. The accused should be present in person at his trial, which would be open to the public, and all statements would be made orally which would enable everyone to decide on the guilt or the innocence of the accused. The decision that the accused was guilty should be made not by judges named by the state but by sworn jurors who would reach this verdict according to their conscience and to their innermost convictions, that is to say freely and independently from all external pressure. In this way the truth and the integrity of the law courts would be guaranteed. To guarantee the juridical truth by these forms of procedure it was essential that the judges themselves should be independent from the reigning power, that is to say that the latter should be unable to influence their decisions. To achieve this, according to the projects of the Decembrists, a strict separation had to be established between the judicial and the administrative powers through the immutability of judges. In a criminal trial the safeguard of the interests of the accused as well as of the plaintiff was to be assured by barristers or, as they were later called, sworn solicitors whose professional activities could be accomplished in complete freedom.

My great-grandmother lived to see the realization of the Decembrists' ideas and witnessed the liberation of the peasants and the introduction in the army of Alexander's statutes in 1863. Fortunately for her she did not live to see the day when, in the conflagration of the October revolution, these statutes were destroyed in the same way as was destroyed the inscription on the facade of the Regional Tribunal of Petrograd; «May Truth and Clemency reign in Russian law courts.»

The Decembrists' ideas on what should take the place of the police dictatorship in Russia at the start of the last century were expressed in legal terms in their constitutional projects. There were several of these projects but the two most

210

important ones were the project of Nikita Muraviev, a member of the Northern Society, and the «Russian Truth» by Pestel, a member of the Southern Society. My great-grandfather Trubetskoy was closely associated with the drawing up of the first one and my great-grandfather Davydoff helped Pestel to write the other. I was told about these projects both by Trubetskoy's daughter, my grandmother Elisaveta Sergeevna, and by my great-grandmother Alexandra Ivanovna Davydova. They both told me about the obstacles that the authors of these projects had had to overcome to achieve these objectives. Along with the other members of the secret societies, they wanted to introduce this system into our country, that is to say give the people complete freedom and civic rights as soon as possible. However, at the same time, they wished to avoid a change of government by force that is to say by a revolution that would lead to bloodshed, civil war and great destructions. They also thought it was essential to guarantee the greatest possible stability to the new structures and to protect them from the attacks of men who might try and gain absolute power and thus transform the reforms into mirages. The only way to avoid a revolution was to maintain the Tsar in power but a power limited by the constitution, and this seemed possible in view of the liberal tendencies of Tsar Alexander I. Nevertheless one cannot say that the majority of members agreed with these decisions. The majority were more in favor of introducing a republican structure, the only form of government that could give total power to the people. Pestel, for instance, who was in favor of this last solution, said that if a person were to be at the head of the state this would lead to despotism whatever guarantees one might try to take. He based his opinion on historical examples and his convictions proved to be so right that he turned out to be a real prophet. Nowadays we can see that in so-called democratic governments with a constitution on paper there reigns in fact either a personal despotic power or the dictatorship of a party formed by another type of «leader», that is to say the worst form of political regime. Finally Pestel's opinion prevailed in the Secret Society.

211

The freedom of thought of the Decembrists that had already taken shape in their youth in their country was developed and strengthened mainly during their stay in the West when the Russian armies campaigned abroad in 1813 and 1814. There they saw with their own eyes what the real right of self-government can give a country. They were able to compare the backwardness of their country in the cultural field with the progress and the high standard of living of free countries and this convinced them even more that a rapid change of government was required in Russia.

Both constitutional projects—Nikita Muraviev's and Pestel's—were inspired in great part by the Western constitutions. In his project Nikita Muraviev states «The sovereign power belongs to the people. The source of supreme power is the people to whom belongs the exclusive right to take major decisions concerning itself. The right to promulgate constitutional rules belongs to the government of the people». The objective of the state, said Pestel, is the prosperity of all society and of each of its members. The state exists only for the good of the people and has no other reason to exist. According to the constitutional projects, legislative power should belong to a Parliament that was known by its historical name of «Vetchy», elected by universel suffrage. The Vetchy could not change the laws of the state. Nobility and serfdom were abolished and all citizens became equal before the law. A clear division was made between the executive and the legislative powers. The law courts became independent from the executive power. A court of justice was created with immutable judges. Every citizen had the right to choose his religion according to his conscience and had the right to express his opinions freely both orally and in writing.

One can easily imagine what well-being would reign in Russia and how freely one could breathe there now if the dreams of the Decembrists that my old ladies spoke to me about with so much veneration had been realized 120 years ago. Alas, they perished in the distant mines of Siberia and for us, the descendants of these pure and unselfish persons, all that is left is the possibility of seeing from afar, from abroad, how much they loved freedom and their country.

Alexander Davydoff concluded this article when he wrote it in 1950 by saying:

«But occasionally history will repeat itself. Today as then the enemy has forced his way into our country and as then he has been chased out by our people. Once again our armies have found themselves in the free countries of the West and have seen in what freedom and well-being these people live. Maybe out of these armies will rise new Decembrists.»

THE DECEMBRISTS
AND THE PEASANT PROBLEM

One would be entitled to think that Russian public opinion had recognized a long time ago the spiritual elevation of the Decembrists' actions and their moral and ideological views on the world, and that there would therefore be no need either to approve or to defend them against critical remarks. Nevertheless one aspect of their deeds is often, even now, subject to criticism both in literature and in public opinion. It all began at the start of the century with the revolutionary fever that took hold of Russian society. Even historical events of the distant past were then judged from an entirely political point of view because the political ideas that predominated at that time were considered to be indisputable truths valid for any epoch. In consequence, the integrity of the Decembrists' political convictions regarding the peasant problem became subject to doubt. People regretted that on this question their actions had not been consistent with their ideas and said that they had been insincere because they had been influenced by the interests of their class and by their own material interests. They were reproached for the fact that, having fought for the liberation of the peasants, they had not liberated their own serfs, and that, on the rare occasions when they had decided to do so, they had not given them any land because this would have meant sacrificing their own materialistic interests to their convictions. Worse still, it was said that, with the exception of Pestel, the Decembrists had been in favor, even in their projects of peasant reform, of liberating the serfs without giving them any land. Consequently, it was said of them that they only wanted to abolish the dependence of the serfs on their master while keeping the land for themselves. In the most favorable of cases, historians like V.I. Semevsky asked that the Decembrists not be judged without taking into consideration the degree of cultural development of society in their time.

Though full of good intentions, these opinions seem to be unfair accusations, even if partially mitigated by the indulgence shown to the accused. In point of fact, a careful study of the history of the peasant problem from the reign of Catherine II up to the emancipation of 1861 shows that the accusations made against the Decembrists by public opinion have no basis whatsoever and that they deserve not only indulgence but a complete rehabilitation.

First of all, a close study of the question shows that, at the time of the Decembrists and in the era preceding it, this problem could be divided into two parts: on the one hand, the liberation of the peasants from the authority of their masters, that is to say from serfdom; on the other hand, the allotment of land to the peasants. The first part was strictly a moral and humanitarian problem. The second could be viewed either from the angle of the government or from the angle of the principle of property, a well-established principle which affirmed that private property was untouchable. It is only later that these two parts were united into a whole and acquired a political character. If one were not to take these elements into consideration, one might be led to paradoxical conclusions such as, for instance, that the Russian Imperial power had much more advanced ideas on the peasant question than the Decembrist «revolutionaries». Secondly, a careful study of the question also shows that the assertion that the Decembrists, except Pestel, did not wish to give land to the peasants is totally false.

In Russian society, the idea of the liberation of the peasants from serfdom matured slowly. For a long time there was only a feeling of commiseration for their fate and for the distressing aspects of their condition, and the desire to lighten their burden. Already Peter the Great, after studying this question of the harsh life of the peasants, had ordered that the estates of tyrannic landowners be taken into tutelage and had expressed the wish that masters should not interfere in their peasants' marriages. After Peter I and until the end of Elisabeth's reign, the peasant question was forgotten and Peter's ukase remained a dead letter. For interest in this problem to be revived in the public mind, it was first of all necessary that, for the first time in Russian history, the public conscience should awaken and that the desire to create an ideal conception of the world be born. This occurred in the last years of Elisabeth's reign. The special circumstances in which this ideal conception of the world was created and the characteristic traits of this conception were to have such an influence on the reaction of Russian society towards the peasant problem that the subject deserves a more detailed study.

It is precisely in the last years of Elisabeth's reign that one remarks among the more educated elements of Russian society a reaction against the realism of Peter the Great's era and the appearance of vague ideological interests. The need to justify and to strengthen the previous moral and religious idealism manifested itself in the use of new rational bases in place of religious authority. The first Russian newspapers to appear at that time are testimonies to the moralizing tendencies of Russian youth. For instance in the newspaper «Useful Entertainments» that was edited by young students of the University of Moscow, we find attempts to create a certain social conception of the world. «The world is nothing but decay and vanity», write the authors. «He who does good by loving his neighbor and his friends will not rot. Love is the only way of fighting vice, and the only objectives of our life are the elimination of evil in the world and the creation of a society that uses love to attain this». Tendencies such as these could not be satisfied by the primitive religious idealism of Muscovite Russia. Compromises had to be found between this idealism and the new influences of the «enlightened» era that had found an echo in reformed Russia. These compromises were found in the interest that was aroused on a moral and religious plane by the first degrees of freemasonry, the tendencies of which were very close to those expressed by the young students in their paper.

People tend to think that Russian freemasonry, which had

217

started under Elisaveta Petrovna and had developed especially under Catherine and at the start of Alexander I's reign, had a political character as in France before and during the revolution. From there stemmed the notion that freemasonry had always played an important role in politics and that it reached its acme when it gave itself entirely to this role. This concept, partly true as far as French freemasonry is concerned, does not apply to the British freemasonry, nor to the German, nor to the Scandinavian. These did not have any political objectives and never formed any «revolutionary cells». In Russia freemasons first came from England, then from Scandinavia, and they were finally subjected to German influence. This determined their conduct for a long period of time. L.N. Tolstoy, who was never a freemason but who devoted a great deal of his time to the study of freemasonry in the archives of the Rumantsev Museum, painted a very true picture of the very essence of freemasonry in what he made Bazdeev (Pozdeev, a well known freemason in the early 19th century) say to Bezukhoff [1]. The only thing that L.N. Tolstoy omitted—and this is an important element of the question of the influence of freemasonry on the formation of the Russian conception of the world—is that, to become a freemason, a man must not only be of good morals, he must also be free. This rule goes back to ancient times and existed long before the appearance of French influence and the theory of natural right. Freemasonry's point of view on liberty is a much broader notion than the political one. Masonic liberty is the liberty from all dogmas, whether religious, political or other. That is why it can only be the prerogative of a man «of good morals».

Freemasonry, as it was created in Russia in the 18th century, being apolitical and not representing in itself a conspiracy, did not require for its blossoming any exterior manifestation whatsoever. Its importance lay in the influence it exerted over its milieu. This influence was above all moral and humanitarian and was completed by the masonic concept of liberty. Until now the importance of this influence on the formation of the Russian concept of the world has remained greatly under-

---

1. In «War and Peace».

estimated. It gave it a particular coloring that created Russian national moralism, characteristic of Russian thought. One of the positive aspects of the ideas expressed by freemasonry was the fact that, as it had no political character, these were adopted by large circles of society, from the Emperor to representatives of the middle classes. Already in Elisaveta Petrovna's time the most cultured people were freemasons. Among these were A.P. Sumarokoff, Prince Chtcherbatov, Boltin, Feodor Mamonov, P.S. Svistunoff, Count N.N. Golovin, Counts Z. and I. Tchernitcheff, Roman Vorontzov (father of Princess Dashkoff), Princes Golitzin and Trubetskoy. In Catherine's time, other representatives of high society entered the ranks of freemasonry, for instance Lopukhin, Master of the Horse Narichkin, Prince Alexander Trubetskoy and Prince P.P. Repnin. Emperor Paul I and, in his entourage, Count N.I. Panin and his brother Piotr, Prince N.V. Repnin and Prince A.B. Kurakin, P.A. Tchaadaev, A.M. Kutuzov and N.I. Novikoff, were either freemasons or martinists. Finally, during the reign of Alexander I, at the time of the revival of Russian freemasonry, many of those who later became Decembrists joined the movement, among them P.I. Pestel and Prince S.P. Trubetskoy.

The moral views of the Russian concept of the world first clashed with the peasant problem. In this problem what shocked most the new ethical-religious psychology of society was the condition of slavery of the peasants, the total power that the landlords had over them and the total lack of rights that the peasants had with regard to their landlords. That is why, from the moment this problem attracted the attention of society and of the ruling power, it was first presented not as a problem of the total liberty of the peasants, that is to say their emancipation from the power of the landlords and from the land they tilled, but as a problem of lightening their state of slavery. In Catherine's time, under the influence of enlightenment and the development of the humanitarian spirit, the question of lightening the fate of the peasants gained strength and took shape. It is precisely at this moment that the first aspirations to abolish the «cattle» condition of the peasants made their appearance and that the shameful procedure of trading people both in lots and individually captured the attention of society. Already in 1763 Count P.I. Panin had suggested forbidding the trading of conscripts and accepting the sale of peasants only if the whole family was involved, thus finally reducing their obligations to more normal proportions. Catherine herself, in her «Order», expresses the idea of giving to the peasants the right of ownership over all movable goods and the right to have their complaints against the landlords examined by itinerant judges. In this «Order» she is also in favor of requiring «the landowners to impose their exactions with a great deal of discernment» and reminded them of the law previously promulgated by Peter the Great and of his wishes. Radishcheff, in «Travels from Petersburg to Moscow», in the chapter «Mednoie», describes vividly and with great indignation an auction sale of a peasant family by individuals. Further on he says that the increasing danger represented by the rising indignation of the people could only be eliminated by improving the fate of the peasants who were living in a state of slavery. In his project Radishcheff, among other measures, gives priority to the distinction between serfs who work the land and those who work as servants. «This distinction», he states, «must be abolished before anything else». It is only after he has enumerated all the measures that should be taken that he says: «After that comes the complete abolition of slavery».

Even Paul I did not forget the peasants and ordered that their unpaid working time be limited to three days a week. If Catherine and Paul had thought about the fate of the peasants, even if without results, one can understand why Alexander I, in the liberal first half of his reign, could not but be especially concerned with this problem. On June 5, 1801, by order of the Tsar, Attorney-General Bekleshoff presented to the State Council a note which stated that «up to this very day people have been used like personal objects and have been traded and sold at public auction» and it was suggested that the sale of peasants without land should be forbidden. This suggestion was not approved by the State Council and did not go into effect. Alexander I's only achievment in the first half of his reign was the law of February 20, 1803 on «the organization of voluntary workers of the land» according to which landowners were authorized to liberate their peasants by entire families with the obligation to provide them with a plot of land. The importance of this measure was that the liberation of peasants without land would become impossible. Again in 1818 Alexander I returned to his idea of lightening the fate of the peasants and ordered Araktcheev to devise a project which would conform to his wishes. One must say that Arakcheev acquitted himself very well of this task inasmuch as he understood the Tsar's basic idea of eliminating the peasants' personal dependence on the landowners, and created the possibility of putting the Tsar's project into practice. According to this project, each year 5 million roubles taken from the state funds were to be allocated by the public treasury to the buying back of peasants with two dessiatines of land per soul. Because of disturbances abroad, this project came to nothing. Speransky, in his attempts at general reforms, dedicated two works to the peasant problem: a memoir of 1802 and the project of law of 1809. These two works have only one objective: «the abolition of the citizen's state of slavery». In them, he divides these reforms into two stages. As a first step he suggests defining the periods of compulsory service of the peasants and instituting special law courts to examine the state of affairs that exists between the peasants and their master. The peasants were to pass from the state of «serf property of the landowner» to «serf of the land» and become only «registered people». Private taxation was to be transferred to the land and the deeds of sale of the landlords were to indicate not the number of souls but the amount of land. At the same time it would be forbidden to change peasants into servants. As a second step, «that could not be soon», it was suggested that the peasants be given back the old custom of passage from one owner to another and thus «assure the certainty of their being bought back». In the 1809 project, Speransky is in favor of real measures and the abolition of civil slavery. Among other things, he suggests that «landowners be deprived of the right to punish serfs without judgment and that the latter should be sent to military service only according to the law and not according to the master's fancy, and that in general landowners should not manage inhabited properties in any other way than according to the law». As one may see Speransky was also guided by moral motives.

In 1824, one year before his death, Alexander I said to L.F. Lubanovsky: «Enough of the glory of Russia, enough of it. Whoever would wish for more is mistaken. When I consider how little has been accomplished inside the Empire, then this thought weighs on my heart like a weight of 10 poods. That is why I am so tired». These words show how much he suffered morally from the peasants' condition. This peasant question also made Nicholas suffer, but, after attempts to solve it had been unsuccessful, he limited himself to a partisan war and to the education of Alexander II.

The Decembrists were children of their time. Their thoughts and their sentiments were in unison with their era. The charter of the «Union of Salvation» is wholly imbued with moralism. The roots of this Union are to be found in the fight against all evil and all lies in Russian life, and for the Decembrists the right to own slaves was the first of these evils. According to Pestel's writings, the liberation of the peasants in a very near future was the sole objective of the Union but the Decembrists did not yet know how to achieve this liberation. I.D. Yakushkin, in his writings, states that, in 1816, wishing to free his peasants «he did not quite know how to go about it nor what the result would be». However, convinced as he was that the right to own slaves was abominable, he was filled with the sentiment that it was his duty to free «the people who were under his dependence». The members of the Union of Salvation were aware of the liberal convictions of Alexander I and of his projects that had the same objectives as their own, and also knew about the suggestions of Bekleshoff and of Speransky. They therefore thought that by propagating the idea of liberation and its advantages they would succeed in convincing a great many nobles that they should themselves suggest this liberation to their sovereign. The charter of the Union of Welfare, which was based on the German charter of Tugendbund, forced its members to give up the sale of serfs as conscripts and in general to abstain from selling them individually, although it contained no specific article obliging its members to free their peasants. It also forced them to arrive at a friendly agreement with the peasants on the procedure of transforming the possession of the land by contract into that of complete private ownership and to act in such a way that the amount of land be sufficient to cover the needs of the workers' families. It was only later, after they had become convinced that they would not succeed in convincing the nobles that they should present to the ruling power the request for the abolition of the right of serfdom, that the members of the Union of Welfare decided to act independently and to approach the Tsar themselves. In that very year of 1818 when Alexander I asked Arakcheef to prepare a project for the liberation of the peasants, A.N. Muraviev presented to the sovereign a note that is an ardent protest against the right of serfdom as being totally contrary to Christian morals, but this note does not indicate the practical means by which serfdom could be eliminated. Because of this omission, or because he was convinced that the initiative of such a liberation should only come from the supreme power himself, the Emperor answered A.N. Muraviev in very unflattering terms, telling him to mind his own business. The fact that Alexander I did not want to leave the initiative of a liberation of the peasants to his subjects was confirmed the following year, in 1819, when Count Miloradovitch, military governor of St. Petersburg, gave N.I. Turgenev the job of preparing a similar project. N.I. Turgenev accomplished this mission and made many useful suggestions for the limitation of the right of serfdom which were all favorably received but were never put into effect. Finally, in 1820, this same N.I. Turgenev tried to create a society that had as its objective «the search for a means of improving the fate of the peasants and achieving their progressive liberation, both their own and that of the servants who are part of Russian society». The sketch of N.I. Turgenev's project for this society and the measures suggested by him are testimonies to the great step forward made by the Decembrists on the road to finding a solution to the peasant problem. Now they no longer limited themselves to their aspirations of abolishing the «cattle» condition of the peasants but searched for a legal and economical statute for

223

these peasants. Turgenev suggested that the landowners and the peasants should be given the right to conclude an agreement on the leasing of the land that should be «freely given for a long period of time, even hereditary», stipulating that the peasants could refuse the contract whereas the landowners could not. As payment for the lease, N.I. Turgenev suggested the possibility of working days that would be fixed by law. Furthermore, the right of passage from one landlord to another was to be granted. In I.D. Yakushkin's project the houses and the kitchen gardens of the peasants were to be transferred to them free of charge and in full ownership and their refusal to take any tillable land did not deprive them of the right to live in their house without any obligation towards their landlord. As far as the servants were concerned, it was suggested that they be freed immediately after having obtained from the government «certain guarantees» according to which these voluntarily freed men would form a special class so that their liberty could not be changed into oppression. Once again, probably because he considered that the supreme power had the right to the initiative for this peasant problem, Alexander I decided that the creation of this society was unnecessary but expressed the wish that any person who was in favor of it work separately at it and present his project to the Ministry of the Interior. The project to establish just such a society was the last attempt to reach this objective during Alexander's reign. Only one road remained: first obtain political liberty, then abolish the right to slavery.

The entry of the Decembrists on the road to revolution corresponds to the end of the activities of the Union of Welfare in 1821 and the creation of two secret societies, one of the North, the other of the South, each following its own road until the uprising, when their members would meet again in front of the Court of Inquiry and would share the same fate. In each of these societies, constitutional projects that included resolutions on the peasant problem were written. In these projects the moral element remains the basis of the propositions of liberation and priority is given to considerations of right and economy. The main question becomes the allocation of land. One of the members of the Northern

224

The SMOLNY INSTITUTE
Aunt Lina and pupils
1905

The SMOLNY INSTITUTE
The ball-room
1905

28 Mai 1915

Chère Olga Alexan[drovna],

Comment vous exprimer tout ce que mon cœur ressent de tristesse profonde en apprenant le décès de votre bien-aimée sœur Lina! Quel terrible chagrin et quelle perte irréparable, pas seulement pour vous, sa famille, et pour [Timotue?], mais

Letter from Empress Maria Feodorovna
after the death of Aunt Lina

pour moi personnelle-
ment qui l'aimais
et l'appréciais tellement
et je leur serai tou-
jours reconnaissante
pour tout ce qu'elle a
fait de bien, et pour
l'affection qu'elle me
portais. Aussi j'étais
si touchée ! Je comptais
sur elle comme sur
son rocher, elle m'était
si nécessaire avec son
esprit et sa bonté de cœur
Je suis heureuse de
l'avoir encore vue hier
et d'avoir pu lui parler.
Elle était si bonne et
touchante et m'a bénie
avant de partir, mais
je ne pensais pas que
c'était le dernier adieu
Pourtant il faut remer-
cier le bon Dieu qu'il
l'a délivrée de ses souf-
frances et qu'elle s'est
endormie tranquille-
ment.
Je pense tant à vous
dans votre douleur
et prie Dieu de vous
soutenir —

Marie

Май. 1884.

The DAVYDOFF brothers
Alexander, Piotr, Vassili
1884

XXIV

Alexander, Piotr, Vassili
1891

YURCHIKHA
1981

The Elisabeth Institute
Moscow — 1981

St. Petersburg
1909

Simferopol
1906

1916

2nd from right :
A.V. DAVYDOFF — 1903

A.V. DAVYDOFF — 1916

SABLY — 1905
A.V. DAVYDOFF in the park

NICE — 1926

In his office at the « Vozrojdenie »
Paris — 1926

Olga Yakovlevna
DAVYDOVA
b. de Miller
the author's wife
1899 — 1975
(ca 1924)

Olga DAVYDOVA — Rome 1966

The author's daughter with Xenia Yurevna DAVYDOVA. Klin — 1973

X.Y. & I.Y. DAVYDOVA. Klin — 1981

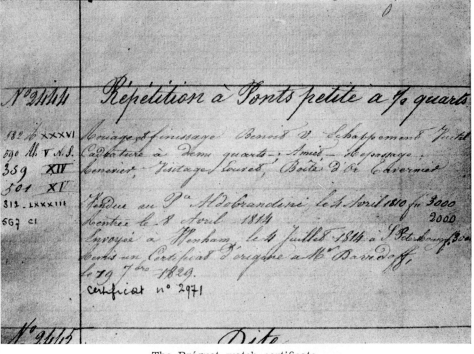

The Bréguet watch certificate

REMBRANDT
St. Bartholomew

SABLY — 1981
In front of the house

SABLY — 1981
The administrator of the sovkhoze
with the author's daughter

The Red Apples
Paris — 1981

Society, N.M. Muraviev, writes in the two projects he made in collaboration with other members of the society: «The state of serfdom and slavery is abolished», but the liberation is made without land. «The land of the landowners remains theirs». In the second project, under the influence of I.D. Yakushkin and Turgenev, he adds that «the peasants homes, their kitchen gardens, their working tools and the cattle belonging to them are accepted as being their property free of charges». The proposal of liberation without land did not meet the approval of all members of the society. For instance I.I. Pushin writes in the margin of the project «If there are to be kitchen gardens then there must also be land». Finally N.M. Muraviev takes another step forward in the account he made of his constitutional project at the request of the Court of Inquiry by adding that the peasants were to be given at the time of their liberation 2 dessiatines of land per soul and the right to acquire land as private hereditary property to enable them «to establish themselves permanently». However, according to the statement of Zavalichin, the majority of members of the Northern Society were for the liberation of the peasants with allotment of land that was to be bought not by themselves but by the state.

As far as the project of the Southern Society is concerned, it seems that it was not drawn up by all the members of the Society but exclusively by its leader P.I. Pestel. One can find no trace of any cooperation of other members in the creation of this project. «Russian Law» gives us the views of Pestel that were formed under the influence of French thinkers and politicians and not of the Russian moralists that we mentioned earlier. Unfortunately the section of the Russian Law concerning the liberation of the peasants remained unfinished and not fully elaborated. The separate notes that remain concerning this question contain some obscure points and contradictions. Its weakness lies in the tremendous complexity of the proposed project. Because of this, one must limit oneself to the exposition of the main thoughts of Pestel and only touch superficially the complicated structure of its realization.

First of all one must define the position of Pestel, who affirmed «that each citizen had the right to a certain portion of tillable land». The state is obliged to assure citizens not only their political rights as citizens but also the material aspects essential to their subsistence. The right to enjoy the land allocated by the state is part of the political rights of a citizen. This proves that P.I. Pestel did not accept the possibility of the liberation of peasants without land. This position is totally confirmed in his later notes. In his appreciations he bases himself on two theories that seem to contradict each other. The first one states that «as man lives on earth he can only live with it and by it and obtain his subsistence from it» and that «the land belongs to the world of man and to any particular individual and that is the reason why it cannot be divided among a few to the detriment of the others». The second theory affirms that labor is the source of all possession and takes into account the meaning of capital in agriculture. The landowner will agree to invest his capital in the cultivation of land only if he is assured of the permanence of his landed property. P.I. Pestel sees the possibility of uniting these two conflicting theories in certain notions he mentions in the Russian Law. In his opinion «the land is the property of the human race and no one can be excluded from it in any way». The notion of private ownership appears at the same time as the constitution of the state. The protection of private property is a sacred duty of the state but the fact of accepting this principle in no way implies the violation of the laws of nature nor of divine laws, for these originate from God and from nature and are therefore immutable whereas political institutions change frequently. With this idea as a basis, Pestel finds an intermediary solution. First of all give the people the necessary means for their subsistence and then acquire the surplus. Every person has the right to the first. The second is only for those who succeed in making this acquisition. Having thus found a middle-of-the-road solution, Pestel assumes that the state must assure to each citizen the land needed for his existence. Therefore it is the state that must get the land for general use but private property can also exist. Nevertheless the general interest must come before all others and landlords must relinquish their rights if these should violate the laws of nature that give each person the right to partake in the ownership of land.

As we know, Pestel assumed that the state would create rural districts that were to form the basis of land reform. He suggested that each rural district be divided into two equal parts: on the one hand public land; on the other, private landed property or property belonging to peasants of the state. The public land would belong to the whole rural population and would form an inviolable property. The other part would belong either to private persons or to the state. This land would be reserved for the acquisition of the surplus. The land of the rural districts must feed those who have no other means of subsistence. To the question of where the funds for the rural districts would come from, only an approximate answer can be found in «the Russian Law» where mention is made of different categories of peasants but only in notes of a poorly developed section. Nevertheless the basis of Pestel's theory is that the liberation of the peasants must not deprive the landowners of the income of their domains. This meant that when the land belonging to the landowners was taken away from them by the state to form rural districts, the state would be obliged to spend a large amount of money. It is obvious that, in Pestel's mind, the liberation of the peasants had to be accomplished with a gift of land and that the peasants were to become an integral part of the citizenry.

«The exposition of the affair», as is said in legal jargon, shows what an evolution had been made in five years in the ideas of the Decembrists on the peasant problem from the creation of the Union of Salvation in 1816 to the creation of the Northern and Southern Societies in 1821. In those five years these idealistic young men who had dreamed of convincing the liberal Emperor and the nobility to accept an arrangement for lightening the fate of the peasants and abolition of their slavery by measures on which they themselves did not have very definite ideas, these Decembrists became revolutionaries plotting the downfall of the existing system and the murder of the Tsar. When forming their constitutional projects they speak already of the rights of the peasants and of their economic organization and not only of the fact that they should be given a more human mode of life. That such a rapid evolution should have been possible is all the more surprising as at that time they could find no approval in their entourage. As always after a great upheaval, weary society craved for peace and had enough of upheavals. For 11 years Russia had fought a desperate war against Napoleon and had lived through all the horrors of 1812. This society could not but be influenced by the recent examples of the French revolution that had plunged France in a blood bath and had ended with the moral decay of French society from which it had been saved by Napoleon's dictatorship only at the expense of another general European conflict and pillage. Also present in everyone's minds were the horrors of Pugachev's revolt of which Pushkin said, though much later, in the words of Grinev, that «may God never see again such a senseless and pitiless Russian revolt». It wasn't only the nobles who were against the liberation of the peasants; certain eminent members of society such as N.M. Karamzin, Derjavin and others were against it as well. For instance, in his famous note «Old Russia and New Russia», where an important place is given to the peasant problem, Karamzin expresses his conviction that although it is difficult to find one's way in the labyrinth of the origins of the peasant class, «peasants of serf origin are, due to that very fact, the property of their master». In any case the peasants had never had any right to the land. The liberation of the peasants is also dangerous from a financial point of view for it would be difficult for them to pay their taxes without the personal help of the landowners. Karamzin asks the question «What does the liberation of the peasants mean to us?» In his opinion it means «giving them the liberty to live wherever they wish, take from the landlords all rights over them and submit them only to the authority of the state». Such a thought scares Karamzin by its possible repercussions. He fears that, not being any longer under the surveillance of the landlord's police, the peasants will get drunk and lead debauched lives. Naturally ideas such as these could not influence the opinions of the Decembrists, but even among the most advanced and liberal members of society, voices were heard against the liberation of the peasants. For instance in

228

the unofficial meetings of a group of friends of Tsar Alexander I in the years 1801-1803, Novosiltsev and Mordvinoff had voted against the suggestions of liberation made by Prince Tchartorisky, Kotchubey and Count Stroganov. It may seem incredible, but the republican Laharpe, ex-tutor of Alexander I, was also against emancipation.

It is only after taking into consideration all that has been said above that one may reach an objective conclusion on the evolution of the Decembrists' ideas that were opposed to current opinion both on a political basis and on the question of the abolition of the rights of serfdom. It seems to me that it is wrong to criticize them and to accuse them of conservatism.

As I said at the beginning of this article, the Decembrists were specifically accused of not having liberated their own peasants themselves and that, when they wished to do so, they then refused to renounce their rights to the land. The first accusation is worthless if only because they were too young to own inhabited properties or personal servants and therefore could not in fact liberate any peasant. The exceptions are Yakushkin, Lunin and Trubetskoy, who wished to liberate their peasants (Lunin did so in his testament) with special clauses giving them the cattle and the tools freehold and in full ownership. Therefore there only remains the second accusation of their lack of progressiveness and sincerity, but in that respect one must ask oneself the question of how, in our time, can one affirm that liberty cannot exist without property, and to what degree can such a proposition be considered progressive? Can one say today that the granting of liberty without goods is a proof of conservatism? If one answers these questions in the affirmative one as good as admits that Alexander I, who had forbidden by an ukase of 1807 the liberation of peasants without land, had then acted as a progressive, while at the same time forbidding the Baltic landowners to do so themselves. By the same token one should consider Arakcheev's project of 1818 to be progressive. And yet neither one nor the other has the favor of historians or of public opinion, which both denounce the Decembrists so severely. In any case this accusation is worthless because both in the Northern and in the Southern Societies the Decembrists

229

in their constitutional projects had decided to grant land to the peasants. It seems that we are confronted with an insoluble contradiction. In truth this contradiction does not exist because the matter is seen from the wrong angle. The question is not progressiveness or conservatism, but the expediency of these ideas and what were the possibilities of the state. It is obvious that at the start of the last century the Russian ruling power wished to give land to the peasants not for reasons of progressiveness but only for reasons of security and finance. It needed the money that the peasants paid in personal taxes. Even if the Decembrists had not been very sincere with their projects, their prime objective was quite different—to achieve by any means the liberation of the peasants. As they were prepared to lose all their rights over their peasants without any compensation they did not feel obliged to give up freely their rights over the land. As we have seen, even Pestel, whom historians and public opinion single out from the mass of the Decembrists, defends the idea that the land of the landlords given to the peasants should be bought back by the state. That is where the major difficulty lay. The state was incapable of doing so because of its financial position. The talks between I.D. Yakushkin and Levashoff at the time of Yakushkin's interrogation illustrate this fact. When Yakushkin mentioned that the government could buy back the peasants from the landlords Levashoff exclaimed «This is impossible! You know very well how miserly the Russian government is with its money!». What Levashoff had said was very true. Following the Napoleonic wars and in the absence of a good management of its finances, all the Russian budgets were in the red and at the end of the Guriev ministry in 1823 the public debt amounted to the considerable sum for that time of 1343,5 million roubles and the serfs formed 45% of the population, that is to say 22.5 million souls.

If we now study the question of whether the Decembrists were sincere and logical or not when they did not decide immediately for the granting of land to the peasants, one must first of all note that in their time this was not considered to be the sign of a progressive mind. This is evident in what Yakushkin had to say around 1850: «The right-minded people, or, as, they were then called, the liberals, wanted above all the abolition of serfdom and because of their European conception of the problem they were convinced that a person who did not belong to anyone was by that simple fact a free person in spite of the fact that he had no personal belongings». The dreadful condition of the proletariat in Europe had not made the enormous progress it has done today. That is why the questions that were raised later on this subject did not disturb anyone at that time, even the most educated and well-intentioned people. Speaking about his conversation with the departmental director Djunkovsky on the subject of the liberation of the peasants without granting of land Yakushkin writes «Djunkovsky often traveled abroad and had a European point of view on the matter. That is why the idea of the liberation of the peasants without granting of land did not make him at all indignant». If during the 19th century and at the start of the 20th and especially nowadays all that is European was and is cited as an example of what is more advanced than anything Russian, this was even more the case when the Decembrists were alive and active. One may simply ask oneself then why in Europe the liberation of the peasants without land was not considered shameful. The answer to this and its explanation is that the problem of the liberty of the individual was not considered under the angle of the personal possession of goods because this was thought to be sacred. As one knows the Decembrists were guided by the example of the West. That is why it is so important to establish what they could learn from it concerning the liberation of the peasants without granting of land. It must be well understood that at that time France was considered the most advanced country in the world and she had herself undergone a revolution, the most profound one there could be, and suddenly the Russians learned that the National Assembly by its decree of August 4, 1789, after having completely abolished the feudal regime, had nevertheless established a distinction between two orders of problems: the rights that stem from the power one person has over another, and the rights linked to the possession of land. The first rights were eliminated without any compensation. The second had to be bought back, but the Assembly

231

could not decide to give this buying back a compulsory and collective character because of the difficult situation of French finances. This question of liberation was only resolved in 1793 when, by a decree dated June 17, all feudal rights and those linked to the social class were annulled without any compensation and orders were given to burn all I.O.Us. This did not mean that the peasants had been given the properties confiscated from the landowners in full ownership nor that they had become national assets. These lands ended up by being sold to speculators who made a fortune during the revolution. As far as England was concerned the liberation of the peasants had in fact taken place there much earlier, already in the middle ages, without any granting of land. Dispossession of the land was a long and difficult process, but the plague and the grazing of the sheep played the most important roles. In Prussia, it was only after the defeat by Napoleon that, by an order dated October 9, 1807, the right of serfdom was abolished, but it was only by the decree of 1816 that the landowners lost the supreme right to possess the land of the peasants, employ forced labor and be paid rent. In the constitution of the Duchy of Warsaw granted by Napoleon on July 22, 1807 the right of serfdom was abolished but no mention was made of the question of land. By the decree of December 21 of that same year, the land was granted to the peasants but not to their advantage. This decision was made in spite of a letter from Kosciuszko to Fouché dated January 22, 1807 in which he gave as a condition for his coming to Poland to help Napoleon the liberation of the peasants and the granting to them in property of the land that was still in their possession.

All that has been said above is sufficient to exonerate entirely the Decembrists from the erroneous judgments made on them. They may leave the tribunal of history not only with guilt mitigated by extenuating circumstances but also with the reputation of clean and honest men who sacrificed everything for the good of their people. The only reproach one may make is their lack of realism concerning the state but this accusation may also be leveled at their accusers. For any governmental structure to be lasting in Russia it is indispensable that it have stable bases represented by its most numerous class—the peasants. Such a situation can only be substantiated if the peasants have full rights to their land. Nowadays this idea may seem «conservative» but what importance does this have in view of what Russia has become! I.D. Yakushkin's peasants were right when they refused their liberation without land and said to him: «Well, Father, let us remain as we were in the past: we are yours and the land is ours».

THE JEWISH DECEMBRIST

Because of their small number in Russia in the late 18th and early 19th century, Jews could play no part in the liberation movement that took hold of Russian society. Furthermore this movement was born and developed among the military nobles who did not accept Jews and who, in spite of their liberal views, were somewhat prejudiced against them. According to Chabade there were at that time in Russia only 152,364 Jews who payed taxes and duties and in St. Petersburg, as Catherine wrote to Diderot, there were only 3 or 4 Jews who, for some unknown reason, stayed with Catherine's confessor. However, fate willed that among the actors of the uprising of December 14, 1825 there was a Jew, member of one of the secret societies, titular counselor, civil servant at the St. Petersburg Chancery under Governor-General Count Miloradovich, Gregory Abramovich Peretz. The fact that he took part in the Decembrist movement is all the more remarkable because he personally never had the slightest trouble with the authorities, came from a wealthy family and was versed both in theological and in business matters.

G.A. Peretz's maternal grandfather, Yoshida Zaitlin (1742-1822) who, in Potemkin's time, lived in Chklov, then the most important center of Jewish cultured society, was a learned rabbi, a patron of the arts and at the same time a financier and a very able merchant. Potemkin needed men who could help him accomplish the great political and military schemes he had in mind and appreciated the business qualities of Yoshida Zaitlin who soon became a sort of finance and supply minister. Having become wealthy in this post, Zaitlin, after the death of Potemkin, gave up his commercial activities and settled down permanently in his splendid estate of Usty in the district of Tchernikov in the province of Moguilev, where he devoted his time entirely to the study of Jewish theology. Already during Potemkin's lifetime Zaitlin had been eager for his daughter Faiguele to marry and had looked around for a suitable husband for her. He finally chose the son, named Abraham, of a respected rabbi from Levertsk, Israel Peretz, an intelligent young man who because of his great erudition promised to become an illustrious rabbi. Abraham Peretz married Faiguele in 1790 but did not live up to his father-in-law's expectations as far as his religious career was concerned. He preferred to go into business and started going to St. Petersburg both for his father's business and for Potemkin's. Shortly after, Peretz settled permanently in St. Petersburg and lived with two other Jews who were under Potemkin's protection, Yehudi Ben Noah and Reb Nathan Noteh. As Catherine had written to Diderot, they all three lived at the home of Catherine's confessor. Once settled in the capital Abraham Peretz started his own businesses and became farmer general. This enabled him to amass an enormous fortune and attain a high position in society. Gretch used to say of him «Farmer general Peretz is a sheeny but he is a kind and truly noble man». Peretz became very friendly with M.M. Speransky and influenced his reforming activities. Because of this friendship, Speransky was subjected to many attacks but he was defended by another eminent Russian, E.F. Kankrin, who had also been able to appreciate Peretz's qualities.

A. Peretz's wife Faiguele and their son Guirch did not follow him to St. Petersburg and continued to live with her father on his estate. Young Guirch grew up there in an atmosphere of wealth and culture. He received his first education as befitted the grandson of Yoshida Zaitlin. Hebrew and the Scriptures were taught him by Simeon Levy, Russian and arithmetic by Seniavin, geometry and algebra by Mendel Stanover, a pioneer of European culture among Russian Jews. In 1803 Abraham Peretz ordered that his son come and live with him in St. Petersburg. The move took place that same year in spite of the opposition of both the grandfather and the mother who did not want to leave their village and remained in Usty. Young Guirch settled in with his father who at that time lived in a beautiful house that he owned and that rivalled in luxury that of his father-in-law, but the people Guirch met there were totally different. St. Petersburg was not a small White Russian borough and the people who lived there had nothing in common with orthodox Jews. Berlin culture reigned in Abraham Peretz's house although he showered gifts on Jews. In his house lived the old professor L. Nevakhovich, the first Jewish writer to write in Russian, who in 1803 had written «The Cry of a Girl from Israel». In that house, Guirch was given a very advanced education by the best pedagogues of that time. What he was most interested in was history, geography, political economy and statistics. In 1810 and 1811 he followed, in the Pedagogic Museum, courses of political economy under Boduyansky. His first notion of world affairs was given to him by his first tutor, a Swiss from Lausanne, Laurent, a freemason and a freethinker. By a strange coincidence the young Jew Guirch and the heir to the Russian throne Alexander had the same source of freethinking.

Abraham Peretz got farther and farther away from the traditions of his ancestors and, mixing with the high society of civil servants in St. Petersburg, he could not escape the attractions of ambition and vanity that were rife in that milieu. The power of wealth was not sufficient for him any more and, if not for himself at least for his son, he aspired to a post in the highest administrative spheres. The only way to attain this was to be given a state function and the earlier the better. In those times this was possible even for young boys. Guirch started his career as a government civil servant at the age of 11 and at 23 he was already titular counselor. His first real post was at the Chancery of the State Treasurer. In 1813 he was posted to the Chancery of the Privy Counselor, Prince Alexis Borisovich Kurakin who sent him to the district of Novorossiisk where there was an epidemic of plague, with instructions to supervise the functioning of the sanitary cordon. In May of that same year Guirch Peretz, who had become in the meantime Grigori Abramovich because his father had become a lutheran, left this

237

post. He was given excellent certificates after leaving his last assignment. At about that time his father lost most of his fortune in some business concerning the delivery of equipment to the army in 1812.

Nothing is known about the activities or the place of residence of G.A. Peretz from the end of his assignment in Novorossiisk to 1818 or 1819. During one of those years he entered the service of the Military Chancery of St. Petersburg under Governor-General Count Miloradovich, where he met Colonel Feodor Glinka. This meeting marked the start of G.A. Peretz's participation in the liberation movement. F. Glinka, one of the prominent members of the Union of Welfare, to the right wing of which he belonged, did not share the republican views of the majority of the members of the Union and was in favor of a limited monarchy. All thought of revolution was alien to him. He did not think it could occur in Russia and was of the opinion that a constitutional government could be set up through a palace revolution such as had occurred frequently in the 18th century. He saw the possibility of achieving his objectives by placing on the throne with limited powers Empress Elisaveta Alexeevna, the wife of Alexander I, who enjoyed the favor of society.

Because of his differences of opinion with the other members of the Union, Glinka decided to found another secret society in 1820, the program of which would correspond to his ideas. This society was to act completely independently from the Union of Welfare and officially have a new head who had not been a member of the Union. It also had no specific name and no written statute. It was founded by Glinka and two of his friends from the Union, S.M. Semenov and N. Kutuzov. Its first member was G.A. Peretz who was named its head and its organizer. Litle by little it started to be known as the society of Peretz. Its aim, as explained later by G.A. Peretz when he was interrogated by the Commission, was to form a representative government with a monarch at its head. Its objectives were «the multiplication of its members, the proclamation of injustices and mistakes of the government and the publication of political news». When they entered the society, members had to take an oath that they would pursue the realization of these objectives and the following words were sometimes used: «I promise on everything that is dear and sacred to me». At G.A. Peretz's request the Hebrew word «heirut» which means «freedom» was adopted as a password.

The first mission that was given by Glinka to G.A. Peretz was the recruiting of members, and it was specified that candidates should be preferably army men. In accordance with this request he enrolled Iskritsky, Seniavin, Dantchenko and Ustimovich. It is interesting to note that during his interviews with candidates G.A. Peretz not only initiated them into the constitutions that existed in the West but also added that a representative government was in accord with the laws of Moses. He probably had in mind Chapter 17 of the Deuteronomy and the First Book of Prophet Samuel, particularly Chapter 8. To a question asked by the Commission of Inquiry G.A. Peretz answered «I told him (Iskritsky), as I truly believed at that time, that for Russia the best thing was a system of monarchal government and that, because of the vastness of the Empire and of other local conditions, the monarch's power should be increased in consequence». To the Commission's question about his conception of freedom of thought G.A. Peretz answered: «When I returned to St. Petersburg in 1817 I had nothing to do so I read Montesquieu, Rousseau, Bentham and Volney.» The discontent in society also influenced him. Colonel Glinka reinforced these ideas of his. To the question about what incited him to join the society and what were his intentions when he did so, G.A. Peretz answered «The injustices and the mistakes of the government provoked in me the desire for the well-being of everyone». The activities of the society were really very modest. There were no meetings. Its members contented themselves with talks when they met by chance and discussed new candidatures, confirmed decisions taken earlier and criticized the actions of the ruling power, among others the disadvantageous conditions of the loans made by the ruling power in the years 1811-1812 when for one rouble of promissory notes one was given bonds worth 50 kopecks in silver.

G.A. Peretz was entitled to think that the society to which he belonged had a large number of members and that besides himself the heads of the society, Glinka, Semenov and Kutuzov, were also busy recruiting. In reality things were quite different. None of the «heads» took any part in recruiting during the time the society existed and it never had more than nine members. Glinka, at that time, created a new society, «Elisabeth», and recruited members for it. After the Moscow Congress of the Union of Welfare to which Glinka was the St. Petersburg delegate when the decision was made to dissolve the Union, he stopped taking part generally in the liberation movement. It was then also that the Society of Peretz fell apart. Drebush and Dantchenko died. Ustimovich left for Georgia. Kutuzov had already left the society a long time before. Peretz himself said to the Commission of Inquiry «I cannot remember when I started to withdraw from it but it was probably already in 1821 for I married in 1822». After leaving the society, Peretz kept his job at the Chancery of Count Miloradovich and at the same time rented the «Ezerk Starost» in the province of Vitebsk that belonged to Duke Alexander of Wurtemberg.

During the days of the interregnum G.A. Peretz became very worried. He went to see Glinka and told him that «nothing good could be expected from a revolution». Finally the day before the uprising, on December 12 or 13 he saw the State Counselor Basil Petrovich Guriev and asked him to let Count Miloradovich know that if Nicholas Pavlovich mounted the throne riots should be expected. «Everyone has more affection for Constantine Pavlovich than for Nicholas Pavlovich», he said. Guriev said to tell Peretz «if he really strongly wishes it I will do as he asks but he must not blame me if he ends up in the fortress». One must not believe that G.A. Peretz wished to denounce anybody. Not being a member of the Society of the North he could not know their plans. He was under the spell of a feeling of self-sacrifice for the happiness and peace of all. Count Miloradovich answered Guriev «We will probably put him in the fortress but what will his wife and children say?» Having said this he expressed his conviction that all would be well which cost him his life the following day on the Senate Square.

On the morning of December 14th, devoured by curiosity, G.A. Peretz went to Seniavin's home and on being told that he was on duty at the Palace went there but did not find him there either. Later, after inquiring about the «events» that had taken place between 2 and 4 in the afternoon, he found himself in the crowd on the Senate Square. He returned there that evening. After December 14th he was afraid he was going to be arrested as people who had been personally linked to the «evil Society» were being taken to the fortress. During those days Peretz wrote a note on urgently needed reforms and submitted it to the Tsar on December 30, 1825. He mentions it in his statements to the Commission: «This was done by me only because I sincerely believed in the justice of these reforms and only because of this». In another passage he says: «I can only say that my sole aims were not the hidden objectives of some secret society but the visible advantage that such a society would have for my beloved country». In the letter that accompanied the note to the Tsar, G.A. Peretz wrote: «Knowing how precious is the time of him who owns half the world, I will be very brief».

Nicholas read the note that was handed to him by the Secretary of State Kikin and wrote on it: «Transmit to the Commission for Criminal Affairs».

Before that, in December, G.A. Peretz had wanted to go to London but after meeting Iskritsky and being promised by him that he would not denounce him he calmed down and decided to stay in St. Petersburg in spite of the fact that Iskritsky himself feared for his own arrest. These fears proved true. On January 26 Ryleev stated to the Commission that «Lieutenant Iskritsky of the General Staff of the Guards belonged to the Secret Society», and Obolensky indicated that he had enrolled Iskritsky a few days before December 14th in the Society of the North. When he learned about the statements of Ryleev and Obolensky, Iskritsky was so shaken that, unable to control himself, he broke his promise and said that he had been enrolled into the society by Peretz. Nicholas wrote on Iskritsky's statement: «Ask which Peretz, the father or the son, and what his patronymic is». Peretz was not arrested immediately but on February 11 and 15 the Commission of Inquiry asked the most prominent Decembrists if he had not been a member of the Society. To this question the answer was unanimous. Not only did they deny that he had belonged to the Secret Society, they also asserted that they did not know him.

G.A. Peretz was arrested on February 18, 1826 and at once presented to the Tsar. Unfortunately the conversation between the «master of half the world» and the grandson of the rabbi from Levertsk has not come down to us. We only know that during his questioning by Levashoff he explained all he knew except for the enrollment of Ustimovitch. After the Tsar had interrogated him Peretz was jailed in the Fortress where on February 22 he was given an inquiry form that he filled out confirming his previous statements. Subsequently G.A. Peretz's fate was sealed by the statements of Glinka and Semenov. These two denied all membership in a secret society and that Peretz had been admitted to one. Arrested on December 30, Glinka was presented to the Tsar and answered him so cleverly that the Tsar stroked his head and said «You are clean, clean». Released, he was nevertheless secretly interrogated by the Commission, who asked him if Peretz had been a member of the Union of Welfare, to which he answered in the negative. However on the evidence of G.A. Peretz's statements, Glinka was again arrested on March 11 and during his interrogation he was asked once more about G.A. Peretz's membership in the Union of Welfare. While trying to erase all incriminating traces, Glinka did not deny his conversations with Peretz but he stated that Peretz was trying to force his way into the society of freemasons and that he had refused because he did not think he was suitable. Instead of the freemasonry, Glinka seems to have suggested to G.A. Peretz «to enter a wonderful society whose members are trustworthy personalities and whose aims are noble». To the question «What was this society?» Glinka answered «of Lancaster». As far as G.A. Peretz was concerned it seems that he spoke to Glinka of the need «to found a society for the liberation of the Jews who were dispersed throughout Russia and even Europe and for their installation in a specific place in Russia such as the Crimea». On March 11, worn out by waiting, G.A. Peretz sent a request to Levashoff reminding him of his promise to save him should he tell the truth. Instead of a favorable answer to this request, Peretz was given another questionaire on March 14 after the persistent

242

denials of Glinka, Semenov and Kutuzov and his own conflicting statements. In his answer G.A. Peretz repeated everything he had said before. The persistent divergence of their statements forced the Commission of Inquiry to bring Peretz face to face with Glinka and Semenov. This did not give any result either. The uncertainty of his situation created in G.A. Peretz a perfectly well-founded fear of possible torture and he sent the Commission a report in which he asked that, if such a measure were taken, it be applied not only to himself but also to Glinka and Semenov. In all probability the Commission already knew that the truth lay on the side of G.A. Peretz and applied with success if not torture at least physical constraint on Semenov by putting him in irons. This procedure broke Semenov's will and not only did he admit everything, he also accused Glinka when he was confronted with him.

G.A. Peretz did not not appear before the Supreme Court. On June 15, 1826, following the report of the Commission of Inquiry, it was ordered that «he be kept another two months in the Fortress, then sent to an assigned residence in Perm where the local police authorities were to watch him secretly and report on his conduct each month».

Compared to the Decembrists G.A. Peretz got off with a very light sentence. In the eyes of Nicholas I his fault was a much lesser one. He had not plotted against the life of the Tsar and had not had in mind a revolution through violence. In his written report on «his Society» there was only the desire to introduce into Russia a representative form of government while maintaining a strong executive power. What is extraordinary is that neither in the statutes nor in the memorandum presented to Nicholas on December 30 is there the slightest mention of the abolition of serfdom. It is typical of a son and grandson of financiers and merchants that in the memorandum a large place should be devoted to professional questions along with questions of justice and calls for clemency. This places G.A. Peretz in a special position among the men who participated in the uprising of December 14, 1825. Maybe he does not deserve fully the term «Decembrist» but in any case he was the first Russian Jew to have suffered for liberty.

ALEXANDER III, THE JEWS AND THE REVOLUTION

In a special drawer of a metal cabinet which, before the revolution, had stood in the office of the Director of Chancery attached to the special section of Credit at the Finance Ministry on the Palace Square in Petrograd, was kept a file which very few people in that section knew about. Today it is difficult to say precisely who knew about the contents of this file but one may say with certainty that all the people who took part in this affair are now dead. The writer of these lines heard about it from the Director of Chancery himself who, one day when he was working at the Chancery, showed it to him and told him its story.

This affair could be entitled «Attempts by the Russian Imperial governement to reach an agreement with international Jewry to stop the activities of the Russian Jews». It started during the reign of Alexander III when S.I. Witte was Minister of Finance.

As everyone knows, Alexander III did not like the Jews and was well aware of the role they played in the Russian revolutionary movement. He realized the reasons that incited the Jews to try and overthrow the Russian Imperial power but, being of an autocratic and wilful nature, he would make no concession to them which might have satisfied their demands and drawn them away from the revolutionary movement.

Alexander III had a very high regard for the capacities of S.I. Witte and had every confidence in him despite the fact that he was married to a Jewess. He therefore decided to

245

communicate his ideas on the Jewish question not to the Minister of the Interior, who was directly concerned with this problem, but to the Finance Minister. He did this in one of the daily reports he was in the habit of sending him. He expressed the wish that the revolutionary activities of the Russian Jews be suppressed once and for all and said that nothing could stop him from accomplishing this project. He asked S.I. Witte to give him his opinion on this matter and to advise him. S.I. Witte answered him that, as he was the autocratic leader of the whole of Russia, he could take, if he wished, the most extreme police measures against the Jews and even order that all seven million Jews who lived on Russian territory be assembled on the shores of the Black Sea and drowned, but that, in his opinion, no extreme measure would achieve the results he was seeking and even on the contrary would, by driving the Jews to despair, increase their revolutionary activities. Furthermore he, S.I. Witte, was convinced that the Sovereign being a Christian, would be incapable of taking the most extreme measure he had mentioned and that in any case such a measure would be equivalent to an act of suicide for the Russian government as it would close its access to foreign financial markets which were all in the hands of the Jews.

The Emperor agreed with S.I. Witte and asked him what he thought should be done. S.I. Witte answered that where force could not succeed, diplomacy might. In his opinion an attempt to reach an agreement with international Jewry could only succeed if it were made not by the Ministry of Foreign Affairs but by the Ministry of Finance and this only in the strictest and most complete secrecy.

The Sovereign agreed again with S.I. Witte and asked him what concrete measures he suggested. S.I. Witte answered that the first thing was to find out where and with whom one should begin negotiations abroad because in Russia there was no valid interlocutor as all the financial aid to the revolution came from abroad. For this, one should, in his opinion, name as Agent of the Ministry of Finance in Paris a Jew who had the full confidence of the Ministry, who had considerable private means and who had relations with the French Jewish bankers.

He thought that the most qualified man for this post was Arthur Lvovich Raffalovitch and the Sovereign agreed to his being named.

A few months after his arrival in France, A.L. Raffalovitch reported to S.I. Witte that, after a long diplomatic preparation, he had been able to have a heart to heart talk with one of the French Rothschilds who was rather sympathetic to the problem but had told him that it was not possible to do anything about it in Paris and advised him to go and discuss the matter in London. However, the interview with the London Rothschild only ended in the same manner except that he stated specifically to the Russian representative that he should see the banker Schiff in New York.

There happened to be at the Ministry of Finance a person who was ideally suited for these negotations in New York, a man named G.A. Vilenkin, also a Jew, who was married to a Zeligman, a relative of Schiff. G.A. Vilenkin was forthwith named agent of the Ministry of Finance in the United States, with orders to start negotiations with Schiff. Thanks to his family relations, Vilenkin did not need to prepare the ground for this interview and it took place very shortly after his arrival in America. It turned out that the indications of the London Rothschild were quite correct and Schiff admitted that it was through him that all the funds passed for the Russian revolutionary movement. However when Vilenkin suggested that an agreement be reached with the Russian government concerning the Jewish question and that, if these negotiations were to succeed, the financial aid to the revolution would stop, Schiff answered that the affair was too far advanced, that Vilenkin's proposal came too late and that, furthermore, one could not make peace with the Romanoffs.

Thus the attempts of the Russian Imperial government to reach an agreement with the leaders of international Jewry ended in failure and this not through the Russian government's fault. This offer was renewed a little later in Paris at a much lower level. A «dame du monde» who was a member of the Finance Ministry's secret service, started to talk about this subject at a ball with Maurice de Rothschild but received the immediate answer: «Too late, Madam, and never with the Romanoffs!».

CORRESPONDENCE BETWEEN
ALEXANDER VASSILIEVICH DAVYDOFF
AND MARK ALEXANDROVICH ALDANOV

Dear Mark Alexandrovich

As I told you at our last meeting I am sending you a short memorandum on a historical event that took place «behind the scenes» in pre-revolutionary Russia. This may be of interest to you. I can personally vouch for its authenticity.

I asked you not to spread this information for two reasons. First I don't wish the note to fall into «rightist» hands—they would use it for their antisemitic propaganda. The second reason is that it may entice «leftist» circles, particularly Jewish ones, to accuse me of being anti-Jewish, which would be totally untrue.

In spite of these apprehensions, I have filed this note because I believe that no historical fact should remain hidden.

Please read my report, dear Mark Alexandrovich, and let me know what you think about it.

Your sincerely devoted
(signed A.V. Davydoff)

Dear Alexander Vassilievich

I have received your letter and memorandum. It is very interesting. It is indeed probable that the antisemites would use it. But history is history. The question is did Davydoff (L.F.) correctly expose the problem to you? Maybe his memory failed him about certain details. I have my doubts about certain aspects of this report and will expose them to you briefly.

Witte himself wrote in his «Memoirs» how he suggested to the Tsar to drown six million Jews in the Black Sea. But it is obvious that he was joking. It was on his part a «reductio ad absurdum». He could not have said this seriously to Alexander III who was not a Hitler. Neither could he have said seriously that «such a measure would be suicidal for the Russian government's credit». During the reign of Alexander III the revolutionary movement was quite weak. Of what use could be Schiff's funds? The revolutionaries of those days had no money and lived almost like paupers. To whom could Schiff have given this money? Most probably to Leon Tihomirovich, but Tihomirovich, after he became reactionary and antisemitic, would have revealed this in his memoirs. Neither could Lavrov have received this money. I may also add that to the best of my knowledge at the time of Alexander III's reign Schiff was not all that wealthy (you may find this information in the writings of Meyers—I don't have them). Furthermore the Rothschilds could not have helped the revolutionary movement in Russia because they never wanted to even hear about a revolution and were always extremely conservative. James was an «Orleanist», Alphonse (Maurice's uncle) from «Orleanist» shifted to being a supporter of Napoleon III who was his guest at Ferrières. Being monarchists, all of them, with the exception of André, boycotted the Third Republic. Besides, the Rothschilds, as early as Nicholas I's reign, were so involved in business transactions with the tsarist government that there was absolutely no question of their giving money for the revolution. Maurice is still living and you could find out from him (in spite of the fact that he is neither nice nor cultured). By the *way, he is a distant relative of yours through the Gramonts. One of the Counts (I think his grandfather) was married to a Rothschild. The rich Russian Jews, as well as some orthodox millionaires, did indeed give money to the revolutionaries. Michael Gotz was himself very rich. For curiosity's sake (and because it is a little known fact) I will inform you that the Jewish millionaires gave money about seventy years ago to the «Counter Revolution» «the Holy Militia». The latter also received quite a little money from Baron Ginzburg, from Poliakoff and from the director of the sugar refinery Zaïtsev, (my maternal grandfather) who had been given that money by Witte. As you may know the young Witte belonged to that «Holy Militia». This is probably the only foolish thing he did in his life. (Such an undertaking was not serious). I think that another Jew financed this Holy Militia, Malkiel, but I am not absolutely certain about this. From all this one may conclude that the main part of the funds came not from the Jews but more probably from Vorontzov-Dashkov. I am quite ready to agree to the fact that in the 20th century Schiff also donated money to the Russian revolutionary movement but I don't think that it involved large sums. Why don't you speak about all this to Boris Ivanovich Nikolaevsky? He is thoroughly acquainted with the history of the revolution and knows everything about it—immeasurably more than I. I have nothing against your showing him my letter. If you ask Boris Ivanovich to keep this matter a secret he will surely do it. I may of course be wrong. B.I.'s address is 417 W 120th St. tel. M021880.*

With best regards and good wishes

Signed: M. Aldanov

New York June 10 1951

Dear Mark Alexandrovich

Thank you very much for your letter of June 6 and for returning my note. I read with great interest your «doubts» about its contents and will now try to clarify certain points. First of all I will say that L.F. Davydoff told me this story long before the revolution when he was Director of the Chancery of Credit and S.I. Witte was still living. It was then that he showed me «the affair». What I mean to say is that all this was still very fresh in his memory and that the joking proposition (he also understood it that way) of S.I. Witte about drowning seven million Jews in the Black Sea was known to him long before Witte's memoirs were published. He knew of it from S.I. Witte himself. He was very close to him when he worked at the Ministry of Finance. It is absolutely true that at that time Schiff was not yet wealthy enough to finance the Russian revolution but this is not what I wrote in my note. I said that it was through Schiff that the money passed. As far as the 20th century is concerned, when the Russian revolution was already in full swing, it was actively supported, according to information given by the Russian political police, by American financial groups and precisely through the intermediary of Schiff. As regards the French Rothschilds, it is correct that they were always monarchists but only as far as France was concerned. They had a different attitude towards the Romanoffs and here the Jewish solidarity played an important role. Yet it is true that they did not control the aid to the Russian revolutionaries, so there was some element of truth in their negative answer to A.L. Raffalovitch. The London Rothschilds, who had suggested sending a Russian agent to America, in what may seem to be a gesture of good will towards negotiations, had a much more negative attitude towards the Russian government and refused to cover this government's debts in England until equality was given to the Russian Jews. The conversation between a dame du monde and Maurice Rothschild occurred much later, under Tsar Nicholas II, when in Russia the revolutionary movement was already on the march. Agenor Gramont, now deceased, father

251

of the present Baron, his brothers and sisters, was married to a Rothschild. I only know the eldest of the children.

I am not at all surprised by the negative attitude towards the revolution of the wealthy Russian Jews. If Baron Ginzburg was a friend of Alexander III, in my time the prominent Jewish bankers supported very loyally the Russian monarchy. The «Holy Militia» no longer existed. It had been replaced by numerous unions of the «Black Hundreds» but no money was given to them, neither by the Jews nor by the self-respecting Russian aristocrats.

In my note to you, I didn't mention, since I didn't think it directly relevant to the historical incident we are concerned with, the consequence of the attempts by S.I. Witte to come to an agreement with Schiff. He was partially successful in this thanks to the efficient conduct of the Portsmouth negotiations. The reason why these negotiations took place was that the Japanese, who had won great victories over Russia, not only had used up all the funds available for the conduct of the war but also could get no further loans from America who had until then very gerenously supplied them with money. The well-known German financier Gelferig in his book «Money in the Russo-Japanese war» concludes by saying that this war that Russia had unsuccessfully waged on the fields of Manchuria had been brilliantly won by Witte at Portsmouth. Thanks to Vilenkin and his connections Witte succeeded in preventing the Japanese from receiving any further funds for the continuation of the war.

And now, as an epilogue, a small personal reminiscence. Some time after emigration, L.F. Davydoff invited me one day to go with him to a ballet at the Paris Opera. After the show we went to dine together at a restaurant in the rue d'Antin. When we arrived the restaurant was empty, only one table was occupied at which sat a group of people we didn't know and Maurice de Rothschild. Shortly after our arrival the Grand Duchess Maria Pavlovna entered with her husband Prince Putiatin and sat at a third table. I said to L.F. Davydoff «Destiny is really strange. There are here right now three persons who know what the fourth one, the one most concerned, does not even suspect». I had hardly pronounced these words *when Maurice de Rothschild got up and went to Maria Pavlovna's table, and after greeting her and her husband, started a long conversation with them...*

I don't know yet if I shall follow your suggestion and show my memorandum to B.I. Nikolaevsky. This is not because I don't trust him but because in a sense I don't want to speak too much about this very sad story which may be judged severely. I would like you to keep my note and therefore ask you to accept it as a present from me.

Now about something altogether different. After our last meeting in Lucerne I had lunch with M.S. Mendelsohn and told him about our plans concerning the publishing of a new bulletin. After lengthy considerations and intricate explanations we finally agreed that we can combine with great advantage your point of view and his. We decided that I would telephone V.A. Grunberg and ask him to discuss with Count B. Zabejinsky the question of convoking a committee. I did this and now we must wait for this convocation which for some reason has been delayed. I hope it will arrive soon which will give me the opportunity of seeing you before you leave, a departure which will, I am afraid, take you once more away from New York for a long time.

Please give my regards to your wife.

Your devoted. Al. Davydoff.

BREGUET

«Until Bréguet's unsleeping chime
Advises him of dinner time.»

A.S. Pushkin

Afew years before the First World War, there arose in the society of St. Petersburg a real craze for Russian porcelain. People, especially women, who had never even thought before of collecting anything whatsoever, threw themselves into the search for old porcelains by Popoff, Korniloff, the brothers Kuznetzoff and others, in markets like Alexander's, or in other places such as antique shops. This craze for collecting porcelains transmitted itself to other old objects such as Empire-style Russian furniture, crystal glassware and engraved portraits. Demand creates supply and the number of antique dealers grew proportionately to the growing number of collectors. If the budding lovers of antiques knew very little about the objects they coveted, the same may be said of the new merchants who knew almost nothing about these matters. People became antique dealers who had never before thought about such a profession but who possessed a small capital that enabled them to purchase cheaply at markets or at auction sales antiques which might interest the public. For this purpose they traveled to Moscow or to the provinces from where they returned with a rich booty of interesting objects.

At the time of which I speak, I was also interested in collecting in an amateur fashion. I became a collector of old engravings absolutely by chance when my grandmother made me a present of some engravings that she had herself inherited from her grandfather count Laval, a great amateur collector, well-known for his love of antiques, who lived at the beginning of the 19th century. I knew very little about engravings and even less about the «art of buying». However, when I learned that my cousin's ex-cook had opened an antique shop in the court of the Aquarium Theater, I decided that an occasion such as this might never repeat itself and that a visit to this shop could not be deferred one minute.

When I arrived at the antique dealer's, I naturally did not mention my family name and asked him if he had any old engravings. After looking through several portfolios, I soon discovered in one of them an interesting specimen and, copying sagacious buyers, I put the portfolio to one side with a disappointed expression. The inexperienced cook did not try to insist on the quality and the rarity of his merchandise and immediately passed on to the second stage of the comedy, that is to say he started to show me objects which were of no great interest to me.

Having bought, as if in passing, for almost nothing, an adorable Elisabethan cut-glass crystal bowl and two gilt glasses of Catherine's period, I returned to the subject of the engravings and finally bought for a very low price the portfolio that contained the engraving which interested me. Having paid, I was about to leave when the antique dealer stopped me and asked me if I was interested in old watches. I answered him very truthfully that I was not at all interested in watches. My sincerity was all the more real as collecting watches requires a thorough knowledge of the matter which I did not possess and only people with considerable means could afford this pastime. However, seeing that the dealer wanted very much to show me a particularly interesting watch and wishing to remain in his good books I agreed against my will to take a look at it.

The antique dealer took out of a special cupboard a flat oblong box covered in red leather and handed it to me. Taking it in my hands I saw on the lid a number engraved in gold which, as far as I can remember, was number 2675. Inside the box there were two small recesses, in one of which was a very flat watch with a chain and a small key, and in the other a spare glass dial and another dial of a different color.

By its chain, which was unusually short, I guessed that this watch was an old Bréguet. I took it out of its box and turned it over. It was then that occurred what so rarely happens in the life of a collector, that great happiness that for many surpasses that of a winning lottery ticket. On the back of the watch was the grey enamel blazon of the Davydoff family! Having with great difficulty overcome my emotion, I asked the dealer what this blazon was and to whom the watch had belonged. The inexperienced merchant did not notice my agitation and started telling me that the blazon was that of the Davydoff family, that the watch had belonged to the poet-partisan Denis Vassilievich Davydoff[1], and that it was an old Bréguet watch. He added that he had bought it at the sale of the Menchikov archives at which twelve letters by Denis Vassilievich had been bought by the Tsar.

Naturally he suggested that I buy the watch and said that he wanted 1000 roubles for it, and that a well-known collector, the wealthy Utaman, had offered him 900 roubles. From this last remark I concluded that if I did not buy immediately this historical Bréguet which had for me, the grand-nephew of the partisan, a very special value, Utaman would end up by getting his own way with the dealer and the watch would be lost to me forever. Without a word, I took out the 1000 roubles that I fortunately had on me and took the watch. When I was already near the front door, the antique dealer said to me: «May I ask your name?». «Davydoff» I answered and walked out of the shop.

Back home I wound up the watch with the little key and was delighted to hear it tick. A few weeks later I went to Paris and, having taken the watch with me, I took it to the Bréguet company which kept old archives. The owner of the Bréguet company glanced at the number engraved on the case and asked that the ledger of the year 1804 be brought to him.

---

1. 1784-1839: well known poet and organizer of the peasant partisan guerillas against the armies of Napoleon. First cousin of the Decembrist V.L. Davydoff.

He read the following extract to me: «The watch number 2675 was sold in 1804 to prince Aldobrandini who never paid for it and returned it in 1810. In 1814, during the occupation of Paris by the allied troops, general Denis Davydoff bought it and asked that his blazon be engraved on the back of the watch in grey enamel. The owner added that general Davydoff had paid 3000 francs for the watch and that, if I wished to sell it to the Bréguet company, he would offer me 9000 francs for it. At the rate of exchange of that time this was equivalent to 3375 roubles.

I did not sell the watch to Bréguet. Along with so many other family objects that were dear to me, it was carried away by the torrent of the revolution...

THE WORLD CRISIS
AND
THE FREEMASONS

Should freemasonry play a role in history and is it able to do so? In other word should freemasonry try and influence events that occur in certain periods of history and, if so how should it go about it?

A positive answer to these questions requires that a great many widespread misunderstandings that obscure the very concept of freemasonry be clarified. There are many different ideas about what freemasonry actually represents. The simple fact that it is a secret society with a structure in «degrees» incites the profane world to spread extremely different notions about freemasonry and even to attribute sinister objectives to it. Being a secret society, freemasonry cannot even try and justify itself without revealing its very essence. This is further complicated by the fact that freemasonry is defined by statutes that do not always correspond to its essence and cover only external appearances. Finally, even in the inner circle of freemasonry many adepts do not know what this essence really consists of.

Independently from any individual appraisal, it is evident that many public organizations of general interest assert that freemasonry is guilty of having played and of still playing an important role in politics, that it manipulates political opinions or seems to be their guiding spirit, and that it makes decisions that are final and compulsory for all brothers whatever their degree.

Without making an apologia for freemasonry nor divulging its secret essence, one should nevertheless try and dispel the most serious misunderstandings concerning it, otherwise it would be quite impossible to arrive at a true answer to the question posed at the beginning of this article. The whole problem resides in the fact that, in contrast to other societies and profane organizations that act on a materialistic plane and pursue materialistic objectives, freemasonry works on a spiritual plane and pursues objectives that conform to this spiritual plane. Its main «raison d'être» is the construction of an ideal temple for the human race, a temple built with elements that have been especially prepared for this purpose. Freemasonry considers man to be an unpolished stone that, in its initial state, cannot be placed next to the other elements that form the ideal temple. The polishing of this rough stone is the very objective of initiation.

From what has just been said it is clear that, as freemasonry seeks a distant ideal objective, it cannot act by itself on events that occur in the outside world, be they majorly serious ones for the human race at any particular epoch of history.

If one considers that the stones polished by freemasonry or by its adepts continue to live and to act in the outside world, one may ask oneself if they could not, and even if they should not, play a special role in this world and if so what should be this role? To give a valid and comprehensive answer to this question, one must first of all consider certain characteristics of initiation that predetermine the role played by freemasons in the outside world or at the very least are essential to it.

The raison d'être of freemasonry is the polishing of the rough stone represented by man. In other terms its main objective is the rebirth of profane man. An ideal human society, called temple by the freemasons, can only be built with people who are capable of defeating their passions and who all aspire to reach a unique goal, the realization of the highest spiritual sentiments that are innate in each human being. To achieve this they must first of all recognize the relative worth of the different roads that face them and by so doing find the road of truth. This can only be achieved by rediscovering the long lost faculty of conceiving unity, that is to say the absolute, and by eliminating many secondary considerations that are characteristic of our epoch.

It is not really essential that freemasonry achieve entirely its objective of polishing each unpolished stone and that it should succeed in creating human beings capable of defeating plurality. It is sufficient that these human beings have their minds fixed on this objective and acquire by this very fact a precise way of thinking that is different from the one of uninitiated man. This way of thinking gives the freemason the possibility of seeing from a different angle the events that occur in the world, of judging them in a different manner and especially of solving the contradictions that arise on the highest spiritual plane by enabling them to see and to define the relativity and the transience of these events. From all that has just been said, one may conclude that a freemason, who pursues the distant objective of building an ideal human society, cannot remain indifferent to all that is happening in this society at each stage of its development. He not only can but also must help to solve the contradictions that are found in this society and that threaten in part to destroy all the primordial values that have been acquired at the expense of much fighting and suffering.

Right now the world is going through one of its periodic crises the outcome of which is difficult to predict at the present moment, but which threatens us with great calamities, the possible loss not only of our material well-being but also of our ancestral culture. Having reviewed the question of the general role played by freemasons in world events, we shall now examine the question of the means by which they can apply this role in our present time.

A precise answer to this question requires that we first examine the problem of today's crisis, the contradictions that arise from it and the reasons for these contradictions.

The latter part of the 18th century and the whole of the 19th was the era of the founding of liberty in all its aspects, and social equality is the theme of the 20th century. The great French revolution had formulated in its triple slogan

261

«Liberty, Equality, Fraternity» the ancient and true aspirations of the human race but it had not achieved all of them entirely. The most complete achievement had been that of liberty which is understandable as, at that time, liberty was the main dominant element of human aspirations, and also because its realization was relatively easy. No economic or social obstacle barred its way. The achievement of equality, on the other hand, was only partial, at least from a political standpoint. The French revolution was a bourgeois political revolution whereas what is happening today is a social revolution.

This is a logical and real state of affairs. After the battle for liberty had been won, it was time for the second element of the triple slogan to be realized—in fact this moment had arrived, or so thought the theoreticians of social equality. It seemed to them that its realization should be easy as, apart from the opposition of those classes whose interests were threatened by it, there could be no other obstacle in its way, especially in the framework of democratic regimes. However, when man attempted to put these theories into practical application in real life, he came up against a very unexpected obstacle. It turned out that the practical realization of social equality created a conflict between itself and liberty. These two concepts could not coexist without limiting each other's actions. This contradiction is such a serious one and goes so deep that attempts to solve it have divided the world into two enemy camps and their mutual hate threatens us in our time with terrible and unpredictable migrations and with the destruction of human culture and civilization. These two camps, while pursuing the same objective, are divided when it comes to the means of achieving it. Both believe that social equality can only be achieved by socialism but they diverge on the means of solving the contradiction between equality and liberty and how to apply them in real life. One of the camps, the totalitarian communist one, affirms that it has achieved social equality in the countries that it controls but remains silent about the fact that this equality is equivalent to the one that was enjoyed by serfs who were deprived of all rights and occupied the lowest echelon of humanity, and that this form of equality was only achieved by the total destruction of any form of liberty and the abasement of the personality of man to the state of a worker ant in an ant-hill. For this camp there is no «sacred theme» and all themes are achieved by force and lies. The other camp realizes that equality without rights cannot give the human race what it has always aspired after and that sooner or later those men who have been abased to the level of serfs deprived of all rights will rise to recover their lost liberty. That is the reason why this camp is trying to find all the possible means that may solve this problem and reconcile the two contradictory elements—liberty and equality. This task is a difficult one and for the moment no solution has yet been found. The free world must continue to defend its liberty against the aggressions of totalitarian tyrannies.

No one knows exactly who was the author of the slogan «Liberty, Equality, Fraternity». Was it taken by the militant French revolutionaries from French freemasonry to which several of them belonged, or did freemasonry borrow it from the French revolutionaries? In all probability the second assertion is the correct one as the slogan only became a part of the ritual of the three first degrees, both for the Scottish lodge and for the Great Orient lodge. It is not mentioned in any of the freemasonries of other countries, nor in the higher degrees of the French Scottish lodge. In truth this is not a very important question as, whatever its origin, the slogan has a typically masonic character. Apart from the fact that its three-faced aspect corresponds entirely to the figure 3 that plays such a capital role in freemasonry, one can, with the three elements that form the slogan, build a triangle which has at its two lower angles the two contradictory elements, liberty and equality, and at its summit the third element, fraternity. The very fact that such a triangle can be built is very significant. It expresses the fact that the answer to the question that the human race is so concerned about, the elimination of the contradiction between the two first elements of the triple slogan, this answer can be found not in the absorption of one by the other but in the third element of the slogan, fraternity, which must form the synthesis of the first two.

This notion seems inaccessible to the profane world that thinks along materialistic lines and looks for the answer to all questions in superficial solutions. Only a freemason knows that the answer to these contradictions can only be found on a very high spiritual plane, in spite of and even because of these very contradictions. That is why there is nothing surprising about the fact that the human race, which has fought and shed blood for the conquest of liberty and equality, in themselves two great principles that can take on the form of material goods, has not so far sought to achieve fraternity. Fraternity is part of a spiritual group that cannot take on a material form and its achievement would not give immediate well-being. It can in no way satisfy the egotistical greed of the individual. Fraternity is love and like all true love it is altruistic. Both in the New and in the Old Testament, the first and foremost commandment is «Love thy neighbor as thyself», in other words be his brother. The human race has not forgotten this commandment but it has formed a great number of wonderful utopian projects that have never been realized and that are now costing it very dear. How could man possibly have such elevated aspirations when he had to fight for needs as essential as bread, liberty and equality? However, it became evident that the partial realization of the triple slogan of the French revolution not only could not give humanity a quiet and happy life and install on earth the reign of truth, but even to the contrary threatened to plunge it into a chaos where it would lose everything it thought it had already achieved. Liberty and equality can only be realized and have their true meaning if they are transformed into fraternity, that is to say love. Only then will the contradiction between these two elements become unthinkable.

From what has just been said one may deduce the role that freemasonry must play in the present critical times. This role can be summarized in the following manner: the totalitarian communist idea of introducing equality on this earth by force and by reducing the human being to a state of slavery must be counterbalanced in every possible way by fraternity, that is to say love.

Such a summary formula may seem quite unreal in our pragmatic era. It is difficult to imagine that in our time it could be possible to propagandize an abstract ideal with any degree of success among the masses. Aren't there already many similar organisations that are busy preaching this type of sermon, quite independently from churches of all faiths and denominations that repeat tirelessly to their faithful how essential it is for them not to forget the fundamental religious precepts? Unfortunately, even when members of the human race do remember these precepts they do not apply them to their acts. What is said in this sermon seems really too difficult to put into practice. The truth is that the realization of human fraternity and of love of one's neighbor on this earth is an essential need and the basic condition not only for the spiritual happiness of man but also for his material well-being. If the preachings of the churches and of other organizations that pursue the same objectives have not had any success, isn't it because their objectives only aim at saving human souls and not at building an ideal human society in which the fundamental principles of liberty and equality would take on their full meaning and would not contradict each other?

One may ask oneself what form the concrete actions of a freemason who pursues the objective of establishing fraternity among men could take. What can he do, and what should he do, so that his efforts do not become a sort of repetition of the moral concepts of the various churches and other similar organizations, but have their own personal characteristics? It is doubtful that the fight to achieve fraternity could be successful in our time, even if it should be strengthened by rational arguments, so that one is forced to look for another way of tackling this problem. When trying to achieve something it often happens that difficulties arise when one fights «for» what one wishes to achieve, and it may be much easier to fight «against» what opposes the realization of one's wish. In the present case, egotism and all the evil sentiments that derive from it are in direct opposition to the altruism of fraternity and love of one's neighbor. The fight for fraternity must

265

therefore become a fight against all the manifestations of egotism both in public and political life. It is quite impossible to enumerate all these manifestations. One can only mention the most important ones, among which class egotism holds without doubt first place and is the primary reason for the contradiction between liberty and equality. This class egotism is especially dangerous in the western world because it is responsible for the fact that population groups, which only think of their own personal class interests, forget the welfare of the state and threaten its security. Second place goes to the egotism of politicians and of other representatives active in public life who see in politics not the realization of objectives of the state but the realization of their own personal interest and advancement. This type of egotism is the reason for the transformation of politicians into politicasters.

The third manifestation, in order of importance, against which the establishment of fraternity must fight, is the phenomenon of racial and religious discrimination which is nothing but another form of egotism. This discrimination arises from the feeling of superiority of a race or of a religion over another and the hate and scorn it engenders. To mention only antisemitism, that exists throughout the whole world, even among groups of a very high degree of culture, not only has humanity been unable to achieve the psychological elimination of this plague for many centuries, but it has even succeeded in cohabiting with a phenomenon that had never existed in distant times, the physical extermination of 6 1/2 million Jews and this by the sole will of one man and the submission of his people to his will. This fact should eliminate from people's minds the notion that there are «superior» and «inferior» people and that Western culture is the only true culture and should convince one that some Western cultures are directly linked to barbarianism and that chauvinism exists even among the most advanced nations of the west. For freemasons the field of action is vast and they cannot do otherwise than attack it.

In conclusion, a saying of Greek orthodox liturgy comes involuntarily to mind: «Love one another and commune in harmony».

266

MY RED APPLES FROM THE CRIMEA

My father's memoirs—how I wish they could interest others as much as they interest me. How can I explain this urge I have felt to go back into the past in search of my roots and of bygone days?

I had been living in a dream world with father and mother always around me, when suddenly, first with my father's death, then my mother's, I woke up to harsh reality, to the fact that they were no longer by me, that I had lost my only link with a country I hardly knew, Russia.

I was an only child, hopelessly spoiled and, in spite of the war, quite happy in my cosy world with father, mother and babushka[1]. Perhaps because of the war I learned to appreciate everything in life and never to take anything for granted. We lived in Paris, in Auteuil, where other Russian émigrés also lived. At home, because of my grandmother, we spoke Russian most of the time. My parents had many Russian friends. Mother played the piano and sang Russian romances and gypsy songs. We always celebrated Easter with the traditional Pascha and Kulitch, and I painted eggs which I tried to make as pretty as those of my governess who decorated them with churches and onion-bulb cupolas. Grandmother prepared delicious Russian dishes. In spite of all that, Russia was like the beautiful portrait of a distant ancestor that hangs in the hall and that one never sees although one passes in front of it several times a day, taking its presence for granted.

---

1. Babushka = Grandmother.

All those Russian customs had, unbeknownst to me, penetrated me very gradually and surreptitiously like something that grows a little each day as years go by.

My father, whom I adored, «my knight» as he used to say, had been near me all these years and was ready and able, with his incredible memory, to tell me all about his past and describe people and events that had taken place before he had left Russia. But I was young and foolish, always rushing to do something else instead of just sitting there quietly and listening to him, always thinking that I could do it another time. Then my father died. How bitterly I regretted the lost time and what wouldn't I have given to be able to listen again to father's stories! Twenty years later, mother died and again this death came as a great shock. We were so close, adored each other and she lived just next door to me. With her disappeared the warmth and the cosiness. There was no one to speak Russian with... and Russia was beginning to attract me more and more. Mother would also speak to me of bygone days. When I used to find her reading a book and would ask her what she was reading, she would answer «a Russian author because it relaxes me more to read in Russian». How well I understand her now when I too prefer to read a Russian book as if by doing so I were finding shelter and peace.

One day some unknown force made me take out of a closet a suitcase that contained all the papers my father had written. Everything was there, untouched since our return from the United States, asleep and forgotten. I began reading them and trying to file them. The more I advanced in my task the more interested I became, like a person who is thirsty and thinks that one glass of water will be sufficient but having drunk that first glass realizes that he needs another and yet another and that his thirst has become unquenchable. It must have been then that I first thought and felt that I had to see for myself this country, Russia, which, although it was no longer as father had described it, might still show traces of what it had been in his time.

So in May 1973, with my husband, in our British car,

I took my first trip to Russia. We drove from Paris to Strasbourg, Baden Baden, Vienna and Budapest, and entered Russia at the Hungarian border town of Tchop. This trip was a particularly wonderful one, not only because it was the first time that I found myself on Russian soil with Russian spoken everywhere around me, but also because I felt so acutely how new everything was to me. Our first stop was Lvov, the second one Kiev, this beautiful city of the Ukraine, so green and luscious with its botanical garden buried in scented lilacs and the deep-blue onion-bulb cupolas of the Vidubetsky monastery in the background, and further away in the distance the Dniepr and its wide banks. I tried to get permission to go to Kamenka which I knew was not far from Kiev but this was refused as we had not applied for it in Paris. So we drove on to Oriol where we discovered, to console us, Turgenev's house and its marvelous park with centenarian birch trees. In Moscow I found the grave, always covered in flowers, of Denis Davydoff in the Novodievitchi convent, and the graves of many Davydoffs in the Donskoy cemetery. I looked for and found Arbat street where father had lived, but I did not then know about the Field of Peas, the Elisabeth Institute or Tolstoy's home that father had written about in his memoirs, which I had not yet read fully. Alas! we could only stay five days in Moscow, such a short time for all I wanted to do. As we drove from Moscow to Novgorod, we discovered Tchaikovsky's home in Klin and stopped to visit it. The walls of the hall were covered with photographs of various concerts and musical events and I was intrigued by the fact that the name Y.L. Davydoff was mentioned several times. When we said this to the administrator who was accompanying us, he asked us to wait a minute and went to make a phone call. A short while later an elderly woman arrived who introduced herself as Xenia Yurevna Davydova, the daughter of Y.L. Davydoff. She had taken over her father's post of curator of the museum after his death. She invited us to her office for a chat and to find out if we were related. Yes, we were! Her grandfather was the brother of my father's grandfather, so we were distant cousins. Tchaikovsky's sister Alexandra had married Lev Davydoff, one of the sons of the

269

Decembrist Vassili, and their son Yuri was this old lady's father. She vaguely remembered my father and she spoke at length about Kamenka. She took us around the house, filled with memories of Tchaikovsky and of his family and with many photographs of my ancestors. Unfortunately time was running short and we had to leave for Novgorod, but we promised we would write to each other. Novgorod with its beautiful Kremlin was only a short distance from St. Petersbourg, that magnificent city where, more so than anywhere else, I tried to walk in my father's footsteps. My father's aunt, Princess Lieven, aunt Lina, had been for thirty years headmistress of the Smolny Institute which, before the revolution, had been a school for the education of young girls of the nobility, and which now was the local headquarters of the soviet party. Father used to visit aunt Lina very often and go to balls at the Smolny. He had been «Kammerjunker» at the Winter Palace, now part of the Hermitage, one of the most beautiful museums in the world. He had known all these streets, the banks of the Neva, the English quay where still stands the house of the Lavals with two lions guarding the threshold. It was from this house that Katacha had left for Siberia to join her husband. On the other side of the river, the University with its lovely red ochre walls stood surrounded by trees. Father used to go to balls at the palaces outside St. Petersburg, Pavlosk, Peterhoff and Tsarskoié-Selo (now Pushkin). Everything had changed but there were still vestiges of the past like the grocery store Eliseef, the Fauchon of olden times, which used to sell caviar, smoked salmon, partridges, quails...

During this trip I thought many times about father's memoirs and the work I still had to accomplish, reading and filing, and these thoughts filled me with joy. Being here, in St. Petersburg, gave me the desire to know more about this country and its history.

On May 25, 1975 mother died and I realized once more how many things we should have spoken about, how many questions I should have asked her about Russia instead of talking about all those trivial things of everyday life.

In January of 1977 we went back to St. Petersburg where

we spent a whole week. It was very cold, minus 25°C, and snow, which suits this city so well, covered everything. It was so easy to imagine the sleighs and the troïkas at the start of the century. It reminded me of old engravings representing life in winter in those days with the Neva all frozen, people walking and ice skating on it, and the children on luges. Everything was so beautiful, so peaceful, and the days being very short the sun at noon was all red like at sunset. There was a special light in pastel shades, so different from the color of warm countries. The sky was that of the far North and at 4 p.m. it was already night. It was fun seeing those eager members of the Walrus club taking a dip in the Neva along the banks of the Peter and Paul fortress, this fortress that I visited again to see the cells where the Decembrists had been imprisoned before their exile to Siberia, and the courtyard where they took their daily exercise. I went to the Alexander Nevsky Lavra and visited the cemetery where many artists, musicians and poets are buried. I found Tchaikovsky's ornate tomb with his bust, also those of Rimsky-Korsakov, Glinka and others. I went to the Nikolsky church of the sailors where several services took place every day. I love Orthodox churches where even the most humble choir is so beautiful and the reflections of the candles on the icons so fascinating. In winter the statues are all boarded up to protect them from the frost and the fountains are closed but the gardens and the parks are beautiful in the icy air with the naked branches of the trees all coated with snow, reminding me of the ballet Cinderella by the marquis de Cuevas where the scenery is in all shades of blues, pinks, and mauves on a snow-white background, so unreal and fairylike. In Pavlovsk park people were skiing or riding in sleighs and one woman was pushing her mother in an «armchair-sleigh»! Snow was everywhere and often fell from rooftops. I think again of father's description of life in Russia in the late 19th century. I remember how he used to tell me about the thaw when, after months of deep sleep, the Neva would flow again and boats could sail once more. Mother used to tell me about Easter, the most important of all Russian religious feasts that also marked the end of the winter, and

271

how it was traditional to wear something white for the Easter Eve service.

One and a half years later I went back to St. Petersburg for the third time, for the beautiful «white nights» in June when the days are so long that night never seems to fall and one is almost ashamed to go to bed. My daughter, who had never been to Russia, accompanied me and I acted as her guide and tried to show her everything I had already seen. I went with her to the landing stage named in honour of the Decembrists where we took a boat to Peterhoff. I photographed her sitting on one of the lions of the Laval house built by Thomas de Tomon, the famous architect, in the middle of the 18th century during the reign of Catherine the Great when many palaces were built. We visited the museum in the Peter and Paul fortress filled with memories of the Decembrists. We went to Tsarskoie Selo where, in addition to the palace and the park, there is also a very rich museum with many pictures of the Davydoffs and a caricature of Denis Davydoff by Pushkin. I wanted so much to show my daughter as much as possible of this town where her grandfather had lived but the seven days we spent in St. Petersburg passed all too swiftly and I had the usual feeling of not having done and seen all I wanted to show her.

Another year went by and yet another. It seemed a very long time since I had been to Russia. At last in 1981, during the month of August, my husband and I flew directly from Paris to Kiev. In three and a half hours we found ourselves in another world. We had left an almost deserted Paris and landed in a city teeming with people. The «dejournaia»[2] on our floor greeted us with «Franzia»? I answered her in Russian and asked if our room was far down the hall. She looked at me with astonishment and asked how I happened to speak Russian. I am Russian, I answered. How and why? Because my parents were both Russian and I am a Davydoff. I apologize if I seem to be bragging about my name but I cannot deny that I am proud of my family name for I know that it carries a little of the history of Russia, that very history that fascinates

_____
2. Woman-guard on each floor of a hotel.

the people of this country and that I have come in search of on this fourth trip, following the traces of my father and of my ancestors to the very places where they used to live.

We left Kiev the following day for Tcherkassy in a drive-it-yourself rented Lada. Tcherkassy is only 54 kms from Kamenka and we drove there the following day accompanied by a guide who insisted on coming with us for reasons that are best ignored. So here I was on the road to Kamenka, that so familiar name that I had heard mentioned time and time again at home during my parents' lifetime. The weather was lovely. The road was crowded with many trucks but only a few private cars. I tried not to miss anything and kept looking right and left thinking that my father, my ancestors and also their many friends, Raevsky, Trubetskoy, Ryleev, Bestujev, Pushkin, Tchaikovsky and many other famous people visiting Kamenka had also taken this same road, in carriages, sleighs or even on horseback. Time went by too fast and these 54 kms did not seem long enough to me. I would have liked to lengthen each verst in order to make my expectation last longer. In a way I was a little afraid that all my dreams and hopes might crumble like a castle of playing cards when I came face to face with reality. It is so wonderful to desire something ardently that I always wish to postpone its realization.

Before reaching Kamenka we found Smela where the river Tiasmin passes that father describes so well in his memoirs, this swampy river that also flows through Kamenka and drives the watermill and generates electricity for the sugar refinery. Everything was so peaceful on this lovely morning.

A few kilometers further on we reached Kamenka, first the village then the estate. We parked the car and entered through a gate on which a sign said «A.S. Pushkin and P.I. Tchaikovsky museum». We walked up a narrow alley through a small park. A woman appeared, came up to me and said in Russian: «Olga Alexandrovna? We were expecting you!» My God! Was I dreaming? Was I really in Kamenka? Was this woman real? To say that I was moved would be an understatement. I would have liked to remain standing without saying a word, without moving, to appreciate and savor this instant like a child in front of Ali Baba's cave

273

waiting for the door to open, to relish this «before» and make it last, knowing that I would shortly be seeing everything. The seconds and the minutes go by and I must move on, on this road to the past.

Maria Antonovna Chkaliberda showed us first around the museum. It was located in the little green house where uncle Kolia used to live. Like all museums in Russia it is very well kept and each object is revered. There were pictures, engravings and paintings of my great-great-grandparents, of the «big house» as it used to look before it was destroyed, of the Nikolaevsky church before it burnt down and uncle Kolia rebuilt a new one, all showing the way it was «then» in 1820-30-40. In spring the lawn in front of the house used to be covered in violets. In the drawing room stands one of the pianos that used to belong to the Davydoffs on which Tchaikovsky played for the first time Eugene Onegin. Everything was there as if waiting for its former inhabitants and I needed very little imagination to feel how gay it must have been when preparations were being made for the picnics in the «Big Wood» to which father also used to go as a small boy, helping to gather brushwood for the bonfire, and where Tchaikovsky used to hear the «carefree laughter of the children».

How can I describe this visit, this place where each object interested me, where I would have liked to linger and where I knew I would wish to return? It was impossible to photograph it all, impossible to remember all the details given by Maria Antonovna who was an unending source of information and knowledge. We visited the grotto where Pushkin, and later Tchaikovsky, used to go and relax, then we went to have lunch, a small intermission in this emotion-filled day. After lunch we walked in the big garden, now a memorial park with a monument to the Decembrists—the one on the left is my great-great-grandfather Vassili Lvovitch Davydoff! There were many beautiful trees of different varieties that must have existed already in father's time. This notion of permanence never leaves me for, although I know that many things have changed and are no longer, such as the small Jewish shops and the synagogue, the sugar refinery and the wine distillery are still there and the bridge over the Tiasmin where a fisherman waits patiently for a catch... Yes, this thought never leaves me during this whole trip. It was already 4 p.m. and Maria Antonovna's energy had never slackened one second. What a pity, I thought, that tomorrow or the day after I would not be able to return and ask her a few questions about details that had escaped me because in spite of all my eagerness and my efforts to remember everything she had told me, I knew that my memory would play tricks on me and that I would forget many of them. But what about Yurchikha? Is it far? Can we go there? Yes, it was only 3 kms away, so we got back into the car and drove to the house where father had lived. By the roadside we saw a grave covered in flowers. It was the grave of Alexandra Ivanovna Davydova, née Potapova, the wife of the Decembrist, my great-great-grandmother! How moving it was to see all those flowers! Yurchikha had been turned into a sanatorium for tubercular children. The one-story house was large but simple, surrounded by a vast garden in the middle of the country with many varieties of high trees, on a small height with a lovely view all around. We were greeted by the doctors who showed us around the house. Though some of the rooms had changed, the general lay out was the same and I caressed the banisters as I was told that the staircase was the original one. What a pity we could not stay longer. The doctors gave us some chestnuts from the estate as souvenirs. We drove back to Kamenka and left Maria Antonovna at the museum. I promised to write to her and send her some pictures and she walked away with an energetic step like herself, a strong character who must have known difficult times.

On our way back to Tcherkassy a host of sensations filled my heart and my mind. If only father could see me! I felt so close to him. The first chapter of this trip, Kamenka, that I have finally seen, is coming to an end. I pray that the photos come out all right; they will be witnesses of this too brief but marvelous visit which I have dreamt about for so long.

We made a pause and spent a day in Kiev, this lovely city that smells of the South. Sadly this time the lilacs in the botanical garden were not in bloom and the blue onion domes needed repainting, so we treasured our 1973 memory of it.

The following day we left for the Crimea. Upon arriving at the hotel we barely had time to unpack, as we wished to visit the town before dark. Alla, the Intourist official, asked what I wished to see and I told her that my only dream was to visit Sably. She said she was not sure this would be possible but she would enquire and let me know. Tomorrow we could go to Yalta, and I answered that I would not be able to live or sleep until I knew for sure that I could visit Sably!

We took a long walk around Simferopol, this town where mother was born and where she once lived with my grandmother and her family. What a pity I did not know where her house was located. Much had been destroyed during the war and much rebuilt but there might still be some places that mother had known. I liked Simferopol although it was only a simple provincial town. It is a southern city and one can feel it in the landscape, the trees, the low white houses and the shaded streets. One realized it must get very hot here and I could well imagine what grandmother used to tell me about, women sitting chatting on their front porches while chewing watermelon seeds. We stopped in a small park where there was a gathering of people standing and talking as if at a cocktail party. We sat down on a long bench next to two old women. One of them suddenly said to me «From the looks of your shoes, you are not from here» and we started chatting. I inquired about Sably and she said that it was on the Sebastopol road and that I should take tram number 5. I felt that there was a hope I would get to Sably even if the Intourist office came up with a negative answer to my request. I could even try and bribe a taxi driver! The old woman told us that the people gathered here were all seeking to exchange apartments. Who could have guessed it? The air was cool and pleasant in this peaceful evening but we had to go and have dinner so we left our two old women and promised we would try and return the following day.

We succeeded with difficulty in getting into the «Ocean», a huge very new and flashy restaurant on the first floor of a building; it was packed. We were put at a table with two men, and very quickly started chatting. The orchestra was too loud. The many glasses of vodka, the excitement of the day, the fatigue, made me feel that I was vibrating all over. We would have liked to prolong the evening but I had to be in form the following day, so our table companions drove us back to our hotel in their car at top speed, left us in front and roared off in the night.

The following day we went to Yalta by taxi with a very nice Intourist driver, Boris Nesterovitch. The weather was beautiful and we loved Yalta and Tchekov's house. I could so well imagine «the lady and her little dog» walking along the boardwalk. Everything was so old-fashioned. It was a resort for ladies with hats and parasols. I dipped my feet in the Black Sea and stared aghast at the crowd of sunbathers on the beach, then walked back to the Oreanda hotel that my parents had spoken to me about. It is true that, as father used to say to me, the coast reminds one of the Amalfi coast, with its cypresses, flowers and balconies filled with plants. I started dreaming... How nice it would be to spend a vacation here, in this hotel. I visited a room with a large balcony facing the sea. It was all very old-fashioned and probably not very comfortable but I liked it. After Yalta we drove along the coast and visited two famous old palaces, Vorontzoff's and the Livadia. I could well understand why Russian princes chose to build their summer homes here. We decided to have lunch at the Chalach restaurant at the Baïdarsky gate and with the help of our driver we very quickly had a table cloth laid out on one of the wooden tables in the garden and had one of the best Russian meals of this trip. We drove back to Yalta where I phoned the Intourist office from the Oreanda and Alla informed me that we had been authorized to go to Sably! How thrilled I am! Hooray!

Next morning, here we are on the road to Sably, driven by another driver. The Sebastopol «chaussée» leads to Sably which in fact is no longer called Sably but Kachtanaya which means Chestnut Road, after being known as Partisanskaia, but everybody still calls it Sably. As when we went to Kamenka I look right and left for fear of missing something. Fears assail me. Will I find the house, this second goal of my trip? Will it still be standing? Will I, thanks to the photographs that hang in our flat, be able to recognize the house, father's last residence in Russia and the site of «the Impossible

277

Kolkhoze»? The road as usual is crowded with trucks but Sably is only 15 km from Simferopol so we arrive fairly quickly. Once again I would have liked to stop time and make these last minutes drag on. We turn off the main road into a smaller one that leads to a long alley lined with chestnut trees. It looks so much like the pictures at home, and at the end of the alley, yes, yes, there is the house! I recognize its large windows. I jump out of the car almost before it has come to a stop and rush into the house, race up the stairs to the first floor, where my husband photographs me looking out of a window, and burst into an office where some women are working. I explain who I am and the reason for my visit and they seem interested and curious. Without my realizing it, I find myself sitting on one of the desks of this large office, speaking, explaining, answering questions from all the people who have gathered around me, 20, 30 or more. I explain to them why I have come here. I tell them about my father. I answer question after question that they fire at me. I tell them how «we» live in the West and what I do. They are all so fascinated by the mere fact that I am here. For them I am such a change in their routine, like a person who has fallen from the moon! How long do I sit there talking and talking? My husband says about two hours! I can't believe it! I could go on and on but I want to visit the house, see the rooms, see what has been changed and what has remained as it was. Evgenia Petrovna, a charming woman who runs a kindergarten which occupies the ground floor of the house, is delighted to show me around. Here are some rooms with the children's white iron beds. Here are their playrooms with all their toys, she thinks these were the dining-room and the drawing-room. I see all this as if in a dream. The excitement does more than ten glasses of vodka! We go outside in the garden where the children are playing, some on see-saws, others on a merry-go-round. The garden is not too well kept but it is full of plants, flowers and lilac trees. Two old women say to me that they remember their parents telling them that the Davydoffs who used to live in this house had been fair and kind masters and that my great-grandmother never failed to give them a gold coin whenever they did anything for her, saying that it was for the wedding, the newborn child or a birthday. Someone suggests that we go and visit an old woman who lives close by and whom they think knew my family. So off we all go and indeed find this 98-year-old woman sitting in a small log cabin peeling potatoes. From the main house, that looked more like a hut, came the delicious smell of chicken broth. What a coincidence! This old woman when she was a little girl used to deliver chickens to my great-grandmother and she too always received a gold coin from the Barinia so she could buy herself something.

We drive off to visit the orchards where father used to grow peaches, pears, apples and many other fruits. As we drive up, the workmen and the administrator of this «sovkhoze», as it has now become, greet us and I explain once more my presence here. The reaction is immediate. They are as eager as the others to find out about me and the West. They bring me apples, which is all they grow nowadays, several kilos of them, yellow ones to be eaten right away and red ones that will be ripe in October and that I will take back to Paris. I admire the landscape and try to visualize my father walking along the rows of fruit-trees. If things had been different I too might have lived here...but such thoughts are futile.

We drive back to the house. Almost opposite is a white stone fountain dated 1857! But we have to leave this estate where my great-grandparents, my grandparents and my father had lived, the last place where my father had resided before leaving Russia for ever, the place where he had hoped to create what was to become «the Impossible Kolkhoze». As we drive away I look back wondering if I will ever return...

On our way back we make a detour to visit Bachtisarai where the Khan's palace still stands. Pushkin described its splendours, its refinements and the sad story of the favorite and of the fountain where even today a drop of water falls like a tear at regular intervals into a basin where two roses bathe. I can easily picture the harem, the long benches covered with the multicolored cushions of different shades and the narghile being passed around...

We get back to our hotel in Simferopol in time to close our suitcases and be ready to leave at 7 p.m. for Tbilissi,

Georgia. (I still persist in calling it Tiflis as my parents used to). What a marvelous day this has been, so filled with emotional experiences of all sorts. We land in Tbilissi at about midnight local time. Though I am unable to know or see anything I already sense that it will be very different from the Crimea and even from Russia. The Georgians have an accent when they speak Russian and they seem an altogether different race, much closer to the Persians. Our hotel is old-fashioned, the room large, very hot and noisy as it gives on to the main street. Tired as I am, I cannot sleep and all the events and emotions of this day pass unceasingly through my mind.

The next morning we go to the Intourist Office in our hotel and a short while later a charming and bright young woman appears, Tzetzo, our guide. She shows us all the places of interest in Tbilissi, then the old capital Mshketa. What a difference in the landscape. For me the dominant color is ochre, and this is actually the color that comes to my mind now when I think of Georgia. The character of the Georgians is also very different from that of the Russians.

Three days later we drive to Armenia which is also very unlike Russia. It is like a very spicy dish, the spices of which I have difficulty distinguishing. The people are very colorful. Their skin is more like the Iranian's and I feel very Russian, very white. Mr. Georg who runs the bar of our hotel in Erevan, the capital of Armenia, a bar where one can sample wines, is a perfect example of an Armenian. He is shrewd, cunning and a wonderful host.

From Erevan we fly to Moscow, the city, the capital, the color of which seems steel grey, cold and uninviting after the sunny skies of the South. Everything is pervaded with the feeling of soviet power. Driving is difficult and in general everything here is much more complicated. The Intourist office at the Metropole where we are staying is enormous. We shall often come here to solve thousands of small and big problems that arise at each moment. I am glad we are staying at the Metropole. Mother also stayed here. At dinner in the huge ornate dining-room I can imagine what it used to be like when the orchestra played waltzes and tangos instead of today's

280

loud rock, so loud that one has a hard time talking and hearing what the other person is saying.

The following day we leave in another drive-it-yourself rented car to Vladimir which we reach after two hours of a nightmare drive on roads crowded with trucks in foggy and rainy weather. Along the road we can see many people carrying baskets filled with mushrooms. The weather is perfect for mushroom gathering and I would so love to join them. It has always been one of my dreams. The landscape around Vladimir is already Northern, the sky pale with everywhere my beloved birch trees, a landscape so different from the hot countries we left less than 48 hours ago. A little beyond Vladimir we visit Bogoliubov and, a little further on, in the middle of fields at the meeting of two small rivers, a beautiful church, the «Pakrova na Nerle», small and peaceful in this hour of late afternoon.

We reach Suzdal at about 6 p.m. Fortunately it is still light enough to take pictures. It is a beautiful evening with a glorious sunset that lights up the onion-shaped cupolas of the churches and convents, the wooden village and the shopping arcade with black wrought-iron signs. God knows what the weather will be like tomorrow. This evening it is lovely, the light tender and velvety and the air clear and fresh. Indeed the next morning the weather is grey and foggy and the churches are all wrapped in a veil of mystery.

The following day we drive back to Moscow, stopping to see Yusupov's palace in Arkhangelskoye. The garden, the park, the birch trees and the lions standing guard along the front lawn, are all more beautiful than the house itself. The birch trees are so lovely that if I lived in Moscow I would often come here for walks. We visit again the Novodievitchi convent, so magnificent with its gold and blue domes framed by the trees of the cemetery where rests Denis Davydoff next to his children and a little further my great-great-grandfather Prince Serge Trubetskoy, the Decembrist. Denis Davydoff, whose grave is even more flowered than in 1973, is a distant relative of mine but I feel a special closeness to him because, like I in my youth, he had a white streak in his brown curly hair. Yes, there is such a thing as heredity! Finally we find the Khamovnitcheski Street where stands Tolstoy's house that father writes about in his memoirs. He used to come here to see his friends the sons of Tolstoy. He had danced in this very living room that I was gazing at now. I have difficulty tearing myself away from this perfectly well-kept museum. I would also like to see the Field of Peas, the Elisabeth Institute and all those places father has written about, but, as usual, there is no time.

The next morning we leave early for Yaroslavl. On the way we stop off to visit Pereslav Zalesky, then Rostov Veliky with its beautiful ensemble of churches and its Kremlin, such a joy for the eye, the heart and the soul. The architecture of these churches is so much closer to me than that, more sober and pure but so much more alien to me, of the Georgian and Armenian churches. How wonderful to discover this unexpected present, Rostov Veliky. We do not tire looking at its beautiful buildings and we leave with regret. We are a little disappointed in Yaroslavl itself, but, a few miles outside the town, in Karabikha, we discover the Nekrassov museum surrounded by a splendid garden with beautiful birch trees. It is here that Nekrassov wrote «the Russian Women», those lovely poems about those two great ladies, Princess Maria Volkonskaia and my great-great-grandmother Princess Ekaterina Trubetskaia, the first wives of Decembrists to follow their husbands to Siberia, their «guardian angels». Yes, everywhere the story of my family is present.

We return to Moscow the following morning and the next day we drive to Klin which we had already visited in 1973. My cousin Xenia, whom we had «discovered» in 1973, and her sister Irina are expecting us. We have difficulty finding their home. They seem pleased to see us and we chat in the salon of their small flat before having lunch in the kitchen with tea, bread-and-butter and a delicious salami, and cookies. The conversation never palls but many things remain unsaid and I do not try to broach certain subjects. It is better that way. Later we go to the Tchaikovsky museum which is as well-kept as ever, its walls covered with pictures, photographs and paintings, a piano in the center of one of the rooms and a charming little verandah where Piotr Ilyich used to drink his morning coffee. The atmosphere is warm and cosy. We are shown around by the curator of the museum and a guide, Paulina Efimovna, a young plump woman, intelligent and talkative, who seems to live for and by the memory of Tchaikovsky. She is charming and we could not have wished for a better guide as she knows so many details of Tchaikovsky's life. Here too the Davydoffs were part of the family and I enjoy seeing all their pictures once more. In the evening we return to Moscow under dark and rainy skies.

The following morning we meet a Russian acquaintance who has managed to obtain authorization for us to see certain files in the Historical Museum of the Kremlin. We enter through a side entrance, walk down interminable corridors, up and down several staircases and finally are shown into a large room and seated at a table on which have been set three albums. Two women who work at the museum open them for us and are delighted to see my expression of joy and amazement. I had no idea that these albums existed and this is such a wonderful finale to this fascinating trip. The albums contain drawings and water-colors painted in Siberia by my great-great-grandfather Vassili Davydoff and some of his children during their exile. They depict scenes of everyday life, their living quarters, portraits of each other and of their friends. They did not then know how precious these small chefs d'oeuvre would be today. Everything had been religiously filed away and I, their distant descendant, have been allowed to see them and may even, so I am informed, ask for photocopies that are of particular interest to me. I could look again and again at these wonderful albums. What a wonderful climax to this «search for the past»!

Later that morning we visit the Tropinin museum, then the Pushkin museum with so many souvenirs, letters and pictures of the Davydoffs, before having lunch in a cafeteria where we are delighted to see a little old lady with her hat on, seated very straight, eating her food very delicately and totally ignoring her uncouth fellow diners who are gobbling up their food as fast as they can. What a contrast and how she reminds us of bygone days!

We spend our final morning visiting once more the Red Square, the Kremlin and its wonderful churches with their onion-bulb cupolas and their golden colors which remind me of Boris Godunov, Ivan the Terrible and Mussorgsky. It is so different from St Petersburg which for me brings more to mind Tchaikovsky's music, the very opposite of Mussorgsky's, although they are both very Russian and I love them both. Finally we admire the splendid icons in the Rublev museum, have a light lunch at the hotel and say goodbye to the women of the Intourist Office, who helped solve many a problem, before boarding a taxi for the airport. Already on the Air France plane that is flying us back to Paris, the contrast with what we have just left is incredible. We are back in the free world of the West, a world of goods and plenty, and Russia seems so very far away...but I have my red apples from the Crimea. How sad that I cannot hand them to father and mother...

A SIBERIAN ODYSSEY

Little did I know when I returned in September with the red apples from what used to be father's orchards that I would be going again to Russia before the end of 1981. To my surprise and joy, my husband gave me as a Xmas present another trip to Russia and to his question «Would I like to go?» there could only be one answer: «Yes, I'd love to!». The Xmas present included two nights on the Trans-Siberian train, a drive in a troïka, Lake Baïkal and last but not least Irkutsk, which I had dreamed of visiting for so many years without ever thinking this dream could come true. With little time ahead of us we had to get busy with passports and visas and especially clothing as all our friends, appalled at the news, tried to dissuade us by mentioning temperatures of minus 30°, 50° and even 70°C.! They were convinced we were completely crazy but nothing could make us change our minds.

So on December 25, Xmas day, we left Paris all quiet and asleep after the Xmas Eve festivities, and joined our group at Charles de Gaulle airport. Unfortunately this time we were not travelling on our own as there had been no time to organize such a trip, but with a group of 38 people, most of them French. The flight to Moscow on an Aeroflot plane was uneventful and, after the usual unending customs and police formalities, we arrived in the late evening at the Hotel Cosmos, unattractive but comfortable, and got to bed early.

The following morning we left our group and went by taxi in search of «the Field of Peas», that part of Moscow that father speaks so much about in his memoirs. We knew more or less from our Baedeker where it was located and found it without too much difficulty, but naturally everything had changed. There were still a few old houses and the thought that the ground under my feet was the same my father had trodden was sufficient to make me happy. The Lefortov Street was still there and the German Street. The Voznecenskaya had become Radio Street, and there was the Elisabeth Institute where father had spent so many years of his childhood and his youth. It stands at the corner of Radio Street and Soldtikovskaya Street, which passes through what used to be the park but is now only a mass of new buildings. The students' rooms are now offices and the chapel that used to exist in the Institute has become heaven knows what! Still, the old building is there and I am happy to have seen it.

From the Field of Peas we went to the interesting Herzen museum where a journalist we had met in September was to join us. One of the museum attendants very kindly let us use Herzen's office on the first floor and we sat at a round table so that I could go over the article that Alla Petrovna had written on our last trip and that she wanted to publish in January. There were indeed certain details that I could not agree to and asked her to change such as the word «motherland» that she made me say over and over again as if I were a soviet citizen and not a tourist visiting the land of her ancestors. I also asked her to change a sentence where she made me put a large bouquet of roses on the tomb of Denis Davydoff at the Novodievitchi convent. Not only was this not true, it would also have been impossible for me to do so as there is no florist close to the Novodievitchi and such a bouquet would have cost a fortune judging by the prices that I had seen at the market in Tbilissi from where most of the flowers are flown to Moscow for sale. All in all however she had written a good article and I thanked her for it. Alla Petrovna wanted me to write my impressions on my coming trip to Siberia but we would have to see about that later. Until then we wished each other a happy holiday season (one does not say Merry Xmas in Russia nowadays!) and a Happy New Year and we left her to meet a friend who was taking us to lunch at the home of

Professor Anatoli Filipovich Smirnoff, a specialist on the history of the Decembrists. We had a very pleasant meal with lots of vodka and champagne and spent a fascinating afternoon listening to Anatoli Filipovich who knew much more about my great-great-grandfathers than I ever would. We left relunctantly to join our group at our hotel as we were flying off that very night for Novosibirsk.

Vnukhovo airport is quite a distance from the city but we finally board our plane which taxies towards the take-off strip. We are suddenly startled by a loud noise and a shock somewhere below the fuselage and the plane comes to a stop. Things look bad and we are taken back to the waiting room by bus. We wait there on hard seats until 5 a.m. when we finally board our plane—hopefully another one—that flies us without any further trouble to Novosibirsk where we arrive at 11 a.m. local time, 8 a.m. Moscow time.

Because of our late arrival we have no time to visit Akadem-gorodok, that new Siberian city reserved for scientists. After lunch the head of the local Intourist Office takes me on a short tour of the town and I see a lovely «active» church packed with people. In the evening we are taken by bus to the station where we are to board the Trans-Siberian train at 8 p.m. The station itself is a tourist's delight. It is packed with a motley crowd of soviets, recognizable as such by their standard luggage and clothes and yet so different from one another by their looks as well as by their idioms and dialects. There are, besides some White Russians, Ukrainians, Georgians, Armenians, Uzbeks, Mongols and so many other nationals, all waiting to board our train. It is very cold waiting on the platform, though I must admit that in Paris, even in summer, I always find railway stations very cold.

Our compartment has just the necessary comforts. I have succeeded, by paying a small supplement, in getting a compart-ment with only two berths instead of the usual four. This may be a little unethical towards our group but we are very glad to be on our own. The two berths are separated by the width of the window in front of which a folding table is covered by a white table cloth. At the end of the coach, a samovar is boiling so we may drink tea whenever we wish.

We may have several other things say Galia and Natacha, our two stewardesses, who occupy a small cabin next to our compartment. All we need do is ask them. A short while later Galia brings us some sheets and pillowcases but we must make our own beds!

Here we are on the Trans-Siberian, this famous train that has haunted me since my childhood, that one reads about in so many novels and that I have always dreamed I would take myself without believing this dream would come true. Whenever a dream does come true, I react differently to what I would have expected. A warm feeling engulfs me and makes me silent for a change. How can I make the best of this wonderful experience and not miss anything of the scenery nor of the life on the train itself and in the stations where we stop?

It is pitch black outside except for a few distant lights here and there, maybe stations too small to stop at, isolated houses lost in this immensity. I try to penetrate the darkness, imagine what is beyond as the silhouettes of scattered trees flash by. In deserted railway stations I occasionally glimpse some human beings, «dead souls» as Gogol would have called them, and when they move I realize that they are alive. The snow and the ice stretch as far as the eye can see and I feel the immensity of Siberia, a different world, a whole new continent that gives at the same time a feeling of desolation and gloom and a sensation of infinite wealth. I can't stop looking, sitting on the edge of the bed and wishing I did not feel so sleepy but I do, so finally I get into bed, pull up the covers and fall into a deep sleep and dream strange dreams of troïkas, deep snow and Katacha struggling through all the obstacles that were set up to prevent her from reaching her husband in exile. Indeed, throughout the whole of the following day and night, I never stop thinking and dreaming of my two great-great-grandmothers who had followed this same route with none of the comforts I was enjoying, riding in their draughty kibitkas in the bitter cold of the cruel Siberian winter. Only love, a great immense love, could have made them overcome all these hardships against the will of their parents, their friends and even the Tsar. When I think of these «Russian Women» as Nekrassov called them, I realize the merit of Alexandra Ivanovna

Davydova who had to leave behind her six children one of whom she was expecting at the time of her husband's arrest, which prevented her from joining him as soon as she would have liked.

The following morning I wake up early as I want to get off the train at Krasnoyarsk which we are scheduled to reach at 8:30 and where we will stop for 15 minutes. The reason I want to get off is that my great-great-grandfather Vassili Lvovitch Davydoff is buried here and I want to ask someone to light three candles I have brought with me from Paris in the church close to the cemetery where he is buried. So I get off the train onto the quay filled with passengers rushing to get off or on the train. I also rush to the station with my three candles. The first two people I go up to are so negative that I feel it is useless to insist. Finally I find outside the station a middle-aged woman to whom I tell my story, that I have just arrived from Paris, that my great-great-grandfather the Decembrist is buried here, that I will not have time to go myself to the cemetery, and that I therefore beg her to light these three candles in the church nearest to where he is buried. She says that she knows all about the Decembrist Davydoff but that she herself does not go to church. However she has an old aunt who does and who will certainly do it for me, so I give her my candles from the Alexander Nevsky Cathedral in Paris. She seems eager to talk more so I tell her all I can but I am aware that the minutes are flying by and that I must get back to the train. There are so many railway lines to cross, the platforms seem so long and the train so far away that I feel a panic rising inside me. I want to run but I dare not for fear of falling as the ground is frozen and slippery. At last I reach our coach, just in time as the train leaves less than two minutes later. The Krasnoyarsk stop-over has meant a great deal to me. It has been too short but fortunately I have at home photos of my great-great-grandfather's grave and of the house where he lived, and maybe another time I could stay longer...

At 6:30 on the morning of the 27th we reach Irkutsk. The station is very busy at this early hour. It is only a short distance from our hotel, on the other side of the river

Angara that is only partly frozen. The little bit we see of the town makes me want to rush off and photograph those small wooden houses I see along the way. The blanket of snow and ice that covers the streets delights me. I love the snow. Winter without snow is not really winter and I miss it in Paris where it melts as soon as it has fallen.

As soon as we get to our unattractive but comfortable room, the phone rings. It is Mark Davidovitch Sergeev and I agree to meet him downstairs at 8 a.m. before breakfast. It is four years already since I last saw him in Paris. He is a well-known writer who specializes in stories about the Decembrists. I have read several of his books and have enjoyed them. He tells me that he is working on a new book that will tell about the wives who were unable to join their husbands and whose life was therefore even more tragic. There are so many things I would like to talk about with him but we have no time. We agree to get in touch again this evening after we return from the taiga.

We first go with the group to visit a fur factory and, although Mark Sergeev said it would be interesting and that we should not miss it, we could have done without it. The same goes for a children's school that we are taken to see. We would have preferred walking through the streets of Irkutsk. On our way to visit the taiga, that forest of conifers that covers most of Siberia, our coach breaks down and we wait around for almost two hours before another coach comes to pick us up. We could have spent that time in Irkutsk, although the two hours did go by fairly quickly with members of the group building and lighting a huge bonfire by the road. The sunset over the taiga is beautiful. We eat a late lunch in a restaurant in the middle of the forest. There is no electricity and we enjoy a pleasant meal by the smoky light of two oil lamps. When we get back to our hotel Mark Sergeev calls to ask us to keep tomorrow evening free as a special reception is being put on in my honor at the Trubetskoy house, now a museum.

The next morning we leave with the group to take a ride in a troïka before driving to lake Baïkal. The weather is beautiful and we are greeted by three pretty girls in local costume who serve vodka and hot blinis in front of a large bonfire. The troïkas are waiting for us and the horses' breath is like steam in the freezing air. The temperature is about 30°C. below zero but there is no wind and the sky is blue and sunny. We have a troïka to ourselves and greatly enjoy the ride in the troïka drawn by three horses and driven by two coachmen in front of us. I only wish we could continue on to lake Baïkal! Alas! we must take our coach. We take a short walk in the snow before reaching the lake. The birch trees, the snow and the bright blue skies make a beautiful sight. Lake Baïkal is not frozen and a light mist rises from its surface almost as if it were steaming. It is a most attractive stretch of water, so vast and so deep that it actually contains one fifth of the whole world supply of fresh water. The restaurant where we have a fair lunch is on a small height overlooking the lake and the view is lovely. On our way back we stop in a small village by the lake, Lusyanka. We walk through the lanes lined by small doll-like wooden houses. It is so peaceful and one feels far away from everything. The sunset over lake Baïkal is superb, a flaming indigo red that shines on the frozen snow and on the water. This is another world, another planet.

On our return to our hotel we just have time to clean up and have a quick dinner before Mark Sergeev shows up to pick us up and drive us to the Trubetskoy house where his wife is waiting for us on the front porch. It is a two-story frame house built after the Napoleonic wars of 1812 and restored the way it used to be in the days of Katacha. A sign says «House-Museum of the Decembrists». We walk in. How can I describe the feelings that grip me? They are so varied and complex. This house too I have dreamed of seeing, and here I am, inside it. Many people—30 or more—are waiting for me in the hallway, all of them interested in the history of the Decembrists. I find myself sitting on a platform with my husband and Mark Sergeev on one side of a large room facing a row of bright spotlights behind which the audience is seated, with photographers and cameramen taking pictures right and left. I am worried that I may not live up to the expectations of all these people. They want to know if I can

tell them any stories about my great-great-grandparents, so I
tell them a few things and they ask more questions and I feel
so inadequate. I only wish I had listened more to my father
and all he had to say about those bygone times that he knew
so well. These people are so keen, so interested to know every
little detail. The conversation never lapses. The atmosphere
is warm and friendly and the evening passes very quickly. I am
given a present of nine books and feel I have gone back to my
childhood to the distribution of prizes at the end of the school
year. All nine books are about the Decembrists. One of them
is signed by most of the people present. Another is on Pushkin's
life when he was exiled to Kichinev. Yet another is that wonderful
book by Zilberstein on the works of the Decembrist Bestujev
that I had looked for but had never succeeded in finding either
in Paris or in Russia. Bestujev's paintings, drawings and
water-colors are small works of art depicting the daily life of
the Decembrists in exile. Nothing could have pleased me more.
We are then taken around the house and shown all the rooms
with portraits of the Decembrists, some of the original furniture
that had belonged to my great-great-grand-parents and even a
piece of embroidery made by Katacha! It was marvelous to be in
this house and feel the reverence that all these people had for
the past history of my ancestors.

The next day, December 31st, our last day in Irkutsk, we
are to spend visiting the town. Mark Sergeev comes to fetch
us at our hotel and drives us to the Znamensky monastery.
It is a grey foggy day and the fog gives everything a certain
aura of mystery. The architecture of the monastery is very
beautiful, the porch a pure arch under which pigeons are
sheltering, and from the outside one can see the lovely domes
and cupolas of the church. We walk into the courtyard and
there, a few yards away, is Katacha's grave surrounded by an
iron railing. There are two graves side by side, that of Katacha
and that of her baby boy Nikita. Here I am at last in front
of this grave where my father had knelt in 1904 during the
Russo-Japanese war when his company had made a halt in
Irkutsk. I remember so well his telling me about it and about
his friend who had taken two pictures of him in front of the
grave which he had sent to his grandmother, Katacha's daughter,

who lived in her estate of Sably near Simferopol in the Crimea, Sably that I had visited in September and where father had been unable to find the pictures when he had returned there at the time of the revolution. I too kneel in front of Katacha's grave and try and collect my thoughts and my emotions. I would like to concentrate all the feelings of respect and admiration that I have for this brave woman and communicate them to her. How I wish that I could come again, at Easter for instance, when I could bring flowers to her grave. The church is open and a few worshippers are present. I light three candles I have brought from Paris and pray. The church is beautiful and the icons shimmer above the flickering candles. The choir sings and I let myself sink into this atmosphere that I love so.

We drive to Urik, a small village about 20 kms from Irkutsk, where many Decembrists lived including the Trubetskoys. The road we are driving on is the same one they took to go to «the city». Small wooden houses line the streets, pastel-colored frame-houses that remind me of the little toy houses we used to hang on our Xmas tree in my childhood when there were candles and no electric lights. They do not have any running water but they do have electricity and television, and are heated by the same large Dutch stoves of olden times. Urik is a very small village that seems to be asleep under its blanket of snow. The Decembrist Nikita Muraviev is buried here. He died accidentally when his house burned down. His portrait hangs in our home so I feel he is not a complete stranger.

We return to Irkutsk and drive through the old streets lined with wooden houses. Here is the White House which, in 1820, belonged to a rich merchant, Sibiriakoff. Here is the two-story frame-house of the Volkonskys', similar to the Trubetskoys', which will also soon be a museum after it has been restored to its former condition down to the smallest detail such as the wallpaper which will be the same as the original one, an original piece having been found by chance. The area around this house is to be rebuilt as it was «then» to form what they call here «a complex» of original old houses. The soviets seem to have realized at last that tourists are less interested in their economic and industrial achievements than in old monuments, churches, museums and all the relics of the past, a past that is good to remember.

To night is New Year's Eve, which we will spend with our group. We have been invited to the home of Mark Sergeev but no taxis are available and furthermore we have to get up at 5 tomorrow morning so we have to refuse their invitation very regretfully.

The following day we fly off to Bratsk. We would have much preferred to stay in Irkutsk and wander around its streets. Bratsk is a brand new town with a cellulose factory that pervades the town with a frightful stink. The only amusing sights are the iced chutes down which slide both children and adults, some on sleighs, others on simple strips of cardboard, all having great fun. The next morning, after a quick visit to a large hydroelectric factory, we fly off to Moscow, which we reach late in the evening.

We spend our last morning in Moscow visiting the Tretiakov gallery with its lovely Rublev icons and walk back to Red Square in a strong icy cold wind that makes us think of Siberia as a warm country! Moscow is grey and gloomy and I miss Irkutsk and the beauty of lake Baïkal. These nine days have been so intense and exciting that I must let my feelings settle before I start dreaming of another trip, maybe Pskov, Mikhaïlovsk, Riga... and possibly Bliden, the birth place of the Lievens, my father's maternal ancestors...

INDEX

Campagna, Joseph, 48.
Catherine II, 12, 21, 22, 23, 26, 39, 45, 76, 216, 218, 219, 220, 235, 236, 272.
Chkaliberda, Maria Antonovna, 274, 275.
Chor, D.S., 97.
Chtcherbatov, Prince, 219.
Chtcherbatova (b. Chtericha), Princess Maria Alexeevna, 47.
Chuvaloff, Cegui, 141.
Constantine Pavlovitch, Grand Duke, 13, 76.
Cossé Brissac (b. Des Cars), Jeanne de, 48.
Cossé Brissac, Marie de (cf. de Robech).

Dantchenko, 239, 240.
Dashkov, Princess Ekaterina, 219.
Daudet, Ernest, 76.
Davydoff, Alexander Lvovitch, 24, 27, 29, 30.
Davydoff, Alexis Vassilievich, 151.
Davydoff, Denis Vassilievich, 257, 258, 269, 272, 281, 286.
Davydoff, Dimitri Lvovitch, 151.
Davydoff, Grigori Alexeevich, 151.
Davydoff, Lev Alexeevich, 151.
Davydoff, Major-General Lev Denissovitch, 22, 24.
Davydoff, Lev Vassilievich, 32, 36, 38, 39, 147, 151, 269.
Davydoff, L.F., 249, 251, 252.
Davydoff, Nicholas Vassilievich, 29 to 39, 56, 146, 147, 148, 153, 274.
Davydoff, Piotr Lvovitch, 24.
Davydoff, Piotr Vassilievich, 29, 30, 31, 32, 56, 57, 58, 65, 67, 174, 201, 203, 204.
Davydoff, Piotr Vassilievich, 58, 64, 101, 102, 103, 104, 105, 108, 141, 147, 157, 172.
Davydoff, Vassili Lvovich, 9, 12, 13, 14, 25, 26, 27, 28, 30, 32, 52, 53, 78, 201, 208, 211, 274, 283, 289.
Davydoff, Vassili Petrovich, 56, 67, 68, 69, 93, 95, 146, 147, 157, 174, 177.
Davydoff, Vassili Vassilievich, 62, 64, 84, 101, 102, 103, 104, 105, 108, 153, 157, 172, 184.
Davydoff, Vladimir Lvovich, « Bob », 40, 41.
Davydoff, Yuri Lvovich, 151, 269, 270.
Davydoff, Adèle Alexandrovna, 25, 30.
Davydova (b. de Gramont), Aglaé, 24, 30.
Davydova (b. Tchaikovskaia) Alexandra Ilyinishna, 36, 38, 39, 40, 147, 151, 269.
Davydova (b. Potapova), Alexandra Ivanovna, 23, 25, 30, 32, 37, 39, 40, 146, 201, 202, 205, 206, 208, 210, 211, 275, 289.
Davydova, Alexandra Vassilievna, 35, 39.
Davydova (b. Samoilova), Ekaterina Nikolaevna, 21, 22, 23, 24, 25, 26, 30.
Davydova, Ekaterina Petrovna (cf. Dolgorukaia).
Davydova (b. Princess Trubetskaia), Elisaveta Sergeevna, 31, 43, 44, 53, 54, 56, 57, 58, 63, 67, 68, 69, 145, 174, 180, 185, 186, 201, 203, 211, 256, 292.
Davydova, Elisaveta Vassilievna, 29, 37, 39, 40.
Davydova, Irina Yurevna, 282.
Davydova (b. Countess Orlova), Natalie, 24.
Davydova (b. HSH Princess Lieven), Olga Alexandrovna, 67, 68, 69, 79, 82, 83, 85, 90, 91, 92, 93, 95, 101, 102, 103, 104, 105, 107, 108, 109, 111, 113, 26, 127, 128, 146, 147, 157, 172, 173, 174, 180, 181, 184.
Davydova, Sophie Lvovna (cf. Borozdina).
Davydova, Xenia Yurevna, 269, 282.

Davydova, Zinaida Petrovna (cf. Dublianskaia).
Demidov, Nikita, 45.
Denikin, General Anton Ivanovich, 196, 199.
Derjavin, G.R., 228.
Des Cars (b. Lebzeltern), Alexandrine, 48.
Des Cars, Viscount Jean Augustin, 48.
Des Cars, Jeanne (cf. de Cossé Brissac).
Diderot, Denis, 12, 235, 236.
Djunkovsky, 231.
Dobrochinsky, General, 160.
Dolgorukaia (b. Davydova), Ekaterina Petrovna, 56.
Dolgoruky, Prince Alexis Yurevich, 56.
Dostoievsky, Fiodor Mikhailovitch, 137.
Drebush, 240.
Dublianskaia (b. Davydova), Zinaida Petrovna, 56.
Dubliansky, 56.
Durassova (b. Miasnikova), Agrafine Ivanovna, 45.

Ekk, General, 160, 164.
Elisaveta Alexeevna, Empress, 238.
Elisaveta Petrovna, Empress, 75, 217, 218, 219.
Engelhardt, Alexandra, 21.

Fouché, Joseph, 232.
Fouquet, Mlle, 91, 92, 102.

Gabrilovitch, 97.
Gabrichewsky, 126.
Gaugreben, Charlotte Karlovna von (cf. Lieven).
Gelferig, 252.
Ginzburg, Baron G., 250, 252.
Glebov, Petia, 141.
Glinka, Colonel Feodor, 238, 239, 240, 242, 243.
Glinka, M.I., 271.
Gnedich, P.N., 27.
Gogol, N.V., 39, 46.
Golenichev-Kutuzov, Count, 53.
Golitzin, Prince, 219.
Golovin, Count N.N., 219.
Gorchakov, V.P., 25.
Gotz, Michael, 250.
Gough-Calthorpe, Admiral Sir Somerset, 197, 199, 200.
Gramont, Agénor de, 251.
Gramont, Aglaé de (cf. Davydova).
Gretch, 236.
Grey, Lord, 77.
Griboedov, A.S., 10, 47.
Gruzinskaia, HSH Princess Daria Alexandrovna (cf. Trubetskaia).
Guizot, François, 77.
Gulevich, S.V., 125, 136.
Guniev, Vassili Petrovich, 230.
Gutienko, Piotr, 175, 182, 183, 185, 189, 190, 191, 192, 193.

Handrikoff, Fedor Fedorovich, 132.
Heine, Heinrich, 123, 133.
Hoffman, 97.

Iskritsky, 239, 241.
Ivanov, S.A., 132.
Ivanov, V.I., 46.
Ivantsov, Nicholas Alexandrovich, 137.
Ivantsov, Serge Alexandrovich, 132, 136, 137.

Jablonsky, Prince Jan, 21.
Juravliev, 97.

Kaiserling, Countess, 111.
Kakhovsky, 14.
Kankrin, E.F., 236.
Kapnist, Dmitri, 141.
Karamzin, N.M., 228.
Khmelnitzky, Bogdan, 20.
Kikin, 241.
Kolochyn, P., 49.
Kolokolov, 123.
Korvina-Kossakovskaia (b. Laval), Countess Alexandra Ivanovna, 48.
Korvin-Kossakovsky, Count S.G.F., 48.
Kosciuszko, T., 232.
Kotchubey, Prince V.P., 229.
Kozitskaia, Alexandra Grigorievna (cf. Laval).
Kozitskaia, Anna Grigorievna (cf. Beloselskaia-Belozerskaia).
Kozitskaia (b. Miasnikova), Ekaterina Ivanovna, 45, 46, 48, 55.
Kozitskaia, Grigori Vassilievich, 45.
Kozlov, P.K., 47.
Kronprinz, 120.
Krym, S.S., 196, 197, 198, 199.
Kurakin, Prince A.B., 219, 237.
Kuroki, General, 159, 163.
Kuropatkin, General, 160, 161.
Kutuzov, A.M., 219.
Kutuzov, N., 238, 239, 240, 243.
Kviatovsky, Nicholas Kasimirovitch, 135, 136.

Laharpe, Jean François, 229.
Latchinov, Mikhail, 141.
Laurent, 237.
Laval (b. Kozitskaia), Countess Alexandra Grigorievna, 45, 46, 47, 48, 55, 65.
Laval, Alexandra Ivanovna (cf. Korvina-Kossakovskaia).
Laval, Ekaterina Ivanovna (cf. Trubetskaia).
Laval, Count Ivan Stepanovich, 44, 46, 47, 62, 256.
Laval, Paul Ivanovich, 48.
Laval, Sophie Ivanovna (cf. Bork).
Laval, Vladimir Ivanovich, 48.
Laval, Zinaida Ivanovna (cf. Lebzeltern).
Lavrov, 249.
Lebzeltern, Alexandrine (cf. Des Cars).
Lebzeltern, Count Ludwig, 48, 50.
Lebzeltern (b. Laval), Zinaida Ivanovna, 48, 53.
Leparsky, General S.P., 52.
Lermontov, M.I., 47.
Levashoff, 230, 242.

Pushin, I.I., 50, 225.
Pushin, Alexander Sergeevich, 9, 19, 23, 24, 25, 27, 28, 30, 31, 36, 39, 47, 67, 123, 152, 228, 272, 273, 274, 283, 292.
Putiatin, Prince, 252.

Radishcheff, 220.
Raevskaia (b. Samoilova), Ekaterina Nikolaevna (cf. Davydova).
Raevskaia, Ekaterina Nikolaevna (cf. Orlova).
Raevskaia, Maria Nikolaevna (cf. Volkonskaia).
Raevsky, Alexander Nikolaevich, 23, 27, 28, 29, 30.
Raevsky, Nicholas Nikolaevich, 23, 27, 28, 30.
Raevsky, Nicholas Nikolaevich, 23, 27, 29, 30, 273.
Raevsky, Nicholas Simenovich, 22.
Raffalovich, Arthur Lvovich, 247, 251.
Razumovsky, Count, 75.
Rebinder, (b. Princess Trubetskaia), Alexandra Sergeevna, 53.
Rebinder, Nicholas Romanovich, 53.
Repnin, Prince N.V., 219.
Repnin, Prince P.P., 219.
Robech, Count de Lévis Mirepoix, Prince Guy de, 48.
Robech (b. de Cossé Brissac), Princess Marie de, 48.
Rogdestvensky, Father, 136.
Romanoff, Ivan (Yogan Christophore), 76.
Rostsichewsky, 147, 150, 151, 153.
Rothschild, 246, 247, 249, 251, 252.
Rothschild, Alphonse, 249.
Rothschild, Maurice, 248, 249, 251, 252, 253.
Ryleev, K.F., 13, 14, 50, 208, 241, 273.

Safanov, Vassili Ilyich, 97.
Samoilov, Alexander Nikolaevich, 21.
Samoilova, Ekaterina Nikolaevna (cf. Davydova).
Samoilova (b. Potemkina), Maria Alexandrovna, 21.
Schiff, 247, 249, 250, 251, 252.
Sebastiani, Marshal Horace, 30.
Semenov, S.M., 238, 239, 242, 243.
Semevsky, V.I., 216.
Seniavin, 236.
Seniavin, 239, 240.
Sergeev, Mark Davidovich, 290, 291, 292, 294.
Skobeleff, General, 89.
Smirnoff, Anatoli Filipovich, 287.
Smirnoff, Serge Nikolaevich, 136, 137.
Sokoloff, Serge Alexeevich, 94.
Speransky, M.M., 221, 222, 236.
Staël, Baroness Germaine de, 47.
Stanover, Mendel, 236.
Strekalova, Alexandra Nikolaevna, 86.
Stroganov, A.N., 46.
Stroganov, Count, 229.
Sumarokoff, A.P., 219.
Sverbeev, A.D., 63.
Sverbeev, N.D., 53.
Sverbeev, Serge Nikolaevich, 53.

The « Bréguet » quotation is taken from a translation of « Eugene Onegin » by Charles Johnston.

The other quotations are translated by Olga Davydoff Dax.

The illustrations are from the A. V. Davydoff family archives except for :

Page VI — « The Davydoffs' home in Krasnoyarsk » and « The grave of V. L. Davydoff » which comes from the Moscow Museum of History.

Page VII — « The three Trubetskoy sisters » which comes from the Russian Museum in Leningrad.

Page VIII — « Lev Vassilievich Davydoff & Alexandra Ilyinishna Tchaikovskaia » which comes from the Tchaikovsky Museum in Klin.

The water-colors which are by Marianna Adrianovna Davydova, by courtesy of her daughter Elena Lvovna Vassiloff.

Page IX — « Kamenka : Early 19th century » and « A. S. Pushkin & Decembrists in Kamenka » which come from the A. S. Pushkin — P. I. Tchaikovsky Museum in Kamenka.

CONTENTS

15